Ecotherapy in Practice

Ecotherapy in Practice reflects the growing interest and research in this field. Drawing on a diversity of experience from the counselling and psychotherapy professions, but also from practitioners in community work, mental health and education, this book explores the exciting and innovative possibilities involved in practising outdoors.

Caroline Brazier brings to bear her experience and knowledge as a psychotherapist, group worker and trainer over several decades to think about therapeutic work outdoors in all its forms. The book presents a model of ecotherapy based on principles drawn from Buddhist psychology and Western psychotherapy which focuses particularly on the relationship between person and environment at three levels, moving from the personal level of individual history to cultural influences, then finally to global circumstances, all of which condition mind-states and psychological wellbeing.

Ecotherapy in Practice will provide refreshing and valuable reading for psychotherapists and counsellors in the field, those interested in Buddhism and other mental health and health professionals working outdoors.

Caroline Brazier is a psychotherapist in independent practice and course leader of the Tariki training programmes in psychotherapy and ecotherapy. A practising Buddhist, she is author of six previous books on Buddhism and psychotherapy. Having loved the outdoors since childhood, she has worked with groups and individuals in many different therapeutic, educational and community settings over the years.

Ecotherapy in Practice

A Buddhist Model

Caroline Brazier

Routledge
Taylor & Francis Group
LONDON AND NEW YORK

First published 2018
by Routledge
2 Park Square, Milton Park, Abingdon, Oxon OX14 4RN

and by Routledge
711 Third Avenue, New York, NY 10017

Routledge is an imprint of the Taylor & Francis Group, an informa business

British Library Cataloguing in Publication Data
A catalogue record for this book is available from the British Library

Library of Congress Cataloging in Publication Data
Names: Brazier, Caroline, author.
Title: Ecotherapy in practice : a Buddhist model / Caroline Brazier.
Description: Abingdon, Oxon ; New York, NY : Routledge, 2018. |
Includes bibliographical references and index.
Identifiers: LCCN 2017005731 | ISBN 9780415785952 (hardback) |
ISBN 9780415785969 (pbk.)
Subjects: LCSH: Environmental psychology. | Buddhism--Psychology.
Classification: LCC BF353 .B69 2018 | DDC 615.8/515--dc23
LC record available at https://lccn.loc.gov/2017005731

ISBN: 978-0-415-78595-2 (hbk)
ISBN: 978-0-415-78596-9 (pbk)
ISBN: 978-1-315-20826-8 (ebk)

Typeset in Bembo
by Integra Software Service Pvt. Ltd.

To George, Owen, Sebastian and Ana
For their future to be possible

Contents

Introduction

Environmentally-based therapies represent a new and developing field. Whilst many people are impressed by the potential of the outdoors for therapeutic work, the contexts in which the work is actually being done, and the forms that it takes, are varied and often on the fringes of the therapy profession as a whole. To work in this area is therefore to be something of a pioneer, and those aspiring to offer ecotherapy, in whatever context or form, are often learning to be adaptive and creative as they draw together threads from different areas of expertise. With increasing interest in the therapeutic benefits of nature, even those working in quite circumscribed situations, who offer distinct activities such as woodland crafts or outdoor sports which have well established practices, are now working with groups who have psychological or social problems. These practitioners are therefore benefitting from developing psychological awareness and interpersonal skills.

With such diversity, there are few blueprints available and it would be foolish for this book to attempt to provide one approach to fit all situations. Whilst the book offers an integrated philosophy of personal change and a consistent model of human process, it is primarily a tool-box of method, theory and praxis from which those working in different spheres can draw. In it I share some of the experience and theoretical principles which underpin my own thinking and that of others in the field. I invite the reader to forage in this material and find support for their own ways of working in whatever setting this may be taking place.

My background in ecotherapy has roots in a number of areas and this broad foundation reflects several different contributory areas and applications which we see in environmentally-based approaches. Whilst I have been offering activities which have been termed 'ecotherapy' for about six years now, mostly through groups and workshops and sometimes in one-to-one situations, I have experience in the counselling and psychotherapy professions, in community education and in taking people outdoors going back over three or more decades. This experience includes a longstanding individual psychotherapy practice, therapeutic groupwork, community work and delivering formal and informal education to both adults and children. In addition, as a Buddhist, I have lived and worked in Buddhist centres and communities for the past 25 years and, during that time, have participated in and led a variety of retreats, ceremonial and classes, sometimes using time in nature as a central feature.

This book provides a framework for thinking about therapeutic work outdoors. Whilst offering a model based on a Buddhist understanding of mental conditioning, it is primarily concerned with practice and so is broad in its approach, drawing on a variety of different therapeutic fields, integrated within an overarching structure. In this, it is informed by both the indoor world of counselling and psychotherapy and the wider sphere of community and outdoor activities, giving models for developing therapeutic working in nature, whether with individuals or with groups. Whilst based on Buddhist principles, the book will be of interest to practitioners from all schools of psychotherapy who are interested in taking their work outdoors, as well as to those already working outdoors who want to develop their skills and understanding in a more therapeutic direction. With its Buddhist roots, the book may also be helpful to those who are running retreats in nature and who wish to broaden their skills and find new ways of engaging with the environment in a spiritual milieu.

Contexts and sources

Although interest in ecotherapy has grown relatively recently, the relationship between psychology, nature and the outdoors has long been explored formally and informally. Indeed, as the biophilia hypothesis (Wilson 1984) suggests, the affinity between humans and the living world of nature has always underpinned our positive mind-states, and, as a consequence spending time in wild places, has been valued throughout history as one of our deepest sources of replenishment. Intentionally or otherwise, mental health and outdoor activity have always been linked.

As humans became more urbanised, the idea of going into nature as an act of self-discovery or an agent of change became more established as a conscious agenda. A number of different cultural influences have fostered this, bringing different aspects of the encounter with wildness to the fore. Some saw our relationship to nature as spiritually and culturally uplifting. The Romantic Movement, for example, encouraged people to seek inspiration from the natural environment, supporting the flourishing of nature-based arts and philosophy. Others saw the encounter with nature as offering the potential to challenge people and so push them to extend their personal limits. Based on ideas drawn from diverse sources such as initiation rites, religious austerities and military training, experiences of the wild came to be seen as good for character building. Approaches based on these outward-bound principles have been used in executive development and team building (Wagner, Baldwin & Roland 1994), whilst it has become customary to take young people outdoors through organisations like the Scouts and Guides, the Woodcraft Folk or Duke of Edinburgh award schemes in order for them to experience the wild and learn survival skills as part of their growth towards maturity.

In the meantime, other groups have been using the outdoors as a way of improving mental wellbeing. Recently, the national mental health charity, Mind, has taken a strong lead in developing outdoor therapies (Mind 2013), as have other groups in the sector such as drug and alcohol agencies, those working with people with disabilities and many small charitable and local authority projects. Many of these groups have established approaches using outdoor activities such as sports or gardening (Diamant & Waterhouse 2010) to create spaces for interaction and encourage service users into a more active engagement with one another and with their surroundings. Such therapies are offered by staff and volunteers from different professional backgrounds. These people bring differing levels of awareness of, or interest in, the psychological processes which their work involves.

At the same time, growing interest in shamanic practices (Knudson & Suzuki 2006; Schaefer 2006) has fired a plethora of popular therapies, workshops and events, attracting a following of people who are looking for paths to personal fulfilment and healing outside the mainstream. These activities may draw on the spiritual practices of different traditions (Straffon 2007; Kirkey 2009) and are sometimes delivered in spiritual settings such as retreat centres (Brazier 2011) or ashrams. Participants may seek transformation and inner peace through solitary and collective practices, sweat lodges, solstice rituals and rites of passage, all of which may involve nature-based activity.

Despite the many developments of this kind, however, there has been considerable concern that many young people today are growing up without much contact with nature (Moss 2012), a situation termed 'Nature Deficit Disorder' by Richard Louv, author of *Last Child in the Woods* (2005). Deprivation and pressurised lifestyles mean that inner-city children do not have much experience of wild spaces, whilst on suburban estates, technology and social media are making indoor pursuits more attractive to youngsters than the outdoor play of previous generations. In response to this, teachers and youth workers are recognising a need to set up more opportunities for outdoor play and young people from the cities are being introduced to nature through the forest schools movement (Knight 2011), and similar ventures.

Whilst these practical developments have been taking place in the field, concern has also been growing among academics, activists and practitioners about the way that socio-economic change is affecting our planet, prompting them to look at implications of these changes for the psychological sciences. As evidence for environmental degradation and negative human impact on animal and plant species, both globally and locally, increases, rather than confining themselves to working with individual neuroses, some are questioning the role of psychology and the psychological therapies in addressing systemic environmental problems. In particular, the deep ecology movement of Arne Naess (1989) and others has inspired some practitioners and theorists to look beyond the personal and try to understand and ameliorate our human embeddedness in the planetary fate. A diverse movement of theorists and practitioners have come together over the past few decades in a field which has come to be referred to using the umbrella term ecopsychology (Roszak, Gomes & Kanner 1995; Sessions 1995; Fisher 2002; Rust & Totton 2012).

Ecopsychology addresses the situation in which, as a species, humans have come to experience disconnection from the environment and the symptoms associated with the resulting malaise. This movement has influenced therapists of different schools, challenging some of us to look for ways of working which give space to environmental concerns, and which recognise how aspects of human pathology arise from, or are exacerbated by, the collective sense of powerlessness, guilt and despair that these ecological problems give rise to. At the same time, in recognising the interconnection between ourselves and our environments, the ecopsychology movement has also advocated the healing power of reconnection to nature in supporting both mental and physical health. This has led to the development of ecotherapy as a distinct practice within, and alongside, other therapeutic modalities (Buzzell & Chalquist 2009; Jordan 2015; Jordan & Hinds 2016). Thus, for many practitioners, ecotherapy is inevitably connected to our position in a troubled ecosystem. Therapeutic benefit cannot be separated from responsibility for seeing the bigger picture.

Closely connected to the deep ecology movement, in the Buddhist world and beyond, Joanna Macy has been influential through her writings and her workshop programme *The Work that Reconnects* (Macy 1991; Macy & Brown 2014). Her ideas, based on Buddhist principles of inter-connection and personal transformation through engagement with despair and affliction, have been widely taken up by activists and others within the field, contributing to a growing literature on Buddhism, environmentalism and ecotherapy (Badiner 1990; Kaza & Kraft 2000; Hanh 2004; Brazier 2011). This seems appropriate, given the origination of Buddhism as a practice of awareness undertaken in the forests and countryside of India (Fisher 2013).

Working with this book

The diversity of settings and practices which are supported under the umbrella of ecotherapy create complexity. Whilst broad principles can be outlined, specific working situations place different demands on the therapist and their practice. For this reason this book includes examples taken from a range of settings. Nevertheless, the practitioner working in the field will need to be creative and adaptive in applying theory or using exercises suggested in it.

The book is divided into five parts according to the Ten Directions model outlined in Chapter 1. The first two parts provide principles for the work, looking at the general area of therapeutic containment and at the core models of other-centred approach (Brazier 2009) in parts one and two respectively. This approach is described on our website www.buddhistpsychology.info. Parts three to five then look sequentially at three levels of psychological conditioning: the personal, the cultural and the collective. These explore both the process of conditioned experiencing and its transcendence through insight, encounter, creativity, energy-transformation and lifestyle. We will look at a wide range of methodologies including empathic accompaniment, imaginative investigation, mindfulness, practical engagement in activities, group and individual process, arts and writing, shamanic practices and encounter. The book includes practical guidelines for exercises and activities as well as more general reflections on the principles behind various ways of working.

On a practical note, because ecotherapy practice is so diverse, and because it is often located in the interfaces between professional fields, there can be difficulties in choosing which language to use. Language is political and carries associations which can be controversial in some professions. In this book, I have tried to maintain neutrality by adopting terms which are as unaligned as possible, but have found myself variously using the words 'therapist', 'facilitator', 'group-worker' or 'practitioner' to describe the person delivering the experience, and 'client', 'group', 'participant' or 'people' to describe those for whom the services might be being provided. I hope that the reader will take these terms in context and appreciate that in most cases the theoretical point being made could be applied to one-to-one work, groupwork or more informal community settings, sometimes with necessary adaptation. Because many ecotherapists work with groups rather than individuals, and groupwork has made up the larger part of my practice in nature, the book does have a bias towards group situations, but it gives guidelines throughout on individual working outdoors as well.

Psychology and psychotherapy have been highly influential in shaping our society over the past century, and the emergence of an environmentally conscious psychology is vital to the times that lie ahead. Working outdoors is an important development in the therapeutic profession and has the potential to contribute to change in society, albeit in small ways. The rift between humans and other creatures, founded on the psychological and spiritual crises of identity and impermanence, has the potential to destroy all of us, so any work which helps to heal that broken link will serve us all into the future. For this reason I believe a Buddhist approach, whether practiced by people who identify as Buddhist or not, offers particular advantages, both in its methodology of mindful awareness and engagement and in its philosophical understanding of our interdependence with life in all its forms.

Abbreviations

Throughout this book, the following abbreviations will be used for Buddhist texts:

MN Majjhima Nikaya
DN Digha Nikaya

References

Badiner, A. (1990). *Dharma Gaia.* Berkeley: Parallax.

Brazier, C. (2009). *Other-Centred Therapy: Buddhist Psychology in Action.* Ropley: O-Books.

Brazier, C. (2011). *Acorns Among the Grass*. Ropley: Earth Books.
Buzzell, L. & Chalquist, C. (2009). *Ecotherapy: Healing with Nature in Mind*. San Francisco: Sierra Club Books.
Diamant, E. & Waterhouse, A. (2010). Gardening and Belonging: Reflections on How Social and Therapeutic Horticulture May Facilitate Health, Wellbeing and Inclusion. *British Journal of Occupational Therapy*, 73(2): 84–88.
Fisher, A. (2002). *Radical Ecopsychology: Psychology in the Service of Life*. Albany: State University of New York Press.
Fisher, S. (2013). *Meditation in the Wild: Buddhism's Origin in the Heart of Nature*. Ropley: Changemakers Books.
Hanh, N. (2004). *Touching the Earth: 46 Guided Meditations for Mindfulness Practice*. Berkeley: Parallax Books.
Jordan, M. (2015). *Nature and Therapy: Understanding Counselling and Psychotherapy in Outdoor Spaces*. London: Routledge.
Jordan, M. & Hinds, J. (Eds.). (2016). *Ecotherapy: Theory, Research and Practice*. London: Palgrave.
Kaza, S. & Kraft, K. (Eds.). (2000). *Dharma Rain: Sources of Buddhist Environmentalism*. Boston: Shambala.
Kirkey, J. (2009). *The Salmon in the Spring: The Ecology of Celtic Spirituality*. San Francisco: Hiraeth Press.
Knight, S. (Ed.) (2011). *Forest Schools for All*. London: Sage.
Knudson, P. & Suzuki, D. (2006). *Wisdom of the Elders*. Vancouver: Greystone.
Louv, R. (2005). *Last Child in the Woods: Saving Our Children from Nature-Deficit Disorder*. Chapel Hill: Algonquin Books.
Macy, J. (1991). *World as Lover, World as Self*. Berkeley: Parallax Books.
Macy, J. & Brown, M. (2014). *Coming Back to Life* (revised Ed). Gabriola Island, BC: New Society Publishers.
Mind. (2013). *Feeling Better Outside, Feeling Better Inside: Ecotherapy for Mental Wellbeing, Resilience and Recovery*. London: Mind.
Moss, S. (2012). *Natural Childhood*. UK: National Trust.
Naess, A. (1989). *Ecology, Community and Lifestyle*. D. Rothenberg (trans.), Cambridge: Cambridge University Press.
Roszak, T., Gomes, M. & Kanner, A. (Eds.). (1995). *Ecopsychology: Restoring the Earth, Healing the Mind*. San Francisco: Sierra Club Books.
Rust, M. & Totton, N. (2012). *Vital Signs: Psychological Responses to Ecological Crisis*. London: Karnac.
Schaefer, C. (2006). *Grandmothers Counsel the Earth*. Boston: Trumpeter.
Sessions, G. (Ed.). (1995). *Deep Ecology for the 21st Century*. Boston: Shambala.
Straffon, C. (2007). *Daughters of the Earth: Goddess Wisdom for a Modern Age*. Ropley: O-Books.
Wagner, R., Baldwin, T. & Roland, C. (1994). Outdoor Training: Revolution or Fad. In C. Schneier (Ed.), *The Training and Development Sourcebook*. Amherst, MA: Human Resources Development Press.
Wilson, E. (1984). *Biophilia*. Harvard: Harvard University Press.

Part 1

The therapeutic container

1 Conditions for change

This chapter explores the concept of 'therapeutic conditions', initially drawing on the work of Carl Rogers who proposed that people flourish when good psychological conditions are in place. Drawing on recent developments in the field of ecotherapy, it then proposes that being outdoors is in itself therapeutic. The chapter then explores the concept of the therapeutic container, suggesting that this has two functions: creating safe boundaries for working and intensifying therapeutic process. It proposes that in ecotherapy containment is provided by therapist and environment working collaboratively. The chapter concludes by summarising the Ten Directions model which underpins the book.

The process of personal change happens within a crucible of conditions. Whether this process is labelled therapy or not, the conditions which produce positive growth and deepening of spirit can be said to be therapeutic. Such conditions may occur by happy happenstance, they may result from coincidences of circumstances, but they can sometimes be cultivated intentionally. Those of us who work in therapeutic professions like to believe we make a difference. We facilitate processes of psychological change and growth. More truthfully, though, at best we can be gardeners, offering the soil in which the spirit of actualisation can work and human potential can grow. We create conditions, not outcomes.

Whether we work in therapy rooms or outdoors, we are not alone. We are but one influence in a person's life, albeit sometimes a significant one. Other factors play a part in the process of change, and most of these are far beyond our control. Like gardeners we can tend the delicate new shoots and protect them to some degree from forces that might otherwise damage them; we can choose suitable locations for planting and provide rich nutrients to build strength, but we cannot prevent the unexpected frost or divert the invasion of insects which may destroy them. More, we cannot touch directly the life force itself, a force which naturally grows towards the light. This force is strong.

Carl Rogers, the well-known psychologist and theorist, wrote of finding a sack of potatoes in a dark corner of his family's cellar. Although they had no soil or water and little light, the old, shrivelling potatoes were covered in a tangle of white roots. They had sprouted. Rogers was struck by the miracle of life-energy represented by those potatoes. This image of resilience inspired him as he started to reflect on human process and on how therapy could best be of help to people. Despite the adverse conditions, the potatoes were striving towards the light. They seemed to have an inbuilt tendency towards growth. Perhaps humans had the same potential.

> The conditions were unfavorable, but the potatoes would begin to sprout – pale, white sprouts, so unlike the healthy green shoots they sent up when planted in the soil in the spring. But these sad, spindly sprouts would grow 2 or 3 feet in length as they reached toward the distant light of the window. The sprouts were, in their bizarre, futile growth, a sort of desperate expression of the directional tendency I have been describing.
>
> (Rogers 1980: p. 118)

Rogers drew a parallel between those stunted potatoes, trying to grow in such impoverished circumstances, and the experiences of the many troubled people with whom he worked in his psychotherapy practice. He recognised that, despite sometimes living in the most awful circumstances, these people had remarkable resilience, carrying on with their lives, albeit sometimes in limited or distorted ways, despite their unhappiness.

Whilst he was a realist and recognised how far short of their potential many people fell, and how, like the potatoes in the cellar, their lives often became grotesque parodies of what they might otherwise have been, Rogers nevertheless believed that the life force, which he termed the *self-actualising tendency*, was ever-present, leading people to make the best of whatever opportunities they had. Whether people flourished did not depend on their innate nature, but, rather, on the conditions in which they lived. Like plants, people needed good conditions in order to reach their full potential. Given the right circumstances, they could be trusted to find this.

Rogers' life-work centred upon identifying, practising and teaching the conditions which he saw as being most conducive to the process of actualisation. It was on this work that his therapeutic model, known as person-centred approach, was based.

Conditions for growth

As we start to explore the therapeutic potential of working outdoors, it is good to remember Rogers' iconic image. It speaks to us especially. We, after all, may be gardeners of the soil as well as of the psyche.

The potato is a tuber; a plant in its dormant phase. Though it carries the potential for the new plant within it, it can exist without the normal requisites for growth. A potato can be dug up, stored, sold and even cut into pieces, yet its capacity to grow is not destroyed. At the same time, for the potato to grow into a plant, it needs the right conditions: good soil, water, sunlight and so on. Indeed, the better the conditions, the better the plant and the better the yield of new potatoes. Potato plants only usually reach their potential when the conditions are right. A drought or an invasion of Colorado beetle will stunt them or kill them completely.

Humans also need particular conditions in order to grow. The conditions we experience affect us in many ways and without adequate resources we do not thrive. On the other hand, even when people are living through very difficult circumstances, human potential is not destroyed. Food and shelter, companionship and occupation, values and beliefs establish the physical, psychological and spiritual environment and thus provide a complexity of conditions, some growth promoting, others less so. For Rogers, the story of the potatoes not only illustrated the power of the self-actualising tendency, but also the importance of having the right conditions in place for positive growth. The potato in the cellar might be stunted and shrivelled, but planted in the earth it could grow into a healthy plant. Likewise, with positive conditions, humans naturally reach their potential. Without them, they are limited.

Rogers' main contribution to therapeutic theory was to identify the set of conditions which he saw as necessary and sufficient for psychological change (Rogers 1957). His original formulation suggested six conditions, but was later refined to the three core conditions of person-centred approach: empathy, congruence and unconditional positive regard (Mearns & Thorne 1988). When humans are listened to with understanding in a warm, appreciative and honest context, their innate tendency to growth emerges, allowing them to find their own way of being the best that they can be.

Buddhism also speaks of the importance of conditions. All things come into being dependent on causes and conditions. Nothing exists without a precursor, and particular conditions combine to give rise to particular objects and outcomes (Thomas 2011). What we experience and what we do, create the conditions for future actions. Each object is formed out of the material of previous objects, according to patterns already conditioned by previous events and formulae.

In this way, Buddhism sees everything as being in a state of flux, a moving kaleidoscope of forms, but, at the same time, as the creation of particular circumstances, produced according to common patterns from that which has gone before. Any process or object exists at the interface of conditions from past and present, and will become a condition for future phenomena. A potato exists as a result of the conditions provided by previous potatoes, as well as the various environmental conditions which we have already discussed. Its presence in the cellar depends on human intervention: the farmer, the householder, the sack maker and so on. There are so many steps in this chain of conditions that to understand the potatoes' existence in the moment would be infinitely complex. On the other hand, conditions can be changed or influenced and the ways of doing this may sometimes be obvious but sometimes not.

Buddhist texts are broadly concerned with exploring the conditions which are conducive to growth. These include instructions for different kinds of meditation, advice on behaviour, principles for ethical lifestyle, and inspirational stories and imagery. In particular, they suggest that it is important to pay attention to the conditions with which we surround ourselves in any particular moment. The mind is conditioned by the objects of attention. We become what we are as a result of the things with which we engage.

Working outdoors provides us with rich conditions for psychological and physical wellbeing, and particularly for cultivating mental health. This has been increasingly recognised in recent years, as we see, for example, in the 2010 report of the Faculty of Public Health, produced in consultation with Natural England (Faculty of Public Health 2010) and in the reports produced by the UK based charity, Mind (Mind 2007; Mind 2013). All of these studies cite substantive research from universities and government bodies which supports the idea that being outdoors in green spaces, close to nature, is good for your mental wellbeing.

Although there is much evidence for these positive effects, many of the activities which these reports describe are not what one might narrowly think of as therapeutic. They do not involve counsellors and psychotherapists in conversation with clients and service users about conscious and unconscious process. Often they involve sports or leisure activities, horticultural and landscape work, arts and social events. Taking people outdoors, it seems, is, in itself, beneficial. The environment provides healing conditions, and those who facilitate the process do not necessarily need specialist skills beyond being an instructor, companion or guide. Going out into wild spaces in itself seems to have a positive effect on people's psychological wellbeing. Nature-contact does you good. The land is the therapist.

This does not, however, diminish the potential contribution of therapist or facilitator. Working with people outdoors, the facilitator herself is a condition for those with whom she works, just as the landscape is. We can hone our skills and develop our ability to offer therapeutic responses. This may mean developing our capacity to listen with more depth and appreciate psychological process. It may involve working alongside people on something practical, chatting informally, or suggesting activities to suit their mood on a particular day. It may involve working in a broad, community-based context or with a more narrowly psychotherapeutic remit. Working therapeutically outdoors creates new situations in which psychological process can be examined, offering natural metaphors for feelings and intuitions and providing experiences which reflect life issues in ways which can then be talked about.

The consulting room outdoors

The idea that a good working environment is beneficial for people is not new. Those working in business or manufacturing, offices or shops have long recognised the importance of the working environment for the wellbeing of staff and customers, as well as for increasing their productivity.

Most therapists create good working environments in their consulting rooms, aiming to make them calm, safe and private. Inasmuch as they have control over these spaces, they may choose colour schemes, décor, seating, lighting and so on, so that the room is welcoming, but also so that it communicates something about their approach. Some therapists prefer professional neutrality, choosing bland colours and plain furnishings. Others are more interested in creating a healing atmosphere, and might prefer lush plants and soft colours. Others might choose bright colour-schemes and provide art materials or idiosyncratic objects to invite creativity. In this way, the therapy room may reflect the style and personality of the therapist or may attempt to conceal it. It may be muted and relaxing or colourful and stimulating. Therapists working indoors thus make many deliberate choices about the kind of working space they want to use.

Being outdoors, the space which we use can be less predictable. Going outside, we enter a working space which is vibrant with life, but also has many uncontrollable factors which have the potential to intrude on the therapeutic process. If we are used to working indoors, we may have to adapt our work to allow for this vibrancy and the changeability of our surroundings. As we will see in this first section of the book, we can make choices about where we go and what we do, selecting places for their healing potential and not compromising basic therapeutic needs. These places will not, however, necessarily provide us with the level of control which we are used to having over our workspace. We may be surprised by weather, by passers-by, by animals and birds or other distractions. Some spaces may lack privacy or even be dangerous. We have the potential to get lost or separated. Plans can go wrong in ways that we may foresee or ways that we may not. There will be practical considerations which we are not used to, like allowing time to return to base at the end of a session. There may be limits to our physical capacities and those of the people with whom we work that require us to stay within safe parameters.

These different working conditions challenge the therapist who is starting to work outdoors to think out of the box (Jordan & Hinds 2016). Sometimes the transition might involve taking therapeutic methods developed in the context of the consulting room outdoors, but other times we return to first principles and ask ourselves what conditions are really necessary for therapeutic process to happen, and how these can be best facilitated in the natural environment. We may try to balance more experimental methods with adaptations of our previous training. This can be an anxious process. We may worry that we are losing therapeutic responsibility in trying to develop new theory and methods (Brazier 2013) and struggle to find supervision and support for our work.

Not every therapy client will take to working outside and some issues are better talked about in the closed, intimate space of the consulting room. For some, the complexity of the outdoor environment is too distracting and for others it lacks the level of containment that is provided by four walls. The move to working outside, if this is our direction, does not necessarily mean that one abandons the therapy room for good. Ideally the two arenas work in tandem.

Therapeutic working outdoors places demands both on the therapist and on those with whom she works in ways that therapy in the consulting room may not. It changes the relationship. In the therapy room, the client enters a space which, as far as he is concerned, belongs to the therapist. It is subject to the therapist's control and reflects her choices. Outdoors the space is more neutral. It does not reflect the therapist's being as completely as the consulting room might. Even if the work is done in a garden owned by the therapist, there is unpredictability. Earth and sky, birds and plants are beyond human ownership. The therapist and the people with whom she works are all guests of their working space in a way that is much more evident than it is indoors.

Not every ecotherapist starts her professional life in the consulting room, however. As we have seen, for some people moving into the field, the outdoors is already home-ground. Many make the transition into more psychologically based therapies from outdoor education, bush-craft, wildlife conservation or mountain leadership because they find that being outdoors naturally evokes psychological reflection and change.

This book is concerned with an exploration of how the conditions provided by the outdoors, in all their many manifestations, can become conditions for facilitating personal change. This is not just a theoretical journey, however. Whichever field we come from, starting to work therapeutically outdoors is likely to first and foremost impact on ourselves. To be able to support others, we ourselves need to be experienced travellers in the field and develop awareness of the impact of nature on the inner landscapes of the psyche, experiencing at first hand both human and non-human forces of uncertainty, change and transformation emerging from the encounter with nature.

The therapeutic container

Therapeutic change takes place within the context of certain conditions. In ecotherapy, these conditions are provided by the therapist and by the environment. As Carl Rogers suggested, if the therapist offers certain conditions, psychological healing is likely to follow. We have also seen that there is a growing body of evidence that the outdoor environment provides a set of conditions which promote mental and physical wellbeing. Thus therapist and environment collaborate, creating a container for the therapeutic process.

We use the term 'therapeutic container' to describe a set of conditions which are conducive to psychological growth. The therapeutic relationship itself aims to provide many of these conditions and thus be the primary source of containment for the therapeutic process. The ethical framework, time limits, confidentiality and other aspects of the therapeutic contract, as well as the physical space in which therapy takes place all contribute to this sense of containment, which is one of the most significant conditions for psychological change. The outdoor environment can also provide conditions. Some of these are deliberately sought out, whilst others occur spontaneously.

Containment works in two ways. On the one hand, it provides psychological safety. This is achieved particularly by maintaining certain parameters of the kind described above, known as therapeutic boundaries. People with whom we work need to feel held and supported by the therapist and by the setting in order to feel safe enough to do psychological work. Then, when people feel held in this way, the feeling of containment enables an intensification of the therapeutic process. The conversation becomes more focused and so mental phenomena are amplified. Personal stories are put under the magnifying glass of attention and difficult aspects of experience are felt more fully.

In this way, therapy is both the holding vessel and the alchemical crucible in which change emerges. The therapeutic container needs strength and flexibility, space and openness for creative forces to emerge. The stronger the container, the more powerful the process it can hold. In other words, we can say that:

- containment is concerned with creating safety and boundaries
- containment is concerned with intensification.

This section of the book explores some of the most basic conditions which the therapist provides and the ways in which these form the container for the psychological work. These reflections are common to therapy generally and, whilst our focus here is on working outdoors, becoming more environmentally aware can also influence the conditions which we provide in our therapeutic practice indoors. Being in nature changes us and changes our therapeutic style as a whole. Since starting to work therapeutically outdoors, I am aware that my work back in the consulting room has changed. The divide between indoors and outdoors is in our hearts and minds as much as in the practicalities of our practice, and we can, as Nick Totton suggests (2011), take our encounter with wildness home.

As therapists and facilitators working outdoors, we may guide the process but we cannot entirely control it. We make choices about place and activity, but we always work within conditions which arise naturally. We can select a suitable location. We can consider weather conditions. We can plan and structure sessions. We can think about our own behaviour as an influence on the process. We can think about what we say, what language we use, how directive we are, whether we allow things to flow or whether we set up activities and so on. We can observe what people do spontaneously and decide whether to intervene or not. In these ways we influence the level of therapeutic containment. We are, however, always working within the bigger context of environmental factors which, though they may be containing, are beyond our control. Further, we too are held by the environment in which we work, alongside those whom we facilitate, relying on the supportive qualities of natural spaces.

The therapeutic container is important to work with both individuals and groups. Whilst in one-to-one work, therapist and environment together create the container, when we work with groups, the group provides an important level of containment for the individuals within it. For this reason, group therapists often deliberately work to support the growth of the group as a therapeutic container.

Creating the therapeutic container: early stages in groups

In the early stages of any therapeutic group, a number of factors contribute to members' sense of containment, allowing them to use the therapeutic space effectively. At this time, group members tend to be preoccupied with questions of safety and purpose. They draw on previous experiences of groups to understand the new situation, and this may sometimes lead to misconceptions. As a result, to prevent misunderstandings, facilitators often provide a basic framework of ground-rules or facilitate group members in agreeing their own ways of working.

A number of factors will contribute to any group successfully establishing a positive basis for future work. These might include:

- the quality of presence of the facilitator(s)
- a suitable location of work which offers a sense of security, privacy and space
- clarity about the structure and purpose of the group
- clarity about ground-rules and boundaries
- an opportunity for members to introduce themselves and get to know one another
- the gradual introduction of activities which are at a suitable level for participants (interesting but not too challenging)
- drawing on the familiar before introducing new or challenging ideas and ways of working.

Groupwork need not be didactic. Group structures can be negotiated by the group from the beginning, but it is often helpful to give the group some ideas, explanation or clarification of what may happen. The group leaders can also invite the group to think about experiences which they have had previously and about what they would like from this experience.

The group thus establishes a sense of possibilities, based on combination of the group leaders' suggestions and participants' prior experience and expectations. From this, some kind of working contract will emerge, which is usually only partially explicit, and which will evolve and change as the group progresses.

Outdoor therapy as a collaborative process

In the outdoors, the therapeutic relationship is collaborative. Nature is not concerned with isolation and the ecosystem functions as a whole, with different elements depending upon one another in different ways. Similarly, therapist, participants and the environment all work together in the therapeutic process. Each plays a role. Different relational dynamics emerge. Sometimes the therapist is proactive, drawing on resources in the environment and inviting participants to take part in some kind of activity. Sometimes therapist and participants explore possibilities together, investigating and working with their surroundings without a preconceived plan. Other times some environmental process, like a sudden storm, becomes so compelling that the session is diverted. Working outdoors, the environment becomes an active aspect of the therapeutic process, and unless what is offered harmonises with the conditions it provides, the work flounders. Many activities just will not work if the weather changes or unexpected circumstances arise. One cannot pre-plan for every eventuality.

We can conceptualise the containment which is offered outdoors in two ways. We can see the therapist and environment as working together to create a containing space for the participant to work in. We can also see therapist and participants as working within the containing ambience of the place in which they work. These two contrasting perspectives reflect a creative tension which we can see running through the whole of our work outdoors. This tension is not unique to outdoor working, but it is amplified by the context. It particularly manifests in a tension between a) managing the therapeutic process and b) following the process with the participants. More simply, it is the tension between knowing and not knowing.

Certainly there are ways in which the therapist needs to be proactive. She takes the main responsibility for the boundaries of the session and for matters of physical and psychological safety. On the other hand, much of the time, the therapist is responsive to the process emerging between participants and the environment, taking her lead from what arises spontaneously. Outdoors, the working conditions are unpredictable and changeable, so this need for responsiveness is greater. The therapist is not all knowing. She too is evidently a child of circumstance, and whilst she may hold a general plan for the work and aim to stay within her own capabilities for the sake of safety, she may be surprised by unexpected events and will sometimes even be visibly vulnerable, and forced to be more explicitly congruent about her limits. Being in nature makes us real.

The relationship between taking control and surrendering to processes which we cannot control is part of any therapeutic relationship, but it becomes more obvious when we move out from the therapy room. It reflects our relationship to nature herself. We are influenced by and dependent on many things in the environment which cannot be controlled, and at the same time we carry responsibility for our actions and for respecting the needs of others, whether human or non-human. Much of the work described in this book involves groups. In groups there is a complex interplay of mutually supportive relationships. If there are two facilitators, they work together collaboratively. Group members support one another. Facilitators support group members who in turn come up with ideas. In this way, the many inter-relationships help to build the therapeutic container.

The Ten Directions model

This book presents a model called Ten Directions which was developed on our training programme at Tariki Trust to provide a methodological framework for therapeutic work in the outdoors. The underpinning theory-base of the programme is grounded in Buddhist psychology, but the framework of ten elements which make up the model is flexible enough to be adapted for use in conjunction with other psychotherapeutic models. The Ten Directions model is conceived as a large scale mapping into which many of the different styles of working outdoors can be incorporated. It can be used for specifically therapeutic work, or in more social or educational contexts. In this way, it can be used for developing environmentally-based approaches to mental health in diverse settings.

The Ten Directions model consists of five fields. The first field, which we are exploring in this first section of the book, establishes the basis for the therapeutic relationship, whilst the second presents the theoretical underpinnings on which we will be drawing. The latter three fields describe three levels of exploration which are found within the therapeutic process: the personal, the collective and the global. The focus of the therapy may move between these latter three fields or be focused primarily in one or other of them, depending on the therapist's style and the client's or the group's needs. All three fields will be implicitly present in any work which is done. Personal associations have their roots in cultural and mythic traditions, and, in turn, lead to the attitudes and beliefs which shape our relationship to the planet. It has been widely recognised that ecotherapy (e.g. Buzzell & Chalquist 2009; Jordan & Hinds 2016) and its seedbed, ecopsychology (Roszak, Gomes & Kanner 1995), have the potential to deepen people's sense of connection with, and responsibility to, the planet and her environment, and this model intentionally creates a bridge between the personal arena of therapeutic practice, and the larger scale issues facing us today. In summary, the five fields are:

- the therapeutic container
- the theoretical base
- personal process
- collective and cultural frames
- global context and wider horizons.

Each of these five fields is made up of two elements which in some way complement or contrast with one another. The chapters of this book explore these fields in more depth, but it is probably useful for us to take an overview of the ten elements here.

Embodied presence and sacred space

The first field explores the therapeutic container and the means by which it is established. This field is made up of two elements, namely the therapist's presence and the working environment itself. The therapist engages with the client or group in the context of place, and this context, particularly when it is outdoors, is naturally healing and supportive. The two elements together provide the container for therapeutic work. The therapist's embodied presence provides the ground for the work as she offers deep, resonant empathy. The working space, referred to as sacred space, is the landscape within which therapy happens. This landscape offers both holding and opportunities for encounter. Capable of evoking cultural and personal associations, it links participants into the interconnected web of life, inviting engagement with the mystery of existence itself.

Therapeutic triangle and object-related identity

The second field explores the theoretical framework of Buddhist psychotherapy and other-centred approach (Brazier 2009) which underpins the model. The model particularly highlights object-related identity, a concept based on Buddhist theory which suggests that the sense of self is maintained by a process of giving biased attention to particular things (objects) through which we define ourselves, either through identification or by distancing ourselves from them. The theory suggests that the activity of the senses is distorted by our need to self-define in this way so that our perceptual field supports a personalised view of the world. Other-centred methodology is grounded in this understanding and involves a collaborative investigation of perceptual experience. The model conceives a primarily triangular relationship between therapist, client and environment in which therapist and client work together to explore the processes of projection, seeking clearer perspectives on the object-world which surrounds them.

Conditioned view and encounter

The third field is concerned with personal psychological process. It focuses on investigating different aspects of conditioned experiencing within the world-view and on holding these up against the real presence of things in the environment. This field is concerned with the way that personal history, childhood events, family relationships and the immediate context all influence perception. The work can involve exploring personal habit-patterns and the emotional and psychological impact of past events. It also involves initiating direct encounter with the immediate surroundings, testing out assumptions and exploring the immediate qualities of things. This can sometimes be practical or even scientific, implicitly bringing into question projections and personal stories. The field of personal process is concerned with particular processes of individuals and the factors which maintain them, as well as enabling those individuals to find new ways to relate to the world.

Myth and ritual and creativity

The fourth field explores the broader cultural aspects of human experience and the ways in which myth and collective stories are evoked by, and act as, conditions for relating to the environment. Working in this field includes exploring metaphor and symbol and their power to hold meaning in relation to ordinary experience, as well as working with traditional themes which weave themselves into our experience of the world. The field draws on the rich human legacy of mythic, spiritual and shamanic traditions and explores the role of these in therapy. It also explores creativity, both as it emerges from these traditional roots and the cultural legacies of human societies in poetry, art and music, and also as it arises from the encounter with the natural world, which provides a catalyst for innovation and expression.

Vibrancy and embedded living

The final field explores active engagement with the environment and with the planet. Vibrancy is concerned with the experience, use and direction of life-energy. On the one hand this element is concerned with practical considerations such as pacing the work, ensuring safety and inclusivity and achieving focus. On the other, it explores ways in which we attune to the flow of energy which naturally occurs both in ourselves and in the cyclical processes of the planet. This element is complemented by the final element, embedded living, which addresses aspects of lifestyle and the personal impact of impending environmental changes. The way that people live not only affects their psychological wellbeing, but also affects the global situation. Working outdoors, has the potential to raise awareness of our interdependence with the planetary systems at many levels, physically, emotionally and psychologically. Thus, in this last field, we explore the way that we are unable to divorce ourselves from planetary survival.

The Ten Directions model offers a framework for conceptualising therapeutic working in the outdoors. We recognise that we cannot separate individual psychological distress from the bigger context of global crisis, but we should not forget that this model is primarily therapeutic. Its intent is not to promote political activism or raise awareness of climate change, extinctions or other environmental issues, but rather to provide a framework for those working in psychological and related professions. The model recognises the inter-connection of human suffering and planetary issues, knowing that we cannot avoid the responsibility incumbent on all of us to connect with the bigger questions that face our age. It proposes that, by helping people to connect more authentically with nature and the environment, it will help them to be less driven by processes of consumption and alienation and bring more awareness of the effects of these behaviours upon the planet.

Concluding

In the Ten Directions model, the therapeutic container is the first level of the therapeutic framework. It is the foundation on which other work is built. The therapeutic container has two elements, reflecting the two aspects of the therapeutic conditions: the therapist and the environment. These two elements are *embodied presence*, the therapist's own presence as a containing factor in the therapeutic process, and *sacred space*, the sense of the physical environment as a place of psychological holding.

Reflecting on therapeutic containment is particularly important to outdoor work because many of the structures which offer containment in regular therapy are not automatically provided when we go outside. We learn to read the psychological landscape alongside the physical ones to be sure that sufficient containment is in place for a particular person at a particular time to do particular work. Whilst in regular therapy, containment is offered by the therapy room, the regularity of meetings, the time boundaries of the session and the continuity of certain routines, outdoors there is often less continuity, less privacy and less predictability. It falls to the therapist to provide the framework for working and to be the point of continuity and stability between places and sessions.

The environment also provides containment. People experience the outdoors as naturally holding, and across generations and cultures the Earth has often been referred to as 'Mother'. The Earth is the womb of life and the container for us all. Going outdoors provides us with real-time encounters and challenges. Whilst the therapy room is to a large extent symbolic space, the outdoors is real. It will always be there and always available to those who participate in environmentally-based work even when the therapy has ended.

Therapy cannot be contrived. We cannot force the process of growth but we can tend the fresh shoots and provide the best conditions that we are able. Therapeutic process tends to unfold organically and, if we are willing to let things happen in their own time in mysterious ways, nature will often surprise us. Much happens almost by chance. On the other hand, we also need to be able to step in where needed and hold the space. We need the courage to be bold.

The therapeutic container is the framework on which the therapeutic process hangs. It is the presence of the therapist and the physical, temporal and behavioural parameters within which she works. Its holding properties intensify the process of therapy. Its spaciousness allows expansive growth to take place. As we proceed in this exploration we will see that there is not one formula to be adopted, but many; no right way, but many potential paths.

References

Brazier, C. (2009). *Other-Centred Therapy: Buddhist Psychology in Action*. Ropley: O-Books.

Brazier, C. (2013). Sacred Space: Different Boundaries in Environmentally Based Therapies. *Thresholds*, (pp. 5–9), Autumn.

Buzzell, L. & Chalquist, C. (2009). *Ecotherapy: Healing with Nature in Mind*. San Francisco: Sierra Club Books.

Faculty of Public Health. (2010). *Great Outdoors: How Our Natural Health Service Uses Green Space To Improve Wellbeing*. Briefing Statement: In association with Natural England.

Jordan, M. & Hinds, J. (Eds.). (2016). *Ecotherapy: Theory, Research and Practice*. London: Palgrave.

Mearns, D. & Thorne, B. (1988). *Person Centred Counselling in Action*. London: Sage.

Mind. (2007). *The Green Agenda For Mental Health*. London: Mind.

Mind. (2013). *Feeling Better Outside, Feeling Better Inside: Ecotherapy for Mental Wellbeing, Resilience and Recovery*. London: Mind.

Rogers, C. (1957). The Necessary and Sufficient Conditions of Therapeutic Personality Change. *Journal of Consulting Psychology*, 21(2), 95–103.

Rogers, C. (1980). *A Way of Being*. Boston: Houghton & Mifflin.

Roszak, T., Gomes, M. & Kanner, A. (Eds.). (1995). *Ecopsychology: Restoring the Earth, Healing the Mind*. San Francisco: Sierra Club Books.

Thomas, D. (2011). *This Being, That Becomes: The Buddha's Teaching on Conditionality*. Cambridge: Windhorse.

Totton, N. (2011). *Wild Therapy: Undomesticating Inner and Outer Worlds*. Ross on Wye: PCCS Books.

2 Embodied presence

This chapter explores the importance of embodiment in the therapeutic process and its relevance to working outdoors. Drawing on the theory of focusing developed by Eugene Gendlin and on Buddhist mindfulness practice, both in the Satipatthana and in recent work of Jon Kabat-Zinn and others, this chapter offers practical guidance on grounding and body-awareness exercises and on the use of embodied presence in therapy. In addition, the chapter contains sections on different forms of walking meditation and ways in which they can be a source of inspiration for therapeutic praxis.

The fundamental quality which the therapist brings to the therapeutic encounter is presence. This quality is at the heart of the therapeutic alliance and the creation of the therapeutic container. To be present means to be embodied. The client's capacities both to receive embodied attention and to attune to his own felt body-sense as it evolves and changes in the moment, are also significant in the therapeutic process. The two factors are not in fact separate. By observing and experiencing the therapist's embodiedness, the client also learns to connect to his own body-sense.

Embodied presence is vital to our connection with the world. It is at the foundation of mental health. We physically inhabit the space of our life-sphere and, at the same time, experience authentically our inner processes in embodied ways. Going outdoors introduces particular opportunities to work therapeutically with the body-sense. Therapist and client are not limited to verbal exchange. Outdoors, they relate to one another in three dimensional spaces, populated by living things. There they are not static and sedentary, but move about and engage in physical activities, and, connecting to outdoor spaces, also connect more deeply to inner ones through body-based process.

As therapists we can develop our capacity for embodied presence, and also facilitate the people we work with in becoming more aware of embodied reactions. We might do this by offering structured exercises, including grounding and body scanning, by example, modelling an embodied way of being, but also, by simply going outdoors and being active.

Reconnecting to the body-sense

Whilst we have all been embodied since birth, our experiencing is often disconnected from the body-sense. In modern life, people tend to focus on cognitive and verbal processes, not valuing body-based experiencing in the way that previous civilisations have done. A shift from the heart-centre to the intellect as the locus of wisdom has left us disembodied and brain-centred.

Also, the body is the seat of emotional reactions. For many people, painful feelings are moderated by dulling body experience. Dissociation from the body can, in the extreme cases, lead to delusional states. For most people, however, it simply means a loss of awareness of the body-sense. Their feelings are distanced, and they distract themselves when body-feelings arise.

Because disconnection from the body-sense is often, at least in part, a retreat from uncomfortable emotions, reconnecting with it can mean reconnecting with difficult feelings. Sometimes if a person has experienced trauma in the past which has not been processed, body-awareness exercises can lead to cathartic reactions. If you are working with groups, whether intentionally therapeutic or otherwise, bear in mind that body-awareness exercises can evoke unexpected emotions and proceed cautiously at first. Mostly, though, connecting to the body is experienced as relaxing, pleasant and supportive. Learning to be more embodied is fundamental to therapeutic containment, but embodiment is not always easy. We have spent much of our lives learning not to feel our body-senses. They can be too raw, too immediate, too compelling. Embodiment is therefore something which people often have to learn in therapy.

Eugene Gendlin, a colleague of Carl Rogers, suggested that being able to observe the felt-sense, as he termed body-based psychological process, is a key factor in successful therapeutic work (Gendlin 1978). According to his research, those clients who were able to connect with the felt-sense progressed much faster in therapy than those who could not. Gendlin developed the technique called *focusing* and taught people to use the felt-sense, acquiring tools to help them make life decisions and face difficult situations.

Bringing awareness to the body can be a deliberate act. Initially developing the felt-sense involves learning conscious awareness of body experience. Gradually this awareness becomes automatic, however, and the felt-sense becomes second nature, a central part of reflexive process.

Grounding

When I am outdoors working with a group, generally the first thing that we do is to connect with the body-sense. In doing so, we also connect to the physicality of the environment. We usually do this through a grounding exercise.

The concept of grounding is widely used in therapeutic contexts. It involves bringing intentional awareness to the body-connection with physical objects, particularly the floor beneath the feet. Grounding redirects the attention. It interrupts rumination and moves the focus of awareness away from anxiety states, into embodied contact with something real and external. Grounding can be thought of as a way to guard the mind against unhelpful preoccupation, and grounding exercises are commonly taught in mindfulness or yoga classes. Originally based on meditation practice, they help people become more focused and less anxious. Grounding can be developed intentionally, but it also often arises naturally when we tune in to the body-sense in the natural world.

Working outdoors, the practice of grounding holds additional significance. Our contact with the ground is real as well as symbolic. When we walk or sit, we feel the Earth's solidity beneath us. We directly experience her support. We connect to the soil, the place and the planet, in ways that go beyond conscious cognition. We bring to awareness something which we have always known intuitively; that we are held by something greater than ourselves, which has always been present if we did but feel it, and which will remain the foundation of our lives for as long as they continue. The connection to the ground thus provides a metaphor. It represents psychological and spiritual holding as well as literal connection. There is concrete and symbolic meaning simultaneously. Grounding unites the mind–body experience, bringing actuality and image together, conditioning our mental and physical states of being. The process is subtle and intuitive.

Before we can teach grounding to others, it is important that we practice it ourselves. Being grounded enables us to offer solid presence to those we work with, affecting the quality of our listening and our awareness. It also invites others to become more grounded through processes of modelling and resonance. Body states are contagious. If someone is anxious, the presence of a therapist who is grounded and not swept away by emotions provides an anchor. It works in two ways, offering a role model, but also helping the person to relax through physical resonance. Whether we are walking or sitting, our physical way of being affects those we work with. The ways we move, how we dress, and our general ease and manner have impact. It is from us that our clients learn to be grounded or not.

Practising grounding is important. If you have not tried it before, you may like to follow this simple grounding exercise or you can find similar scripts recorded on the internet.

Grounding

Make sure you have at least fifteen minutes of uninterrupted time. You can do this exercise indoors or outside, depending on what feels comfortable. Once you have learned to ground yourself, you can use a shortened version of this method outdoors before you start a walk or other activity. Grounding is ideally done with bare feet, but you can wear shoes if necessary.

Stand still. Feel the soles of your feet touching the earth (or the carpet). Close your eyes and give your attention to the felt connection between your feet and the ground.

Notice the detail of sensation. Feel the sole of your foot in contact with the ground, observing particularly the edges of the meeting space between skin and floor. Feel the gradations of pressure within the area of contact. How is weight distributed across it? Which parts of your foot carry the heaviest load and which are only lightly pressing down? Gently sway your body, feeling how the pressure shifts and changes as you do so.

See if you can explore the texture and qualities of the ground on which you are standing by continuing to shift pressure of your feet. Keeping your eyes closed, what can you discover about the material on which you stand through the contact with the soles of your feet? Is it earth, grass or pebbles, carpet, floor boards or tiles? Notice temperature. Notice damp or dryness. Notice the sensitivity of your feet. Are they as sensitive as your hand?

Keep your eyes closed or look at the ground in front of you. Tune out from the visual sense. Keep awareness with your foot-sense but also bring awareness to your breathing. Focus on each out-breath. Let your breaths gradually slow, thinking of each exhalation as a release of downward energy. Feel energy passing down through your body, into to your feet, strengthening your connection to the ground.

Use your imagination to deepen and develop a sense of connection extending down through your feet into the ground. Imagine your breath-energy as the roots of a tree. Tree roots extend as far beneath the surface of the Earth as the tree's branches extend up into the sky above. Imagine you are a tall tree with roots reaching deep down into the soil. Feel the depth of those roots and imagine them drawing up nutrients to support you as you grow. Feel the flow of the Earth's healing energies coming up into your body from the ground.

Now notice how the felt-sense of your body changes as you do this grounding exercise. Stand and enjoy the feeling of calm and solidity. When you have finished, you may like to go for a walk outdoors. Observe trees as you walk, noticing how they are rooted in the ground, solidly connected to the soil. Imagine their root systems going deep down into the ground and your own roots doing the same.

A grounding exercise like this can be practised regularly. You might want to make a recording of the instructions to help you. If you do this, leave spaces between the steps so that you have time to really experience each stage. It is good to start off by taking time to really feel your way into the exercise through the imagery, but once you are familiar with grounding and recognise the body-sense it evokes, you can learn to ground yourself more quickly.

One way to become grounded quickly is to breathe out slowly and consciously, and as you do so, focus on the downward energy of the breath and feel your body-connection with the ground beneath you. You can use this simple technique to relax and ground yourself in a variety of circumstances.

Grounding can be useful at the start of a session to help participants become focused and present. If you are leading grounding exercises, start by grounding yourself using the out-breath. Tune in to your body experience as you do. You will probably say something similar to the script shown above, but it is best to work spontaneously from your own experiencing. Reading a text lacks immediacy and can spoil the process. In reading, the focus is taken away from the body-sense and people often find their voices become too harsh and the pacing goes wrong. Pacing is important, so practise beforehand as people tend to rush when they are nervous. I usually close my eyes whilst leading grounding exercises so as to tune into my own body-sense better.

Mindfulness

Secular mindfulness has gained popularity in recent decades through a movement inspired by the work of Jon Kabat-Zinn (1990) and others. This movement has described mindfulness as involving intentional present moment attention, applied without judgement and in a particular way. Mindfulness is now being introduced into many settings including business and government, as well as mental and physical health services and wellbeing centres. In the UK it is particularly associated with the work of Mark Williams, Zindel Segal and John Teasdale (Segal, Williams & Teasdale 2013). Mindfulness has been used for relaxation, sharpening awareness, pain reduction, improving concentration, helping clear thinking and many other purposes.

When we examine this Western interpretation of mindfulness, we can see that much of what has been discussed so far in this chapter can be thought of as mindfulness practice, though grounding and working with the body-sense are also widely used in other contexts. Mindfulness involves bringing the attention to immediate embodied sensation and giving focused awareness to everything we do. This includes observing the actions of the senses and the mental processes associated with them.

Mindfulness enhances our contact with nature because it involves slowing down, sharpening awareness and giving attention to things around us. It means seeing trees and vegetation in their particularity, hearing the birdsong, noticing dew on grass or ripples on a pond. It also means moving consciously, aware of where we step and what we touch, feeling wind on our skin and subtle changes of temperature. Being outdoors, there are constant reminders to come into the present moment. If we become preoccupied with thoughts or let our minds drift onto auto-pilot, some experience usually brings us back to awareness before too long.

Kabat-Zinn's interpretation suggests that mindfulness helps people develop embodied awareness and become less judgmental. As already discussed, many people are distanced from the body-sense because they are avoiding difficult feelings such as fear, distress, but also because they feel shame or embarrassment over having these feelings. People often judge themselves for experiencing strong feelings. They may believe that such emotions are weak, humiliating or overwhelming or may judge negative feelings such as anger, dislike, greed or lust because they believe these feelings are bad. Self-judgement often leads people to close down the body-sense.

Cutting off from emotions and the body-sense is functional in the short term. It lets us get on with our lives. It is not helpful, however, if it becomes a habit. When we are cut off from the body-sense, we lose the capacity to reference the felt-sense and live in emotional shut-down, experiencing neither grief nor joy. As mindfulness teaches people to give non-judgmental attention to mind and body, people become more honest with themselves about their thoughts and impulses. They censor their reactions and emotions less and live more fully in their own experiencing. They become more caring of themselves and less self-critical. In this way, mindfulness and self-compassion, a practice also based on Buddhist principles which has been developed by Paul Gilbert (2009), complement one another. Indeed, this self-directed mindfulness functions rather in the way that Rogers suggests unconditional positive regard does.

Mindfulness has its roots in Buddhism and the teaching of mindfulness is common to many Buddhist schools. Whilst some secular mindfulness practitioners are keen to distance themselves from the spiritual roots of the practice, others are looking to these roots to find ways to enhance and expand their definition of what mindfulness is. There is an emergent literature (e.g. Bazzano 2014) which is re-evaluating mindfulness as taught in secular settings in the light of other aspects of the original teaching and I have myself contributed several papers and chapters on the subject (Brazier 2013, 2014). Whilst we do not here need to engage with the various controversies which this debate has revealed, we can draw on the Buddhist teachings to find a broader understanding of mindfulness in order to deepen our therapeutic work.

The Buddhist text which provides the fullest explanation of the practice of mindfulness is the *Satipatthana Sutta*. This text is so central to Buddhist thought that it is found repeated in two places in the Pali Canon, which is probably the earliest collections of Buddhist scriptures, in the *Majjhima Nikaya* (MN10) and *Digha Nikaya* (DN22). The *Satipatthana Sutta* is divided into four sections, the first of which explores mindfulness of the body. This underlines the importance of direct body experience in mindfulness practice. In the *Satipatthana*, the practitioner is given a series of detailed instructions for meditation. These firstly encourage him to focus his attention on breathing, observing the length and quality of each breath. He is then to focus on movement, observing the body in stillness and activity, walking, sitting, and lying down.

As therapists working outdoors we can immediately appreciate the relevance of these early writings. For one thing, the setting in which the mindfulness practices are described is outdoors. The text begins with the practitioner going into the forest and sitting at the root of a tree where he meditates, observing his breathing. The Buddha lived and taught in Northern India about 2,500 years ago and, for the most part, he and his followers practised in the open air (Fisher 2013). Spiritual practice mostly took place in the forest or under trees in the centre of the village, not inside buildings. Experiencing natural sounds, smells and sensations outdoors was inevitably part of the context of these early meditation practices, and, although not explicit, the instructions imply that the practitioner is developing awareness of being in nature as well as simply investigating mind-states.

The sutta continues, describing practices of observing body functions and processes, its anatomy and the substances of which it is made. The practitioner observes the body as an assemblage of elements. These basic elements make up all things. The practitioner thus realises how his body is deeply and materially interconnected with other living and non-living things. The section on the body ends with meditations on the death and decomposition of the body, reminding the practitioner that the body itself is impermanent and vulnerable to change.

Although these meditations on the elements and on impermanence are not commonly used in mindfulness courses, they have obvious relevance for those of us working outdoors. The ecopsychology movement has often emphasised the inter-connectedness of human and other-than-human life (Macy 1991). In my previous book, *Acorns Among the Grass* (Brazier 2011) I gave a number of examples of how the elements meditations and the meditations on decay and impermanence can be used as the basis for working outdoors. In the natural environment we often become aware of processes of life and death, change and dissolution. We will return to these topics later in this book.

Mindfulness is important to creating the therapeutic container. If the therapist is mindful, her presence is focused and embodied and the quality of attention which she gives will be good. Inasmuch as she is non-judgmental, she will not demand that those whom she works with conform to particular conditions or to her world-view. The therapist respects that people function in their own way for their own reasons, whilst at the same time recognising that they function in ways that are subject to conditions and thus ever fluid and changing.

Presence

What does it mean to be present to another person? Earlier, we explored the concept of groundedness, a state of deep, experiential connection to the Earth or to solid objects. In grounding we give attention to the Earth and inanimate things. Presence, on the other hand, primarily involves giving attention to other people. Also body-based and intentional, calm and focused, it is our outward face which others experience. Grounding is a private activity. I can be grounded and completely absorbed in my personal connection to the world, but when I am present I am definitely in connection with the other. I sense his being, the quality of his emotions and he is able to connect with me. Sometimes presence is receptive and non-intrusive, dropping into the background, and giving space for others to work. Other times it is active. It may involve reaching out to others, responding to their emotional expressions and offering something of myself to them.

Presence leads us not only to connect but also to be affected. The first level of presence is receptive. The orientation of the felt-sense is to the other. We welcome whatever is expressed with stillness and composure. We may respond with concern and compassion to the other person's story or feel sympathetic joy at his achievements. As empathy develops, however, we start to notice a feeling-sense which, to some extent, mirrors the emotional tone of the other person's experiencing. This second level of response mirrors emotions and is sometimes called empathic resonance. Other felt responses may be reactive, being responses to the other person's conscious or unconscious process. If the person loses confidence, the therapist may feel protective. If they feel child-like, she may feel parental. This third category of responses might involve transference or counter-transference processes in which historic relationship dynamics are replayed.

In contrast to these different reactive responses, active presence involves intentional engagement with the other. Reactive presence is based on empathy, but active presence is often openly congruent. We may share views, encourage, teach, advise or challenge. Active presence reaches out. It questions, instructs, holds or comforts the other. The great orator has active presence. So too has the saint or the healer. Active presence intervenes for better or worse. It takes a lead.

Working outdoors, a therapist who has strong, active presence can inspire confidence. Many of those working in difficult terrain – wilderness work or mountain-climbing for example – have strong presence, inspiring people who would otherwise be timid and nervous to try difficult physical challenges.

Most importantly, though, having presence often involves holding the space for others. We are present, creating a safety-net without interfering in what they are doing. Although this may seem like doing nothing, such presence is very important to an individual or group's process. Paradoxically, when people know that the leader is around they often feel more freedom to explore. If a leader goes off site, they tend to become unsettled and stop working. Young monkeys cling to their mothers as the troop moves on lest they get lost in the melee, but, once the troop settles, they run off to explore. Similarly, the settled presence of the facilitator creates a held space for the group, but if the facilitator disappears insecurity can creep in. Therapists are gatekeepers for the working space and reference points if things become difficult, but they do not always need to be in the forefront of activity.

Working outdoors, therapists will offer different kinds of presence on different occasions, and different facilitators develop different ways of operating. Some therapists will tend towards one or other end of the spectrum. This may depend on personal style and circumstances. In general it is best to be flexible, and in order to be present to others, we need to let go of our own emotional baggage as far as we are able as this will tend to make us more rigid. In the immediacy of the moment we can do this through grounding, but longer term we need to find places and people with whom we can share the things which trouble us so we can become more at ease with our own embodied process, and so become more ready to listen to others in an embodied way. This is the foundation of presence.

Embodiment

Embodiment and groundedness help to create the therapeutic container. Often in the background of awareness, body-awareness develops gradually over time, eventually becoming part of how we spontaneously experience the world rather than something that we consciously do. If we are preoccupied with trying to be self-aware, we will focus too much attention on our own process and not give enough to those we work with. Although it is good to consciously check body process from time to time, mostly the therapist has only a peripheral awareness of it.

One way of developing awareness of the body-sense is through a method called body scanning. This involves systematically examining sensation in different areas of the body in turn. Body scanning is commonly taught in mindfulness classes, but is also used in other body-based therapies. You may well have done it before. Body scanning can be done in any position. When you're working outdoors you may prefer to do this kind of work standing, but you might also do it lying on the grass. The following script is designed for lying down, but you can adapt it to other positions.

Start your body scan by finding a place where you can lie comfortably. Choose somewhere firm like the floor rather than a bed. Make sure that your body is straight.

Let the ground support you, just as you did in the grounding exercises. Because you are lying down, you will be able to feel the points of contact in your head, shoulders, arms, spine, pelvis, legs and heels. Stretch out comfortably.

First take your attention to your feet. Without moving, take your awareness into the soles of your feet. Notice the way your feet are lying on the ground. Probably they are splaying outwards if you are relaxed. Take your awareness systematically through the whole foot: into the arch, the ball of your foot. Stretch your toes, and feel the spaces between the toes. Slowly bring attention up to your heel and then your ankle. Bring awareness into the joint. Try to clench the muscles around it so you experience some movement and then relax it. Feel the contact between the back of your heel and the floor.

Gradually bring awareness up your leg to your knee, slowly tensing muscles and moving the joint so that you feel it consciously. Remember to breathe as you do this. Then move attention to your hips and the back of your pelvis.

Bring awareness to your back, feeling your way up your spine, one vertebra at a time. Feel the contact between your back and the floor. Tense muscles and then relax them as much as you can. Work your way up past your shoulder blades to your neck and the back of the head. Press your head down onto the floor and then release it.

Now bring your attention back to your shoulders and down your arms to your hands and finger tips, once more repeating the sequence of tensing and relaxing.

Finally bring your awareness back to the centre of your body, giving feeling attention to your chest, stomach and belly. If you notice a feeling, sensation or emotion at any point, just hold it in awareness for a few minutes and then move on. Try not to judge or push away experiences.

When you have scanned your whole body, relax for a few minutes. Focus on your breathing in the centre of your body. Notice whether it is smooth or jerky. Sometimes focusing on the breath can bring up emotions. If this happens to you, be gentle with yourself and let them flow.

After your body scan, roll over onto your right side and then slowly get up.

As with the grounding exercises, once you have learned body scanning, you can lead others through the process. Remember, however, that body scanning can evoke more difficult emotions than grounding exercises do, particularly when attention is drawn to the central body area. Working with a new group, I usually start with grounding exercises, and only move on to body scanning if people seem comfortable with these. If you have not led body scanning exercises before, practise with a friend or colleague before doing it with participants. Follow your own body-sense as you give instructions to guide yourself in pacing the process, but avoid allowing yourself to become so deeply involved in your own process that you get emotional.

The body-sense can put us in touch with the subtle feeling tone of our experience, but it can also put us in touch with our wildness. Through it, we can tune in to our instinctive selves and our animal nature. Animals respond to basic instincts for food, comfort, hunger, sociability, survival and curiosity. Working in nature, we inevitably become more aware of our physicality. Whether doing something strenuous which stretches our bodies physically, engaging muscles and the cardio-vascular system, or being still and quiet, feeling the wind in our hair or the sun on our skin, we experience our surroundings impacting on us in ways that just do not happen indoors. Environmental conditions affect our embodied senses, our energy levels and our mood.

Walking

Humans became bipeds between four and six million years ago. Although the capacity to walk on two legs is not unique to the human species, it has been hugely influential on our development since those early times. Walking has changed our focus, freeing our hands to become tool using and making our faces more visible for communication. It has raised our vantage point and extended our reach. As our brains have become further removed from the ground it is easy to forget that we are still terrestrially based creatures.

Walking is often a means of travel. It gets us from A to B, and we are not particularly aware of the walking process itself unless we go further than usual or have ill-fitting shoes. Other times we walk for pleasure, strolling with a friend or challenging ourselves on hard terrain. Walking can reconnect us to the Earth, slowing us down and making us more aware of our surroundings. If we walk to a place, we feel more closely connected to it than if we travel there by car or public transport. We get a sense of distance and experience the lie of the land. We see the in-between spaces of our route, and notice the weather and the changing seasons. Walking is also used in ritual and ceremony. It can be solemn or exuberant. We walk the catwalk or the red carpet, the royal road or the way to the scaffold. We connect to the Earth as we walk. We also walk towards something. Walking brings us to our destination.

Walking is fundamental to environmentally-based therapies. When we go outdoors, we tend to walk a lot. Sometimes walking is our main activity. Other times we walk between activities, but, although this getting from place to place may seem functional, it is still part of the session. We can walk consciously using the process to ground ourselves or as an interlude to reflect and assimilate work which has been done. We can walk in silence, going inward and shifting gear, preparing for the next activity, or we can walk together, sharing experiences. We can walk fast and energetically if we need to cover a distance or warm up. We can walk slowly, concentrating on body sensation, or focusing on our surroundings, tuning in to sensory experience. We can walk sociably, talking with companions.

Walking can play an important part in creating the therapeutic container. At the start of sessions, after a grounding exercise, we commonly start with a walk to the location where we are going to do the first exercise of the day. This walk is often, but not always, done in silence. It creates a division between the arrival time and group time, demarcating a boundary between world space and therapeutic space. This walk is a small rite of passage. In marking the transition, it changes the rules of interaction, drawing the group together and framing the private space of the group.

Walking as meditation

Walking meditation is a spiritual practice. In Buddhism, there are different forms of walking meditation in different traditions. Sometimes walking is alternated with periods of sitting, but other times it is used as a method in its own right, helping people develop focus and mindfulness. In the *Satipatthana Sutta* referred to above, one of the exercises described is walking mindfully.

In Theravada Buddhism, walking meditation is generally done along straight lines. These are marked out on the ground, using two objects, such as a couple of stones, as end points. These are placed a fixed distance apart – often thirty paces. The practitioner starts at one end of the line, centres himself then slowly walks to the other end, focusing attention on the contact between his feet and the ground. Reaching the second marker point, he pauses, centres himself again, then turns and walks back to the first marker. He continues walking to and fro like this between the two markers, keeping attention on the process of walking and the contact between his feet and the ground. Sometimes whilst walking, the practitioner repeats a sacred phrase or mantra. Other times he simply keeps awareness on the sensation of the foot making contact with the ground and the breath entering and leaving the body.

In general, this form of meditation is done as solitary practice. Even when a number of practitioners are walking at the same time, each of them walks individually at their own pace. Theravada Buddhism claims to follow practices dating back largely unchanged to the time of the Buddha. There are many references in Buddhist texts to the practice of walking as a form of meditation so, although the method may have developed over time, walking with awareness as a spiritual exercise has its roots in the earliest practices of Buddhism.

In Japanese Zen, walking meditation developed a different form. It is done very slowly, usually by the whole community together. Practitioners take small steps, keeping intense focus and awareness, moving almost imperceptibly around the shrine-room in a line. This practice, known as *Kinhin*, creates breaks in the periods of sitting meditation. Everyone walks at the same pace. The emphasis is on posture, the body kept straight and hands folded at the heart. The breath is timed with the walking pace, in on one step and out on the next. Although originally developed to allow practitioners to extend their periods of sitting meditation, this highly ritualised form of walking has now become nearly as characteristic of Zen meditation as sitting zazen.

In contrast to the formality of Kinhin, Vietnamese Zen master Thich Nhat Hanh teaches walking meditation as a mindfulness practice (Hanh & Nguyen 2006). On his retreats, until recently, he commonly led large groups of people in mindful walking. This practice is freer than either of the forms of walking meditation described above. It involves developing awareness by walking slowly, paying attention to the moment by moment experience of touching the Earth and breathing the air. This meditation is intended to be enjoyed, and practitioners are encouraged to take conscious pleasure in the things which they see and touch: trees, flowers and the Earth. The emphasis is on sharing and people often hold hands as they walk together. This simpler, more secular approach to walking meditation can easily be adapted to ecotherapy groups.

Another form of meditative walking is circumambulation. Used in other faith traditions, including Christianity, circumambulation means 'walking around'. It usually involves circling a place or object of significance – perhaps a stupa, a Buddha statue or a holy site. Circumambulation can include repeating a mantra or other devotional practices. The focus is less upon the act of walking itself, and more on venerating the object which is being circumambulated, so this kind of walking meditation is associated more with place than with body experience.

Walking meditation can inform our work outdoors. We may choose to walk meditatively in similar ways to those described above, but we can also experiment with different focuses of attention. We may, for example, deliberately adopt a wide-focused attention, expanding the field of vision to incorporate the full hemisphere in front of us. This can be done by means of a trick – hold your two index fingers together in front of your nose and then slowly move them outward, to each side of the head, allowing your eyes to soften focus and keep both in the field of vision as long as possible. This wider field of vision can be especially useful on night walks.

Another method which we sometimes use is to 'walk like a camera' holding our gaze in a fixed direction, letting the things which we pass move through our field of vision without letting our attention be caught by anything in particular. As we pass them, branches, tree trunks, grasses and so on, all slide past with alarming speed as we resist following them with our eyes. The attention is indiscriminate and the effect surprising.

Other times we walk without agenda, allowing nature to engage us in the 'soft fascination' identified by Kaplan and Kaplan (1989), whose research demonstrated the restorative power of just being in nature and the many emotional and physical benefits which came from it.

Walking together as therapy

When someone is troubled, it is not uncommon for a friend, mentor or acquaintance to suggest going for a walk in order to talk things over. Similarly, in therapeutic contexts, whether as part of an on-going therapeutic relationship or as a one-off, taking someone outdoors for a walk gives space to talk. People are less self-conscious outside and this kind of informal walking can be helpful if they are anxious and find communication difficult.

As groups move between working locations, the time spent walking can be used for sharing. This can be done in partners and can be formal, with members instructed to pair up and divide the walking time between them, one talking and the other listening, or informal with each pair being left to find their own style of conversation. Participants may be given specific instructions and prompt questions to work with, or may be encouraged to talk in a more spontaneous way. Sharing in this way allows space for consolidation and integration of insights and for emotions to be expressed. It also gives participants a space to talk about more personal material with one other person in relative privacy. For this reason some discussion of ground rules for the sharing may be important. It is common to agree that things shared in pairs will not be brought back into group discussions without the permission of the person whose material it relates to. In this kind of walk-and-talk exercise, facilitators will generally not participate, but will keep an eye on the process in case any pair becomes overly distressed or needs support.

For therapists who work predominantly one-to-one outdoors, walking together can be fundamental to the process (Marshall 2016), yielding a multidimensional relationship in which verbal and embodied exchanges take place in the wider context of a journey through a landscape. This complexity enriches the interaction, bringing immediacy to issues which might otherwise only be described in reportage in the therapy room. On the other hand, in established therapeutic relationships, switching to outdoor work and going for a walk with a client can bring complications. Boundaries may feel compromised even where nothing has technically gone wrong. Walking with one other person can feel overly intimate and may be experienced as threatening and uncomfortable. It may give rise to fantasies and feed into transference issues for some clients. This means that the therapist needs to judge what is wise in any particular therapeutic relationship and it is often sensible to discuss the idea of going outside, and possible pitfalls, with one's supervisor and with the client in advance of doing it. For therapists whose practice is established as predominantly outdoors, however, fewer problems seem to arise because this way of working is anticipated from the beginning.

Walking together can feel informal, so it is worth reflecting on boundary responsibilities in advance. The therapist usually takes responsibility for negotiating practicalities, such as how far to walk and what time to return, and for keeping to these agreed arrangements as far as possible within the unpredictable circumstances of the outdoors. They may also need to monitor the content of conversation and the wider setting in which the walk takes place, checking for possible intrusions or breaches of privacy. She may ask whether the client would prefer to talk about some topics in the therapy room. With the move outdoors, however, some norms of the therapeutic frame and its boundaries are inevitably challenged and despite the irreducible asymmetry of the therapy relationship, a move outdoors increases mutuality (Jordan & Marshall 2010) and this may bring benefits or problems.

Moving towards interdependence

This chapter has focused on the establishment of the therapeutic container and in particular on the practice of embodiment as an aid to this process. The therapist offers grounding and presence to those with whom she works and they rely upon her presence to feel psychologically safe. With time, however, participants become more grounded and embodied themselves and experience a gradual transition from dependence on the therapist to trust in their own resources.

This may seem like a move from dependence towards independence, but in fact it is probably more accurate to say that people gradually move from dependence on another person (in this case the therapist) towards a deeper confidence in, and interdependence with, or even dependence on, the environment. We become more grounded and less locked into patterns of resistance and avoidance. We start to trust the Earth, becoming active participants in the ecosystem.

References

Brazier, C. (2011). *Acorns Among the Grass: Adventures in Ecotherapy*. Ropley: Earth Books.
Brazier, C. (2013). Roots of Mindfulness. *European Journal of Psychotherapy and Counselling*, 15(2): 127–138.

Brazier, C. (2014). Beyond Mindfulness: An Other-Centred Paradigm. In M. Bazzano (Ed.), *After Mindfulness: New Perspectives on Psychology and Meditation* (pp. 23–36). London: Palgrave Macmillan.

Bazzano, M. (2014). *After Mindfulness: New Perspectives on Psychology and Meditation.* London: Palgrave Macmillan.

Fisher, S. (2013). *Meditation in the Wild: Buddhism's Origin in the Heart of Nature.* Ropley: Changemakers Books.

Gendlin, E. (1978). *Focusing.* New York: Everest House.

Gilbert, P. (2009). *The Compassionate Mind.* London: Constable.

Hanh, N. & Nguyen, A. (2006). *Walking Meditation.* Boulder: Sounds True Inc.

Jordan, M. & Marshall, H. (2010). Taking Counselling and Psychotherapy Outside: Destruction or Enrichment of the Therapeutic Frame? *European Journal of Psychotherapy and Counselling*, 12(4), 345–359.

Kabat-Zinn, J. (1990). *Full Catastrophe Living: Using the Wisdom of Your Body and Mind to Face Stress, Pain, and Illness.* USA: Delacorte.

Kaplan, R. & Kaplan, S. (1989). *The Experience of Nature: A Psychological Perspective.* Cambridge: Cambridge University Press.

Macy, J. (1991). *World as Lover, World as Self.* Berkeley: Parallax Books.

Marshall, H. (2016). A Vital Protocol: Embodied-Relational Depth in Nature Based Psychotherapy. In M. Jordan & J. Hinds (Eds.). *Ecotherapy: Theory, Research and Practice*, (pp 148–161). London: Palgrave.

Segal, Z., Williams, M. & Teasdale, J. (2013). *Mindfulness-Based Cognitive Therapy for Depression.* UK: Guilford Press.

3 Sacred space

This chapter introduces the concept of sacred space, exploring both experiences of space and notions of the sacred as applied to a modern and often secular world. Developing the theme of conditions, it explores how personal conditions affect experiences of spaces. The sense of home is explored as an archetypal and personal theme. After some discussion of ritual, the chapter concludes by proposing three types of sacred space which may inform our thinking in therapeutic work, the circle, the shrine and the pilgrimage, showing how each represents a different relationship between client and spaces, the immersive, the relational and the linear.

The therapeutic container can be considered to consist of two elements: the therapist and the therapeutic space. These elements work together to provide holding, safety, stimulation and intensification of psychological process. They enable participants to engage in self-reflection and in encounter. Within the therapeutic context, each participant experiences his own patterns of thinking and behaviour. His idiosyncratic perceptions are mirrored back to him both by the space and by other participants as they evoke his habitual reactions. He is also led to acknowledge the reality of others—the therapist, other participants and the environment—as his habitual ways of seeing them are challenged. We can identify a number of aspects of the therapeutic container such as the therapeutic contract, the ethical framework, supervisory arrangements and the wider organisational context, but all are mediated through these two primary elements: the therapist and the working space.

Having looked at the role of the therapist in offering holding and embodied presence, this chapter considers the role of the working space in co-creating the therapeutic container. We will discuss how going outdoors can be conducive to psychological growth and will think about how places in which we work can be more than simply locations, forming part of the therapeutic alliance. Spaces often hold associations, and our reactions to them are both embodied and embedded in our personal mythologies. Some feel containing whilst others carry more difficult associations. Choosing our working spaces well and being aware of their impact on participants can support and extend the therapeutic process.

Particularly, as we reflect on working in outdoor spaces, we will explore the concept of the sacred. We have already discussed how being in nature is widely recognised as a healing experience. For many people this experience has a spiritual or quasi-spiritual dimension. One only has to look at the covers of popular books on spirituality, with their soft focused images of waterfalls and sunsets, beach pebbles and autumn leaves, to see that for many people nature and spirituality are closely entwined. Popular spirituality draws widely on the commonly felt connection to the Earth which has been part of human culture since time immemorial. In this chapter we will reflect on ways in which spiritual traditions have experienced and drawn on this connection, seeing how they can inspire our work, attuning it to themes which appear to have universal human significance. We will also explore some Buddhist practices, looking at how we can incorporate these in a therapeutic frame.

Our relationship to spaces is not only conditioned by the past. The ecopsychology movement (Macy 1991; Roszak, Gomes & Kanner 1995), besides drawing on tradition, has also spawned new questions about our moral, ethical and religious relationship to the planet. In investigating what it means to be human we are forced to look at what it means to take our place in the ecosystem in a more responsible way (Maiteney 2012).

Fluidity and therapeutic space

When we work indoors, using the same room each week provides continuity and creates symbolic as well as physical 'walls' for the work. The consistency of the space provides a stable backdrop against which therapist and client can perceive one another in fluid and changing ways. The unchanging space allows complexity in the therapist–client relationship. Going outdoors changes the dynamic between therapist, client and working space. Outdoor space is more unpredictable than the therapy room. There are more distractions and unexpected interruptions: people, changes of weather, animal life and so on. The outdoor environment can be inviting or scary, interesting or uncomfortable and can change quickly from one minute to another.

Working outdoors involves movement. We use different spaces for different activities. In this, the therapist provides a continuing presence whilst the surroundings change. Instead of the room offering continuity, the therapist becomes the constant factor in the process, providing psychological and practical continuity for participants, protecting the working space, mediating intrusions and facilitating therapeutic activity. Despite this constancy, however, the therapy relationship too is changeable in quite practical ways. Whilst in the consulting room, the therapist is usually seated a constant distance from the client, outdoors participants are sometimes in close proximity to the facilitator but other times, they work with other group members or alone. Hence, sometimes the environment offers a more immediate presence for participants than the facilitator can. As we have seen, the role of the therapist also changes with changing activities.

Even in such circumstances, however, the therapist is still responsible for maintaining the therapeutic container, holding the wider boundaries of the session, and offering a constant background presence which can be returned to at the end of exercises. Also, because a therapeutic relationship is already established, she remains an internalised presence for participants even when out of sight.

The space and the boundary

Working outdoors, facilitators develop an ability to recognise therapeutic potential in different spaces, taking into account both practicalities and psychological impact. The balance between psychological and practical considerations will vary according to the group or individual and the style of the therapeutic alliance, as well as with the terrain in which they are working. As we saw in Chapter 1, the therapeutic container provides holding and safety so that therapeutic work can take place. When the right conditions are in place, therapy happens and the containment creates trust and intensifies the psychological process.

The therapeutic container depends upon the creation of a boundary. This boundary is artificial. It is negotiated through the therapeutic contract, which is both explicit and implicit, and is maintained through a variety of means, most significant of which is the therapist's behaviour. Confidentiality, restrictions on intimacy, role definitions, time limits, frequency of session, privacy of the therapy room, and so on all play a part in maintaining the therapeutic boundary. Guidance on these is set out in the ethical frameworks of professional bodies or recognised as good practice within particular therapeutic models.

In the outdoor environment, the defining characteristics of the therapeutic relationship are inevitably different. Many of the boundaries which are accepted as normal, and even essential, in the regular therapy setting just do not work in outdoor settings. This provides a challenge to the therapist. In his book, *Nature and Therapy: Understanding Counselling and Psychotherapy in Outdoor Spaces*, Martin Jordan (2015) discusses how the therapist who moves out of the counselling room has to take an adaptive approach to these matters. The general principles of containment and safety still remain essential to the process, and counsellors need to reflect on the same questions of professional integrity and good practice, but working outdoors also invites a more emergent frame, negotiated in the specifics of situations as they arise. This organic process seems appropriate to the natural environment:

> everything becomes a more fluid and unfolding relational process. This seems to mirror nature itself which is defined as a vital, relational, unfolding dynamic process. So indoors what may be a static agreement, mirroring the containment and confidentiality offered by the room space, becomes more of an evolving and negotiated process when moving outdoors.
>
> (Jordan 2015, p. 79–80)

A few years ago I wrote an article for *Thresholds*, the journal of the Spiritual Section of British Association for Counselling and Psychotherapy (Brazier

2013). In it I discussed how, in outdoor work, therapeutic boundaries are different, but still fundamental to the work. In environmentally-based therapy, boundaries arise out of a collaborative process between the two elements being discussed in this section – the containing quality of the natural environment, and the therapist's embodied presence.

Space as a condition

The spaces which we inhabit affect us at many levels. Mostly we are not conscious of the impact our surroundings have on our mental states, but occasionally we realise they are affecting us. Perhaps we feel depressed working in dirty conditions or energised by a bright, new colour scheme. Designers and architects, as well as advertisers and planners, know that colour, light, spatial layout, furnishings, planting, building materials and so on all affect mood and behaviour. People can be persuaded to move faster, spend more or watch out for dangers by changing aspects of their surroundings. Whilst generally unaware of these effects, their actions are affected by features which might be dismissed as simply aesthetics.

Spaces create conditions which evoke emotions or associations. Mind-states are conditioned by many factors, including the physical qualities of the places where we live or work, which influence our moods and patterns of thinking. Though this impact can be subtle and unacknowledged, moving house or going on holiday can affect our predominant mind-states profoundly, despite the fact we tend to carry life-scripts with us from one situation to another. We are rooted in places, formed by early environments and re-formed by the different landscapes and buildings inhabited over a lifetime.

Our choice of living and working spaces is also conditioned. The mind tends to seek out familiar experiences. This tendency is ultimately concerned with supporting the sense of identity. We gravitate to places that are similar in some way to those which we have known in the past, and we avoid places which challenge our feeling of personal integrity and our sense of who we are. The person who feels at ease in the art gallery or theatre may feel out of place in a downtown bar and vice versa. Living spaces reflect cultures, and these cultures tend to evolve fashions in decor and architecture and even create landscapes which intimately reflect their values and ideologies. We shape our environments into reflections of ourselves, just as we were shaped by the places in which we grew up.

In Buddhist psychology mind and body are not separate. The mind-state is closely linked to the body-sense, and it is predominantly through the body that we experience the influence of places. Imagine stepping out of an airport in a tropical region and smelling the scent of oleander and frangipani in the air. Notice your body respond to the experience, even in imagination, before the mind can put this reaction into words. The felt-sense is not discerned through reasoning or calculation. It is conditioned by our history and personal associations, which are often unconscious.

Taking people outdoors sometimes exposes them to new places and experiences. This can affect their predominant mind-states. Some years ago, when doing community work in North East England, I took a group of women camping at Keilder Water for a weekend. Although the idea of a weekend away had seemed good before we left, when we arrived at the camp site, the women were less than impressed. They hated the midges, of which there were a lot, and demanded to go home straight away. With difficulty I persuaded them to stay.

Over two days we explored the forest and the lake. Fortunately, the sun shone on us, and gradually the women relaxed and became much more enthusiastic. By Sunday afternoon when we drove back into the city they didn't want to go home. As we entered their estate, we passed an old boat, planted with flowers by the council. The women must have passed that flowerbed many times, but on this occasion it seemed they saw it for the first time. 'I never noticed those before, aren't they lovely!' one commented. After the weekend in nature they were seeing their own environment through new eyes. Their senses had tuned in to growing things and suddenly they appreciated them.

Home spaces

When we go outdoors, often one of the first things we do is to find a place in which we can sit together in a circle. This sitting circle can function as a home base for the group. It needs to be secluded enough that people feel able to talk, and comfortable enough that they can sit there for periods of time. Choosing a suitable place is generally part of the facilitator's role, though as groups become established they may sometimes choose their own spots. Sometimes the home circle will have fixed seating and be used by different groups, but other times it may be more ad hoc and temporary. Either way, it gives a point of continuity where sharing and touching base between activities can happen.

Groups often have more than one meeting place. In our own garden at Tariki, though we usually start our sessions standing in a circle outside the house, doing a grounding exercise before we begin work for the morning, our main base is a circle of benches in an enclosed corner of the garden where we sit to debrief and share experiences. We sometimes also create circles in other places when we are working off site, perhaps in the corner of the field or on the river bank, but these never feel quite as home-like as the circle in the garden.

Meeting spaces are usually more or less circular. Apart from its practicality, the circle is symbolic, representing equality and inclusion in many cultures. These values are transmitted to the group through the rituals of conversation, perhaps going round the circle, speaking in turn, using a talking stick or stone. Such forms connect us to our collective past and add significance to our process.

The idea of home is more or less universal for humans, symbolic as well as actual. Home is contained. You can enter it or leave it. It feels welcoming; an owned space, bringing together those inside and reflecting their identity. Setting up a home base gives participants a sense of belonging. The home base needs to work practically. Seating should be dry and suitable for sitting for longer periods. Ideally the space should offer natural containment, for example under a tree or near a hedge or wall, and perhaps some shelter in case of rain – a tarp or overhanging branches. The space needs good acoustics so people can hear one another whilst at the same time not being overheard or intruded upon by outsiders, and to be small enough to be intimate but big enough so that people are not crammed together.

For individual therapy, having a regular starting place provides continuity between sessions, offering a feeling of continuity and safety. One-to-one therapy may be done in a secluded place like a summerhouse or on a garden seat where therapist and client can sit and talk. Other times therapist and client may meet at a regular place before walking. This initial meeting place does not necessarily need to be outdoors. Sessions may start in the therapy room. For this to work, there needs to be an easy route outdoors so continuity can be held in the move between indoors and outside. It can be good to start sessions in the consulting room, going outside if it seems appropriate and returning to the therapy room for the end of the session. This means that therapist and client can negotiate whether or not they want to take a particular session outdoors.

The concept of home carries associations which are deeply embedded in cultural and human experience. Home is where we have our roots in the land. It is where we start our lives and commonly where we finish them. Home is ordinary, comfortable and taken for granted. It is also the mythic place for which people can search throughout life, to which they long to return. It is a place where, in principle, people feel unconditionally loved and supported, and although for some the reality of home has been painful or disappointing, most of us are still at some level programmed to think of home in an idealised way, redolent with personal and archetypal associations, cognitive and embodied. We want to go home.

Home draws together the sacred and the mundane. Early religious sites were often modelled on the houses of their times, the homes of the deities or of the dead, and, in return, the ancient gods protected human homes. Vesta, the Roman goddess of domesticity, for example, was very popular, especially amongst women. Goddess of the hearth, she was symbolised by the sacred fire which was maintained in her temple by the Vestal Virgins. In Roman times, keeping a fire in the hearth was an important task, and the fireplace was more than simply the cooking place. It also served as the family's meeting place and centre of the home. The Latin word for 'hearth', *focus*, has come into our language to mean the most significant or important point on which we concentrate our attention.

So, as we come into our home space, perhaps seated round a fire pit, we connect to earlier times. The traditional roots may not be conscious, but we still feel intuitively linked to peoples through the ages by the power of precedent. As, in the past, others gathered to share and make sense of their lives, so others will in years to come. Sitting in a circle we connect to our deep humanity and the commonality of cultures.

Sacred spaces

The sacred and the mundane are interconnected. The second element in the Ten Directions model is 'sacred space'. This terminology is deliberate, though perhaps provocative to some. We venerate the sacred, respecting it and treating it with devotion. Sacredness is a quality which is hard to put into words, that is felt rather than defined. More closely associated with what we do not know than with what we know, it is intuited rather than understood. Sacredness is embodied, sensed in tingling skin and the flutter of breath. It is expressed in action, through ceremony and religious practice, walking meditatively or prostrating on the ground. Although difficult to describe, it is reflected in sacred stories, poetry or song, and other holy writings. At the heart of the sacred, is the space beyond words. In Buddhism this wordless space is referred to as Dharmakaya, pure essence, or one-ness, but it has other names in other spiritual traditions. Even names and images are merely fingers pointing to the moon of direct experience, indicators signposting us towards the truth, rather than the truth itself.

The sacred is to be related to. Even when the sacred is within us, it is rarely identified as part of the self. It is seen as the 'not I', the core of God within our being, the spirit that enters into us, greater than ourselves. It is the immeasurable, the infinite and ultimately mysterious force of what we do not fully know.

At a time when the resources of our planet are squandered and other-than-human life is often treated as dispensable, the concept of the sacred provides a fitting antidote, pointing to what our relationship to the planet should be. It reminds us of the truth, that we are dependent upon the Earth for all our needs and pleasures, and that without her we would not survive. The sacred relationship to the Earth has fascinated humans since the earliest peoples committed their dead to the ground or made offerings for the fertility of crops and animals. As modern people we often seem to have lost our connection, yet an instinctive bond with all living things, referred to by Edward Wilson as 'biophilia' (1984), still draws us back into reverential connection with our planet.

Buddhist psychology and sacred space

Buddhist psychology suggests that our relationship with the world in which we live is coloured by the distortions of personal agenda. Our ordinary perception is limited as we see things through layers of projection. It is as if we live in a glass box, constructed out of previous experiences and prejudices. Although the world outside the box is real enough, our perception of it is always contaminated by reflections. Instead of seeing out, we see our own stories reflected in the glass, superimposed on the real objects beyond the window. This is what is meant by 'conditioned view' (Brazier 2003: p. 60–78). It is the reason why, even when we move house or change our work in order to feel happier, we do not always experience the change of mind-state that we hoped for. We often carry our old mind-sets and habitual perceptions with us.

Some Buddhist practices are, in different ways, concerned with cleaning the windows of the box. Other Buddhist approaches are about letting the reality beyond the window speak to us (Brazier 2007). In either case, it is our ability to experience the real world that lies beyond our projected illusions, albeit in limited ways, which is important. Moving beyond the self-preoccupation and delusion which cloud our view brings creative energy into our lives. Stepping out of the box entirely, if we could do it, would mean engaging directly with reality. In practice, however, we always mediate our experience and never get this degree of clarity. Fully engaging with reality remains a hypothetical aspiration which we can move towards, not something that can be realised in an absolute way.

Thinking of the world of reality that lies beyond the window of the glass box in this way, we can start to understand why that world might be described as sacred space. The sacredness is in the mystery of the reality which we never fully experience. We can try to imagine the radiance of a world which would be visible if we could just get beyond the limits of our human minds, but we do not reach it. Relating to the sacred involves narrowing the gap between the actual and the absolute, so, in this respect we can say that all space is sacred space. In addition, when we go out into the world, the sacred speaks to us. Nature can be a voice calling from beyond the windows of our box, reminding us that our perceived world is too small, and bringing promise of other horizons.

Sacred space and embodied ritual

The therapeutic container is maintained in part through ritual activity. This ordinary ritual might include the arrangement of the therapy room, handing over money, starting and finishing sessions and other formalities. These actions are ritual because they are symbolic as well as practical. They provide continuity between sessions and add solemnity and structure to the work. They demarcate a separation between ordinary life and therapeutic space. Ritual is repetitious action, often conducted to achieve an effect. It can be powerful and transformative. Ritual is commonly connected to the sacred. It deepens and develops our relationship with what is meaningful and has the capacity to heal and change us (Scheff 1979).

Some rituals are complex and choreographed, but others are simple and spontaneous. The capacity for ritual is innate, a universal human faculty that is both instinctive and embodied. Although it can be ordinary and secular, ritual particularly offers us a language to express our sense of the sacred. This language of actions – bowing, prostrating, making offerings, receiving blessings and other forms common in religious practice – crosses boundaries of religion and culture, reflecting universal themes.

Sacred ritual is often associated with place. Some places seem to particularly put us in touch with the symbolic, the mysterious and the spiritual. Their power may derive from associations with stories or events. Often fostered over the centuries by the practices of particular religious or kinship groups, they may have grown over time, fed by generations of people. Other places seem to have intrinsic natural power. From earliest times, peoples have identified certain types of place like unusual rock formations, ancient trees or springs, as holy. Such places allow people to relate to the spiritual. Because it is externalised, the power which devotees invest in them can be encountered, touched or even entered. It can also be left and returned to so that the place becomes the repository of the sacred. The holy place thus frees us to be ordinary.

Although in therapeutic work we do not engage in religious ritual, appreciating the power which ritual exerts can help us develop secular ways of working, drawing on the psychological processes involved. Ritual therefore offers tools for working creatively and therapeutically.

Some therapeutic work does draw directly on shamanic traditions, and is based on ritual, often involving rites of passage. Although looking at these in detail is beyond the brief of this book, the forms of these practices can inform and inspire our work. In borrowing from such traditions, however, we should take care not to diminish the power of ancient practices by reducing them to therapeutic techniques. Rather we should respect their origins, and, if using them in the secular field, stay true to their intention of achieving spiritual, as well as mundane, transformation.

Three types of sacred space

Our sensing of the sacred is embodied. It is also outwardly directed. We perceive the sacred in our surroundings. This sense of sacredness can be generalised and broad. All life is sacred. It can also take specific forms. Specific places can hold particular powers. Throughout history people have placed the sacred in the landscape, and have used particular forms for doing so. These ancient ways of thinking about the sacred can inform our work, so let us identify three such forms and explore how each represents a different relationship between the person, the sacred and the landscape. Drawing on these we can develop meaningful activities for those we work with.

The sacred circle

We have already reflected on the place of the hearth at the centre of the home, and the way that both home and hearth have informed spiritual practice. Sitting in a circle around a fire has been part of human life since time immemorial. The circle consolidates the collective identity, a place for stories, shared celebration, and transmitting the tradition. It can host political discourse or social gatherings, law giving or initiation, religious or secular meetings. In modern life we still meet up in circles around the dinner table, in party games, or crowding round the victor on the sports field. In circles we cement relationships, establish equality and create new bonds with one another.

Whilst the home circle is familiar, other sacred circles are valued for their remoteness. They may be distanced from habitation, only visited by a selected few or used on special days; places where sacred mysteries happen or magic is performed, awe inspiring and even frightening. They may be the dwellings of spirits where initiates face trials and challenges. Circles can be places where powerful forces are restrained, separated from the ordinary life, or they can be places of refuge where people can find help. Many of our ancient holy sites such as standing stones, henges are circular. The origins of such places are often lost in the past, and holy sites evolve over time. Pagan sites become Christian churches, but the tradition of sacredness continues.

Circles are also created in movement. People walk or sit, dance or stand in a circle. They might circumambulate a shrine, a stupa or burial mound or even a mountain, or dance around a maypole or a standing stone. The earliest European cathedrals were built with space behind the main altar where people could walk, allowing pilgrims to circumambulate it. Other holy places, like the cathedral at Chartres, have labyrinths which could be walked on special days. Circles create safety. The shaman casts a protective circle to keep the dark forces at bay. The meditating practitioner guards his mind by reciting mantras whilst walking round the stupa and circling his rosary of beads. The medieval church offered sanctuary to fugitives fleeing the clutches of unjust laws. Such practices create boundaries, keeping dangerous forces away and protecting the vulnerable.

The circle is symbolic. It commonly represents unity, eternity and wholeness. We find many circles in Buddhist iconography. The teachings are represented by the wheel of Dharma but conversely, ordinary life, in the grip of karmic forces, relentlessly turns with the wheel of Samsara. Thus delusion and enlightenment circle one another in an unending dance. Zen Buddhism uses the circle to represent emptiness and one-ness, whilst in Tibetan Buddhism the circular mandala, like the labyrinth, provides a kind of mind-map, showing the path to the centre of everything.

Working in nature we can find and use circles in many ways. We can look for spaces which are naturally circular: nestled between scrub-land or trees, secret clefts among rocks or hilltop vantage points from which we can see in all directions, echoing the iron-age hill forts. These places can reflect the mood of the group, offering us safety and protection or space and perspective. We can build circles with stones or logs, or walk crop-circles in the grass. We can create circles of driftwood on the beach or stand hand in hand in a grassy meadow. We can be the circle or we can place ourselves within it. The group is a circle, its process a sacred mystery and we return to circles again and again in our work.

The shrine

Whilst the circle can be entered, the shrine provides a focal point. It draws us into connection with the holy. A shrine is approached. Even when entering a shrine, we still approach the holy of holies within it. Whilst the circle invites us to inhabit it, the shrine invites us into relationship. Thus the circle is the womb, the shrine the mother. Many shrines are places of devotion, where we engage with what is central in our lives. We can make offerings or requests. Some shrines are memorials, commemorating loved ones or events. Thus shrines meet two purposes: they commemorate and they provide tangible representation of the spiritual.

Shrines exist within landscapes. They are often found on ancient routes, on rocky crags or in hidden valleys, off the beaten track. Sometimes the shrine is a natural place, not modified by humans at all. On Mauna Kea, one of the highest points on Hawaii's Big Island, the sacred Lake Waiau was a holy place for native Hawaiians who took the umbilical cords of their new born babies there as offerings to Pele, goddess of the mountain. Climbing to this lake is not easy, for the air is thin at that altitude, making walking difficult. Reaching the lake, however, is awe inspiring: a featureless circle of water nestled between peaks of volcanic rock on the barren mountain-top. Hardly anything grows, just the occasional stunted clump of grass. Nothing distracts from the presence of Pele, spirit of the volcano, embodied in the red dust landscape.

Other holy shrines are transformed by generations of devotees. This is often true of sacred springs. Water is commonly associated with the sacred. Sacred streams and springs and rivers are found all over the world. Iron Age peoples in Northern Europe threw artefacts into bogs and ponds and rivers as offerings to the spirits. Once a place gains renown, people visit it looking for healing or miracles. The original spot is embellished and a cult grows up. Some such places become great pilgrimage sites. The shrine at Lourdes, for example, began as a natural spring but is now surrounded with churches, hostelries and shops selling all sorts of religious devotional objects.

Being close to water can be healing and sitting beside a river gives space for contemplation. The flow of water evokes reflections on passing time, and invites emotions to flow more freely. Sometimes it can be good to sit beside a river to talk, mulling experiences from the past or sharing sadness and grief at recent losses. The water is a constant presence, both comforting and a reminder that nothing remains for ever. Sometimes such conversations lead to a desire to do something to symbolise letting go. We might leave flowers on the river bank or throw them onto the surface of the moving water, or we might devise a more elaborate ceremony. On a recent ecotherapy intensive we made a small boat out of twigs and bark. Participants put small objects into it to represent things which they wished to let go, then we placed it in a nearby river to float away downstream.

Roadside shrines have been created since earliest times: a cairn of stones, a crucifix or a row of prayer wheels. In the past, travellers prayed at these places and left offerings. These days we often see makeshift roadside shrines, ad hoc memorials to people killed in road accidents. These simple expressions of grief can also inspire our work. It is common for themes of loss and grief to emerge in groups and, when working outside, a natural development may be to create a place where people can express their feelings by making a shrine. Once we have chosen a suitable spot, reminders can be placed there of those who are grieved and participants can symbolically and emotionally express their feelings. Such shrines will usually be non-aligned or secular, but they can help people express their sense of the spiritual, however they identify it.

Other times, I have worked with groups who have created a shrine at the end of a workshop. This gives closure and allows participants to celebrate their work together. Usually I suggest that participants walk around the area in which we have worked, each finding an object which speaks to them, reflecting particular insights or experiences which they have had in the group. These objects are brought back into the circle and placed on the ground in the centre or in a chosen spot. Recently we used the foot of an old apple tree, growing in the middle of our garden, as the place for our closing shrine. We stood around it and each person added their object in turn, talking about why they had chosen it. After each contribution the meditation bell was sounded.

Although it may be dedicated to a purpose, a shrine is always a place of mystery. It represents the otherness of the spiritual and the complexity of human experience. Our offering at a shrine is symbolic. We never fully know what it really is that we give or what we are addressing, so, in making an offering, we experiment with our relationship to the unknown. When we are devotional, we explore awe, respect, adoration, and sometimes surrender. We can rage at unseen gods and demand help from the universe. We can express our grief for loved ones who have died or gone away. The shrine is invested with power and can receive our projections or mirror wholesome qualities which we find hard to own.

Pilgrimage

The sacred circle and the shrine are both static spaces. They can be visited or they can also be left behind. The third form of sacred space which we will look at in this chapter is the sacred path or pilgrimage. This is not a static place but rather is characterised by movement. It is framed by places we pass through and places we arrive at, a journey and a route to a destination. Sometimes the greater importance is placed upon the endpoint, the arrival at a sacred place. Other times no ending is in sight, the process of travelling is its essence and the outcome yet to be discovered. A pilgrimage is a quest, a search for significance. It offers time for silent reflection in a changing landscape. This spiritual travelling mirrors the therapeutic process. When we walk, things move and change, walking helps us to think, and walking together in conversation, our anxieties often seem less stuck.

Ancient peoples used long distance pathways, many of which passed religious or ceremonial sites. Some early track-ways have been enshrined in our landscapes as ghostly lines on maps, linking old churches, holy sites, standing stones and barrows. Sometimes they are still visible as sunken lanes, criss-crossing the countryside. These routes remind us that in the past people travelled great distances on foot or pony. Not all early pathways were religious routes, but many were. Spiritual and secular life was less divided in those times. People lived closer to the land and to their spirits.

The idea of the sacred journey or pilgrimage is common to most cultures and most of the major world religions have some form of pilgrimage tradition. Some routes, like the Hajj to Mecca, the pilgrimage of St Jacques de Compostelle, or the Pilgrims Way to Canterbury became established through their links to significant people or events, and though some have been lost, many pilgrimage paths persist to this day.

Pilgrimage is important in a number of Buddhist traditions. As with other traditions, these pilgrimages often include visiting shrines or stupas, and pilgrims undertake devotional or ascetic practices along the way. These can be arduous. For example, on some pilgrimages practitioners prostrate at every step. One Buddhist pilgrimage route covers a 750 mile circuit of Shikoku Island in Japan, linking the eighty-eight temples associated with the Buddhist monk, Kukai, founder of the Shingon tradition.

Making a pilgrimage can be a life transforming event. Although we would not think of religious pilgrimages as therapeutic experiences in the ordinary sense, they create a bridge between the therapeutic and the spiritual. Some people are currently developing religious retreats and pilgrimages tailored to the more psychologically aware, exploring the interface between liberal religion and therapy. Such pilgrimages commonly combine meditation, spiritual reflection and introspection with facilitated space for personal sharing, drawing both on traditional sources, such as the Ignatian spiritual exercises, and therapeutic practice. Those who work in this way often draw inspiration from a number of spiritual traditions including some which have nature-based practices such as East Asian Buddhism, and Celtic Christianity. These may connect with ideas currently emerging in the world of environmentally-based therapies.

Pilgrimages can be solitary journeys, but more often they are made in groups and led by a guide. This leader has both practical and spiritual functions. She knows the route and accompanies pilgrims, giving spiritual advice, support and protection. Therapy could be described as a metaphoric pilgrimage, an inward journey and search for personal roots, and there are parallels between the role of the spiritual guide and that of the therapist. The therapist, like the spiritual guide, draws on her own experience to foresee some of what might be encountered along the way, but also gives those she assists space to make their own discoveries.

The pilgrimage route generally has stages and features. So, in therapy, the image of the pilgrimage can provide a framework, rather like a lifeline drawing exercise, to map out and explore events over a period of time. In this kind of exercise, we can locate events along a route of perhaps some distance as a sequence of exercises or encounters, and use the metaphor of pilgrimage to reflect on experiences and changes over a lifetime, or to review a period of therapy or group process, revisiting events from the past, or exploring possibilities in the present or future. This kind of exercise could be pre-planned or could emerge spontaneously.

Pilgrimage can involve revisiting places which were significant in the past. They can provide opportunities to reflect on memories of events and relationships, honouring things which have been precious to us. Three years ago, when I left the centre in France where I had first started to develop therapeutic work outdoors, I decided, as part of the process of letting go and grieving for a place that I had loved, to make a personal pilgrimage around the site. Over the course of an afternoon I revisited many of the places which had been most important to me. In each, I stopped and recalled memories and associations that I had with it. I felt the intimacy of connection to trees and plants and soil. In some places I re-enacted some part of the experience associated with that place. I chanted in the woods where I had done solitary retreats. I kindled a small fire in the fire circle. I sat in meditation in the outdoor shrine and left small tokens of meadow flowers there. In other places I just sat, allowing the feeling sense of the place to settle in me. It was a cathartic experience, and at the end of it I felt that I had said my goodbyes to this special place and let go of some of the grief which I had at the prospect of leaving.

Concluding

This chapter has explored the connection between space and the sacred. The land we work on is central to the work we do and as therapists we are guardians of the therapeutic process. We hold the space so that the conditions which the environment offers become available to those with whom we work, creating opportunities for participants to encounter themselves, one another and the infinite possibilities for change which being outdoors affords.

In this section we have explored the principles of therapeutic containment. A container is a vessel. It is as strong as its walls and these walls are created and held by the therapeutic boundary, a boundary based both in space and behaviour, which offers holding and challenge to those within it. The therapeutic space is enabled by the womb-like matrix of empathic understanding and the hard-edged limits of congruent reality. In creating this vessel, the roles of therapist and environment are complementary and, whilst the style of containment which each offers is different, together they create a solid and enriching context for the work.

References

Brazier, C. (2003). *Buddhist Psychology*. London: Constable.

Brazier, C. (2007). *The Other Buddhism: Amida Comes West*. Ropley: O-Books.

Brazier, C. (2013). Sacred Space: Different Boundaries in Environmentally Based Therapies. *Thresholds*, Autumn, (pp. 5-9).

Jordan, M. (2015). *Nature and Therapy: Understanding Counselling and Psychotherapy in Outdoor Spaces*. London: Routledge.

Macy, J. (1991). *World as Lover, World as Self*. Berkeley: Parallax Books.

Maiteney, P. (2012). Longing to be Human: Evolving Ourselves in Healing the Earth. In M. Rust & N. Totton (Eds.), *Vital Signs: Psychological Responses to Ecological Crisis*. London: Karnac.

Roszak, T., Gomes, M. & Kanner, A. (Eds.). (1995). *Ecopsychology: Restoring the Earth, Healing the Mind*. San Francisco: Sierra Club Books.

Scheff, T. (1979). *Catharsis in Healing Ritual and Drama*. US: University Of California Press.

Wilson, E. (1984). *Biophilia*. Harvard: Harvard University Press.

Part 2

The theoretical base

4 Concepts, models and practicalities

Commencing the section on theoretical frames, this chapter begins by exploring the role of theory in framing therapeutic practice. It introduces other-centred approach as the underlying model for the book. The chapter then explores settings where ecotherapy takes place, noting that these include group and community based work as well as one-to-one therapy. General principles are proposed around confidentiality, time boundaries, personal boundaries and safety. Since groupwork is a common medium for ecotherapy work, different styles of groupwork are explored including pre-planned, structured, unstructured and solitary working within a group frame. The chapter concludes with general reflections on facilitation and co-working.

There are many different ways to think about working therapeutically outdoors. The environmental therapy movement has its roots in a number of quite different disciplines. *Edge of the Wild*,[1] the annual UK ecopsychology gathering, for example, attracts people from a wide variety of backgrounds including those who identify primarily as psychotherapists, counsellors and psychologists with an interest in working outdoors, but also people from other disciplines including environmentalists and activists, mindfulness practitioners, community workers, people who offer wilderness experiences or take groups out into challenging environments, shamanic practitioners, artists and musicians, people who work with animals or are involved in horticultural therapy, academics and philosophers, conservationists and nature rangers. All of these people bring with them a personal concern and enthusiasm for the environment, practical skills, and theoretical frameworks which are, to varying degrees, therapeutic.

Even within the narrower field of those who practice psychological therapies outdoors, different models of psychotherapy and counselling are used to inform therapeutic work. These models, drawn from humanistic, psychodynamic, cognitive-behavioural and other approaches, have been adapted and cross-fertilised with one another in the move from consulting room to the outdoors.

When we work outside, the relationship to the environment is inevitably a central aspect of the therapeutic process. Whether or not it is overtly discussed with the client or group, the experience of being in a different setting is what distinguishes the work from indoor therapies. As we saw in Chapter 3, the outdoors in effect becomes the co-therapist, and once we expose our practice to nature, we cannot help but be changed by it.

Frameworks for working outdoors

There are many different ways to think about therapeutic work outdoors. Most people who work in environmentally-based therapies have to be flexible in their approach and integrate their different influences in a fluid, multi-dimensional way. The following list of statements show us something of the range of different ways that people think about working out of doors:

- Taking people outdoors facilitates positive mind-states. Being outside does you good.
- Being outdoors provides a particular set of conditions in which spontaneous therapeutic process can unfold.
- The natural environment creates a catalyst for conversation for people who find it hard to connect to others.
- When people have an experience of connection to growing things, it helps them to develop a fuller relationship with the natural world as a whole.
- The outdoors provides a safe environment for building confidence by allowing people to learn new skills such as gardening or woodcrafts.
- Nature provides metaphors for change, loss and death.
- Outdoors we can practice mindfulness and explore direct experience of the 'here and now'.
- The environment is a source of challenge and new experiences, facilitating problem-solving skills and the development of positive qualities such as confidence, courage and stamina.
- Being in nature brings the spiritual dimension into therapy.
- The natural world functions as a transference object. Working outdoors allows us to explore personal process through projective work.
- In nature there is space for catharsis and emotional release.
- There is plenty of scope for creative and expressive work out of doors.

As this list shows, the diversity of approaches which can be used in environmentally-based therapies owes its origins to many fields. Different approaches tend to influence one another, often leading to creative new ways of thinking about the work. If nothing else, working in nature forces us to consider other ways of approaching our therapeutic practice. Because the field is as yet embryonic, most therapists who go outdoors are stepping outside the remit of their original training, and are having to learn ways of working 'on the job', sometimes alone, but often in dialogue with others. The process is, as one might expect, organic.

The map and the road

The psychology and psychotherapy professions have generated large amounts of theory. The fact that so many different schools and models have grown up over the past century and a half perhaps reflects the difficulty of reducing human process to one set of concepts. Despite the perennial desire for a 'theory of everything', the models that we create never show the whole picture of human process. Our understanding is always incomplete. However good our theoretical understanding, it never does full justice to the complexity of human thought and communication. Each model is simply one window through which to look at a wider picture. At the same time, the fact that we have models helps us expand our thinking and see what might be going on in particular situations. Without models, we have no framework from which to begin. If we have no concepts with which to work, we often take a rather impoverished view of things.

The question of conceptualisation and model-making is itself more complicated than we have space to fully explore here, however it is useful to reflect on some of the advantages and disadvantages of engaging in theoretical discussion before we embark on it. When we look at a map, we gain an overview of the territory which is being described. We do not see all the qualities of the land and cannot usually tell things like what sort of trees grow there or how beautiful a view is, but we are given information which helps us to navigate across it efficiently and purposefully. Different maps offer different things. The map which one would use for walking is different from a roadmap. Some maps show particular features of the landscape such as its underlying geological structure, zones of vegetation or historic buildings. If you are interested in wines, you would probably choose to follow a map which shows the vineyards routes. If you are on holiday, a tourist map with campsites and hotels and places of interest would be useful.

Sometimes maps can give us surprises too. If, for example, you live in a mountainous region, you might think that a town in the next valley is a long way away because to get there by road you have to drive a long distance. Looking at a map, however, might show you that, as the crow flies, the town is only a short distance away. This could be worth knowing if you are planning a ballooning trip, or if the inhabitants of the town across the ridge are building a new incinerator, but it would be less useful if you are thinking of driving there for a day trip.

From these examples, we can see that theory can help us to challenge our assumptions. It can give us a more objective way of looking at what is going on because it gives us a different framework to look through. Theory can also help us to look in specific ways. It is not neutral, but is developed with certain agendas in mind. It brings our attention to particular things, leading us to look out for certain features, but it also creates bias, drawing our attention to one aspect of the landscape at the expense of others, or even leading us to see things which are not present because we expect to see them. Theory is always partial. It is a starting point. People who try to make life conform to a text book often find they struggle to make sense of the world.

Other-centred approach

The map presented in this book is based on Buddhist psychology and particularly on other-centred approach (Brazier 2009), a Buddhist inspired therapeutic model. This theory, which will be explained in more detail in the next two chapters, offers an understanding of the way in which human psychology is built upon distortions of perception and selective attention, which in turn are based on a retreat from the existential challenges of mortality and loss (Brazier 2003). This approach puts particular emphasis on appreciating the way that humans relate to reality, how this relationship is conditioned by prior experience and circumstances, and on how reaching a more direct experience of others, whether human or environmental, is likely to be a route to better mental health.

Other-centred approach offers a particularly appropriate framework for working outdoors. The environment in all its richness is populated by a plenitude of others, mostly in the form of non-human life, to which we connect in different ways and at different levels. The landscape is other and so are the trees, plants, animals, birds and insects within it. Weather is other and so are the processes of growth, change and decay. Working outdoors, relationships with this diversity of others can be explored in an immediate way. Other-centred approach has a methodology which facilitates this exploration, and it is this methodology which we are exploring in this book.

Other-centred approach is grounded in Buddhist thought. In this way, it is compatible with mindfulness-based methods (Brazier 2014). Mindfulness is important to other-centred methodology. Being mindful encourages careful, respectful attention in the moment to the immediate surroundings and to the reactions which they evoke in the person. Other-centred approach is also respectful of the mystery of the other, acknowledging that, whilst we can enquire into how others locate themselves in the field of existence, we can never completely know them.

Other-centred approach sees people in the context of the conditions of their lives. It sees the way that people identify themselves as being intimately linked to their perception of things. The method focuses the attention of both therapist and client on this perceptual world, conceptualising the therapeutic relationship as effectively triangular (the client, the therapist and the client's perceptual world). Working outdoors, the approach maintains this triangular understanding of the therapeutic relationship, recognising that the field of the client's perceptual world includes both real places in which the work is taking place and the world of associations, interpretations and interests which have been projected onto it.

As we will see in Chapter 5, exploring the interface between this personal world-view and the reality of the environment is important to other-centred work. The actual presence of the environment is a strong facility in this respect. All other-centred therapy is concerned with discerning, as far as is possible, the reality of the people and things which make up the client's personal world, as well as investigating the client's conditioned view and the way that his sense of the world is coloured by scripts, assumptions and other habits of thought and perception. In outdoor work, the therapist and the people with whom she works are all present in their surroundings and so can directly explore the reality of the things around them. They can thus reach some understanding of how and why things are viewed in particular ways, exploring different perspectives of different participants. This process of investigation is collaborative. The therapist also recognises that her view is conditioned and a clear perspective is elusive.

Exploration of the irreducible gap between the thing which is seen and its objective reality is central to other-centred work. Although coming from a different theoretical perspective, Martin Jordan also reaches similar conclusions about the importance of exploring the interface between the clients' projections and the reality of the environment. He writes, 'I became interested in the space between subjectivity and objectivity and how it can be understood in outdoor therapy experiences' (Jordan 2015: p. 4).

Other-centred approach offers a model of human process founded on the understanding that people construct their world-view based on personal stories, and that in some respects this world-view is a reflection of their sense of identity. By exploring, and sometimes deconstructing, the assumptions embedded in perception, this approach provides a way of exploring people's psychological make-up without directly enquiring into the sense of self. Since the latter is basically defensive, this makes the approach a gentler way to investigate the psyche.

Settings and boundary issues

The scope of ecotherapy is broad. It encompasses, on the one hand, one-to-one counselling outdoors, and, on the other, a variety of group activities which are more akin to community work than psychotherapy in their style, though still therapeutic in their intent. It is therefore hard to generalise about approaches. There are basic principles of triangular relationship, accompaniment, empathy and mindful attention which are relevant to the work in whatever setting the therapy takes place. At the same time there are issues of facilitation specific to different settings. As we have already discussed, we can broadly categorise ecotherapy into three fields, each of which has a number of sub-fields.

Individual work: including counselling and psychotherapy conducted outdoors; less formal one-to-one sessions conducted in settings such as community projects; dialogue between individuals and their mental health workers or other key workers; coaching.

Groupwork: including therapeutic and personal development groups of varying length and intensity; personal growth workshops; training groups and courses; team building exercises and other team-based organisational work.

Community settings: including community gardening projects; forest schools; conservation projects; activities in country parks or nature reserves; nature-based arts; sports and other outdoor activities for people with mental health problems; community gardens; shamanic gatherings; festivals.

Of these settings, some have a primarily therapeutic intent, whereas others are not solely identified in this way, but may nevertheless have a role to play in supporting people's mental wellbeing through being outdoors. In any of these settings, individual workers may find it useful to reflect on their work in terms of the principles we are discussing in this chapter.

Besides having different working styles, different kinds of activity require different boundaries and have different norms in the way workers and service users or clients relate. Whilst no one would suggest that community workers should adopt the kind of inter-personal boundaries that counsellors and psychotherapists normally do, situations often arise in these less formal settings which are even more complex than those encountered by those working in conventional therapy sessions. For this reason, reflecting on the broad principles which operate with regard to behaviour within the therapeutic professions is valuable, and individual professions and settings may choose to draw up their own more specific guidelines on these matters.

Among the things to consider in this context is supervision. Psychotherapists and counsellors are required by their professional bodies to have regular supervision in which to discuss their work. In this, they would normally be expected to reflect on inter-personal dynamics and boundary issues which might be arising. Those coming into the field of environmentally-based therapies from other disciplines may not be used to the idea of using supervision in this way, but are well advised to set up supervision arrangements. Supervision has supportive and educational functions and working with the right supervisor can help you to expand your understanding of the therapeutic process and learn from experience as well as watching out for potential pitfalls.

Even for the counsellor or psychotherapist moving from indoor to outdoor work, a reconsideration of boundaries becomes necessary. Situations arise which are not covered by the usual protocols and ethical guidelines, and boundaries become more complicated. Because of this, the therapist needs to have a strong internalised sense of boundaries which is flexible enough to allow for different scenarios, but still upholds the principles of client safety.

Confidentiality and privacy

Confidentiality is centrally important in any therapeutic work, and it is particularly important to reflect on issues which may arise when going outdoors. Leaving the seclusion of the therapy room can make it harder to ensure absolute confidentiality and privacy for clients. Whilst we would generally choose working spaces which are relatively quiet and unpopulated, unless the therapist is on private ground, there is always the possibility of unexpected interruptions. Even in a private garden, work may be overheard by neighbours or passers-by, and noises from the surrounding area may intrude. This kind of situation is to some extent self-regulating, since participants will themselves be able to see or hear anybody who is within earshot, and will, in most cases, make choices about how loudly they speak and what they say. This natural awareness of when it is appropriate to share sensitive material and when not, however, cannot be relied upon and some people may be completely unaware of their surroundings, particularly when they are highly distressed. To some extent a person's level of self-awareness in this respect can be indicative in itself of their mental state.

The therapist has a responsibility to monitor the level of privacy in the different working locations, to choose suitable places for sharing sessions and to warn people if it seems they are not aware that what they are saying is being overheard. In doing this, the therapist needs to avoid conveying an implicit suggestion that emotions are shameful or that the person has shared something taboo which should have been kept hidden. Basically, therapists need to choose places which are private and contained so difficult emotions can be talked about and expressed as freely as possible. Sharing emotional material in the natural environment feels appropriate and spontaneous, but human factors can be limiting, particularly in urban settings.

In addition to these general risks, if working near to home, there is always the possibility that the therapist or client may encounter someone known to one or other of them. This sort of situation can be complicated, as it can be difficult to walk past a friend or acquaintance without some kind of greeting. It is worth discussing such eventualities in advance if they seem likely to arise. On the rare occasions when this has happened to me, I have offered a brief greeting to the acquaintance then excused myself and walked on briskly. If something of this kind happens, it is important to discuss the incident later, checking out how the client has reacted and asking whether anything needs to be done. In Chapter 11, I give an example of an incident which occurred when I was working with a training group. Two community support officers arrived in the middle of a session and asked what we were doing. On that occasion I took charge of the situation and spoke with them a little way away from the participants, who were engaged in an activity, in order to prevent an intrusion into our work.

Whether working with individuals or groups, the outdoor environment creates challenges to the norms of privacy and confidentiality. In summary, we can address these challenges by:

- choosing to work in places which are less populated
- negotiating in advance what to do if either party encounters someone they know
- being aware of when conversations may be overheard, especially if there are people out of sight (e.g. beyond a garden wall) and making allowance for this.

Time boundaries

Whilst in the consulting room, time boundaries are usually considered crucial to the therapeutic process. When working outdoors the timing of sessions may need to be more flexible. For example, it is not always possible to judge the amount of time that a particular person or group will take to do a walk and there can be unforeseen delays or interruptions, meaning that some sessions may run over. To some extent it is a matter of personal style and therapeutic model how tight on timekeeping a therapist aims to be when working outdoors, but, even where the intention is to be rigorous, the situation is not entirely under their control. Since flexibility around finishing times may be necessary, the therapist working with individuals may need to leave longer breaks between clients to allow for delays or changing wet clothes.

Managing time boundaries with groups can be particularly difficult outdoors, though the level of fluidity which is possible may depend on the type of group. Sometimes groups start and finish in the working space, but other times people meet at a neutral point, like a community centre or train station and walk together to the location where they plan to work. In this case a good deal of time can be lost whilst people are assembling. If a session takes place within a limited geographical area, timekeeping is usually easier, but if the group is going further afield, there may be all sorts of eventualities which slow things down. This means that flexibility may need to be written into the group contract but also that the facilitators need to be aware of particular time constraints, for example if group members need to catch trains or meet children from school.

Working outdoors can also create ambiguity about when sessions actually start and finish. If there is a walk from the meeting point to the working place, this may create a stretch of time which is neither fully within the session, nor outside it. Though this might seem problematic, it can provide an opportunity for a different kind of conversation which is more relaxed. Even though this may be more casual, however, it is still part of the process of the session and will influence its dynamics. It is important for the facilitators to be aware of this and of their own behaviour, and what they say, during this and other 'off duty' phases.

In one-to-one work, such transitions are particularly tricky to manage. It is a five minute walk from my consulting room to the meadows where I sometimes work. If we decide to go outdoors, my clients and I often walk through the village. There is always a small possibility of bumping into someone that one of us knows, so I avoid talking about substantive subjects until we have reached the footpath. Instead I usually initiate a more neutral conversation about our surroundings. This creates a buffer around the working part of the session. I find that the walk actually contributes positively to the therapeutic relationship as it seems to make it more mutual. My sense is that the walking time builds trust between us as we talk more conversationally. I am always conscious of my therapeutic role, however, and am careful not to reveal personal details which might affect the therapy process. Inevitably the therapist working outside is more personally visible, and the client is bound to see her in a more complex way. Conversely, the therapist will also notice things about the client's behaviour that she might not see in the therapy room.

In summary, then, we can manage time boundaries in outdoor therapy by:

- being clear about time contracts and realistic in what is agreed
- anticipating that sessions may run late and being prepared to be flexible

- allowing time for changing clothes or cleaning up after sessions by not booking clients or groups too closely together
- using transitional spaces for lighter conversation or for pair work; getting to know individual clients in a different way
- maintaining the therapeutic role during transitional times and avoiding inappropriate disclosure
- considering meeting in the location where you plan to work
- being aware of absolute restraints on the finishing times.

Personal boundaries

Working outdoors, many of the conventional structures of the therapeutic relationship, such as the consistency of the consulting room and the reliability of the time boundary, necessarily become more flexible. As a result of this, the personal boundaries maintained by the therapist become even more important when working outside as these create the primary boundaries for the therapeutic container.

There are many things about working outdoors which could contribute to ambiguity in the therapeutic relationship, and unless the therapist is conscious of these, problems may arise. Working outdoors may feel less formal and this means that the relationship with the therapist or facilitator could be mistaken for friendship or even occasionally romance. Whilst it can be tempting for the therapist to share more openly in outdoor settings, and sometimes such openness is appropriate and useful, being aware of the effect of sharing personal information or feelings is part of the professional responsibility. Having such awareness is important in protecting the client, maintaining the therapeutic container, and ensuring the safety and privacy of the therapist.

As a therapist, there is an absolute restriction on inappropriate relationships with clients or group participants, whether you work indoors or out. Such eventualities are covered by the ethical frameworks of the professional bodies and by most workplace guidelines. There is also a professional duty to be aware of the unintended impact of one's behaviour on those with whom one works, particularly if it invites participants to have expectations that the relationship is other than just a therapeutic one.

When the therapist and client work together outdoors, some elements of the relationship have the potential to invite fantasies and transferential projections, particularly when working one-to-one. In part, this comes down to practicalities. In the therapy room, there is less room for ambiguity. Chairs are a fixed distance apart and certain formalities are in place. Outdoors, by contrast, one may walk side by side with someone or sit together on a bench. This can feel more intimate, and more similar to something one might do with a friend or lover. There may even be points of physical contact, working together on a practical project or helping one another across a stream, for example. In such situations, the therapist needs to be aware of potential misunderstandings, avoid unnecessarily creating such dynamics and address matters appropriately and sensitively if they arise. For this reason, it is probably wise to meet and assess individual clients for suitability prior to a first outdoor session, being conscious of the potential for such dynamics of the relationship. In summary, we can reflect on these personal boundaries by:

- being conscious of the overt and implicit messages which your behaviour may suggest
- choosing places and activities which are appropriate to the therapeutic relationship and being clear about boundaries of time, place and personal sharing
- being aware of the potential for clients to misconstrue the relationship they have with you
- avoiding giving unnecessary personal information, being aware of the impact of personal sharing and reflecting on the effect of any personal disclosure
- being aware of issues relating to personal space and physical contact and reflecting on the meaning that the client might attach to any such contact
- dressing appropriately for the activity, and for your role as therapist or route leader
- using supervision to discuss any issues which are arising and exploring your own reactions to group members.

Safety and physical limits

Being outdoors brings with it different considerations from those of the therapy room. Much of the work described in this book is done fairly close to home in ordinary, often suburban, environments, so that major safety issues rarely figure. Anyone doing wilderness work, water pursuits or taking people into difficult terrains, however, should make sure that they are properly trained and equipped and have the appropriate safety measures and insurance in place. This book does not address the practicalities of these more specialist situations. In all settings, and especially if children or vulnerable adults are involved, it is wise to do a risk assessment before starting. In suburban areas, this may be quite simple, but it is important to explore the places you will be using and look at potential dangers. In some circumstances, doing a risk assessment may be necessitated by insurance or legal requirements.

Assessing risk involves considering the planned activity, the capabilities of those taking part, the location in which the work will take place, the particular circumstances of the day, such as weather or tides, and any equipment to be used. In addition you may wish to use the following check list to reflect on safety:

- With groups, work with a co-facilitator if possible. It is generally unwise to take groups into wild places on one's own unless one is confident that participants have a high level of capability. Even working close to home, things can go wrong and if someone has an accident, is taken ill or becomes badly distressed, one facilitator may be needed to hold the group process whilst the other deals with the situation.

- Carry a phone and basic first aid kit. Be well equipped. Take maps if you are going anywhere you do not know well. Ideally, one facilitator should have first aid training.
- Advise people to dress properly for the conditions with good shoes, warm clothes, and/or sun-screen. Carry water and high energy cereal bars if going any distance from base.
- Check in advance whether anyone has any physical problems which may affect their ability to participate. Ask people to tell you if they are having difficulties en route.
- Check routes in advance where possible. Make sure that access to working spaces is suited to participants. For example, if a field is accessed by a style, can everyone climb it?
- Make sure you are entitled to use the spaces you plan to work in. Check you are not trespassing and do not need permission. With bigger groups there may be restrictions on using a park or nature reserve.
- Stay within the physical capabilities of the least able participant and well within your own physical capacity. You need to have reserve energy in case of emergency.
- If you are planning a longer walk, identify points where you could take a short cut home if necessary.
- Review activities which you may be undertaking such as fire lighting, tree climbing, swimming or other activities involving water and conduct specific risk assessments for them. Take safety equipment and set ground rules to ensure safe practice.
- Consider getting group members to fill in emergency information sheets. These should include personal contact information; details of doctor, next of kin and any medical conditions that might affect their participation. In the unlikely case of someone being incapacitated or hospitalised you will then have information to pass on to medical services. Such a sheet must be treated as confidential and destroyed after the event.
- Use supervision sessions to debrief and discuss issues of physical and psychological safety.

Styles of groupwork outdoors

So far we have been taking a broad look at general principles behind taking therapeutic work outdoors. Much of this work is done with groups. This book is intended to address both group and one-to-one therapy, but because they are more prevalent, in this section we will focus on groups and look at the different styles of groupwork.

Whilst individual therapy is commonly client-led and facilitative, working with groups can take a wide variety of forms (Douglas 2000; Ringer 2008).

These range from pre-planned sessions, involving exercises or activities, to open-format sessions in which the participants are invited to explore personal and inter-personal process. Different styles reflect differences of purpose, and ecotherapy groups vary in this respect. Some are specifically geared to therapeutic work, others are more focused on general wellbeing, some are educational, others more practical, expressive or creative. Whilst this book is primarily concerned with therapeutic activity, the boundaries between these different areas are often rather blurred. If we look at ecotherapy activities offered by Mind, for example, we find that few fit directly into traditional ideas of psychotherapy or counselling (Mind 2013) and most are more recreational or community based.

Groups may combine different formats, and their style or intensity can be varied at different times or in different sessions. In general, long-term groups tend to become less formal over time, as the group becomes less dependent on the facilitators' lead, but much depends on the group agenda and on the orientation of particular facilitators.

Here, then, are some different group styles you may encounter.

Pre-planned structured sessions

Many groups are run using pre-planned sessions. The facilitators introduce exercises and activities, based on an overall plan. Content will be specific to the group, but sessions typically follow a pattern of introductions and warm-up exercises, followed by the main activities, and finishing with a verbal debriefing and review. Sometimes the whole session is pre-planned. Other times the facilitators use exercises to seed the process, then allow more open sharing and discussion as themes emerge. This structured style of facilitation involves a more proactive leadership style, but facilitators still need to work empathically, giving space for responses. They may then adjust their plans and attune activities to the group's mood and preoccupations, abandoning exercises if they seem inappropriate.

Process-led structured activities

Whilst many facilitators start by introducing exercises into the group, it is also possible to work in a process-led way outdoors. As the group checks in, the therapists connect empathically to emerging themes, listening to the preoccupations behind participants' contributions. They then work spontaneously to develop activities, often in negotiation with participants, exploring these themes through interaction with nature. This style of working demands skill and experience. It is an effective way of working; however, the facilitators need a good repertoire of exercise structures in mind which can be adapted to the needs of the group. The style is organic and gives space for creative responses to situations as they occur. Sometimes the natural environment itself will suggest themes. For example, activities could be devised in response to a sudden change in weather, or the discovery that a tree has fallen over night. Such unforeseen events might lead to spontaneous work or might be overtly linked to themes already being expressed in the group.

Unstructured and semi-structured process-led sessions

Therapeutic groupworkers, working indoors, commonly use an unstructured style, exploring 'here-and-now process' and interpersonal dynamics (e.g. Bion 1961). These process groups are usually suited to indoor settings because by nature they tend to be intense, requiring high levels of containment. The facilitators hold the boundaries and reflect individual, inter-personal and whole group processes as they observe them. Outdoors, this kind of unstructured process group is much less common. Outdoors, unstructured groups tend to be collaborative. Participants may initiate and develop their own activities whilst the facilitators largely confine themselves to making process interventions. This kind of self-directing group can emerge from facilitator-led groups as members become more capable of directing their own ways of working.

Solitary work with group briefing and debriefing sessions

Some ecotherapy consists of solitary activities, embedded within longer group experiences. These might include vision quests, solo retreats or other individual activities. In this kind of experience, although participants may be apart for a good part of the time, the group often develops strong coherence due to the challenging nature of the central activity. Participants might start the process together doing preliminary exercises and sharing their feelings of anticipation or anxiety, then go into the solo period, coming back together at the end to debrief. The initial phase and the debriefing may include elements of group ritual as well as sharing. In such experiences, the group leaders' role is to hold the boundaries and provide an anchoring presence whilst group members are dispersed in their solo activities. They will usually remain in a central place whilst the participants work in separate locations, providing a psychological and practical safety-net.

Although these forms of working have been presented as distinct styles, in practice, groupwork styles are often fluid, and experienced facilitators will move between different approaches over the life of a group.

Facilitation in outdoor groups

Within the types of group described above, facilitators may adopt a number of different styles of working. They may offer supportive facilitation and reflective listening, mediating ideas and negotiating with group members. They may develop themes and suggest exercises, giving practical instructions, setting limits and holding boundaries. In some of these activities facilitators may take a directive stance whilst in others they may hold back and let the group be more self-directing. In all these roles, they have ultimate responsibility in holding the group boundary and providing a solid presence for participants.

Negotiation and direction

Achieving the right balance between negotiation and directiveness for a particular group is important. Sometimes it is useful to discuss ideas for activities with a group but other times the facilitators need to take the lead. Their suggestions may be pre-planned or based on empathic observation. Being able to take charge and be decisive is important, because verbal negotiation can itself interrupt the group's process when something more experiential is needed. The group may get lost in discussion rather than addressing what is going on and may start talking about what they should do in a more distanced way rather than working with experience in the 'here and now'. Negotiation can thus highjack the group process. There are different possibilities to juggle. When group members get into negotiation with one another or with the facilitator, they may be acting out dynamics that are in the group but not necessarily apparent. The facilitators may at this point observe inter-personal exchanges and reflect issues of power, alliance and sub-grouping. Alternatively they may consider that it is important for participants to take the lead. Negotiation can be empowering to group members and play an important part in establishing an ethos of mutuality and shared experiencing.

Empathic facilitation

Many of the responses which we make in groups are empathic. When people share their experiences, the facilitators commonly respond with empathic reflections. These encourage participants to say more about their experience and express deeper levels of feeling. Empathy is foundational to any therapeutic interaction. The introduction of exercises into the group process can also be seen as somewhat akin to an empathic reflection when the activity suggested is attuned to the underlying issues of the group. If exercises are offered tentatively, the group can then accept or reject the proposal, rather in the same way as a client in therapy might accept an empathic response or not. As the facilitator suggests an activity to the group, she watches people's responses and either proceeds with the activity or backs off, letting something else emerge. At such times, there is a balance to be struck between giving instructions with clarity and authority, inspiring a sense of confidence and safety and being willing for the suggestion to be withdrawn if necessary and something else be suggested in its place. This can be a two stage process. The therapist suggests an activity tentatively, but once the invitation has been accepted (or, sometimes, no one has dissented), she changes her mode of speaking, giving instructions clearly, in a more assertive tone. Making this shift from a tentative invitation to assertive direction conveys clarity and confidence to participants. This open-handed facilitation allows the group to become more self-determining, whilst drawing on the facilitator's skill and experience. At the same time, the style is only really collaborative when participants are confident enough to reject activities which do not fit for them.

Co-working

In most contexts, as already discussed, it is better to have two facilitators when working outdoors with groups. Both facilitators will probably be involved in the process of planning the group and recruiting or screening members. This in itself gives them a chance to get to know something of each other's approach and agree broad parameters for the work. If they have not worked together before, it is a good idea to spend time at this stage discussing working styles and methods, planning exercises and attuning to each other's ways of thinking professionally, as well as getting to know each other more personally. This may include discussing roles and how you will divide the functions of leadership and facilitation. Sometimes facilitators will keep distinct roles, perhaps alternating in leading exercises, with the person who is not in the lead role keeping an overview of the group, picking up any problems that arise or offering facilitative interventions if needed. Other times, the two facilitators will work more collaboratively and spontaneously. Whatever style is adopted, it is useful to spend time debriefing afterwards and to have shared supervision sessions in order to review and learn from the process.

Confidence and trust

The confidence which participants have in the group process comes in part from their perception of the trustworthiness and reliability of the facilitator, and in part from their experience of being together over time, and the dynamics of the group itself. In particular, the way that the groupworker holds the group boundary, her trust in the process and her style of leadership all help the group gain trust. Experience of previous groups will also contribute to participants' willingness to stay engaged through difficult phases in the group process. Within any particular group, trust has to be earned, and, as the group progresses, its members gradually acquire deeper confidence in the facilitator and in one another. A number of factors contribute to this process.

Trust can be built in a number of ways. This often requires holding a balance. It helps if members can share feelings about planned activities before doing them, but if too long is spent talking about risks and anxieties, people may just get more nervous. Participants are generally more confident if they have clear instructions about what they have to do and know that there is going to be debriefing afterward. These practicalities are important, in part because they show that the therapist knows what she is doing. It is reassuring to know where to go, what to do, how long is available for an exercise and to have the right equipment provided. These details show that things have been thought through and planned. Knowing emergency procedures also helps. Other factors which we have already discussed, like assertiveness and clear boundaries are also important in inspiring trust. Confidence, however, is largely built up through experience and getting to know each other, so groups need to be introduced to more challenging situations in easier steps, allowing time for inter-personal trust to develop.

Note

1 https://wildgathering.wordpress.com/

References

Bion, W. (1961). *Experiences in Groups*. London: Tavistock.

Brazier, C. (2003). *Buddhist Psychology*. London: Constable.

Brazier, C. (2009). *Other-Centred Therapy: Buddhist Psychology in Action*. Ropley: O-Books.

Brazier, C. (2014). Beyond Mindfulness: An Other-Centred Paradigm. In M. Bazzano (Ed.), *After Mindfulness: New Perspectives on Psychology and Meditation* (pp. 23–36). London: Palgrave Macmillan.

Douglas, T. (2000). *Basic Groupwork* (2nd ed). London: Routledge.

Jordan, M. (2015). *Nature and Therapy: Understanding Counselling and Psychotherapy in Outdoor Spaces*. London: Routledge.

Mind. (2013). *Feeling Better Outside, Feeling Better Inside: Ecotherapy for Mental Wellbeing, Resilience and Recovery*. London: Mind.

Ringer, M. (2008). *Group Action: The Dynamics of Groups in Therapeutic, Educational and Corporate Settings*. London: Jessica Kingsley.

5 Object-related identity

This chapter focuses on Buddhist psychological concepts of conditionality and identity formation. Drawing on the teaching of The Four Noble Truths, it shows how processes of clinging and attachment arise in response to perceptual objects. These power (*rupa*) objects influence mind-states and maintain the sense of self by upholding a distorted world-view. This process of identity formation is basically defensive, fundamentally driven by existential fears of impermanence. The chapter continues by exploring the three types of attachment, known in Buddhism as greed, hate and delusion, or, in therapeutic language, clinging, aversive and ambivalent. These operate at both personal and collective levels. The chapter concludes by explaining the importance of impermanence in giving space for change and growth.

According to Buddhist psychology, the mind is conditioned by the objects to which it gives attention. Put more simply, this means that our mentality is closely linked to our surroundings and particularly to the habits of attention which we have developed over a lifetime. We are intimately connected with our environment, but, more accurately, we are intimately connected to the things in that environment to which we give our attention.

Working outdoors has positive effects on our mental states not least because we are surrounded by nature (Wilson 1984). Exposure to the abundance of growing and living things itself creates conditions for the mind to settle and become more wholesomely based (Nyanasobhano 1998). In this way, being outdoors can be a significant way of re-training habits of attention, leading to lifestyle changes and changes in the sense of self.

Attention is sense-based. It is made up of the moment by moment activity of eyes, ears, body-sense, taste, smell and imagination. What we experience through our senses conditions our way of thinking at any given time and this in turn conditions our sense of self (Harvey 1995; Brazier 2003).

Continuity and change

The process whereby the senses condition the sense of self is not as fluid as it sounds. If it were, we would change moment by moment and have no feeling of constancy in our being. This is because identity is based on habits of perception, and perception itself is conditioned by the person's sense of identity. We tend to choose surroundings which are supportive to our sense of who we are, and to view things in habitual ways according to our interests and preoccupations. If I think of myself as someone who loves the outdoors, my attention will gravitate to birds in the hedgerow and the play of light on the river. If I see myself as a cityite, I probably just see mud and stinging nettles. In this way, whichever identity I adhere to, I am likely to reinforce it even though I might be walking in the same meadow. The senses, the organs of perception, work in a mutually conditioning relationship with the sense of self, continually bringing it into being anew. This process is known, in Buddhist terminology, as 'becoming'. Through the preferential grasping of our senses at particular sensory experiences, we, as we understand ourselves to be, come into being. The process is cyclical. It draws on a repertoire of habits of attention and behaviour which we have built up over a long period of time and provides consistency in how we experience things and also in how we appear to others.

There are other conditions which provide continuity in our lives. Our genetic make-up remains more or less constant throughout life. We commonly associate with the same people over long periods of time and may live and work in the same places for years. We mostly stay within the cultures that we are born into; we speak the same language and are subject to many of the same influences. The continuity in these practical conditions also makes it likely that we will behave consistently and that many aspects of how we experience the world will continue over long periods of time.

On the other hand, other conditions are changeable. We change jobs, move house, have new friends, new partners, new babies. We grow up and become adult. We get sick and we age. We are affected by changes that happen around us, and we make changes for ourselves. In addition to these external changes, our inner worlds change too. Sometimes our psychological make-up evolves almost imperceptibly and our predominant moods and views shift gradually as we develop maturity. Other times, a sudden event like a death or redundancy can rock the foundations of everything which is familiar to us.

Buddhist psychology suggests that most of who we think we are is illusory and subject to change (Brazier 2003). In different circumstances we behave differently, feel differently and even hold different views of our surroundings. As life moves on, there is both continuity and change in our sense of self.

Nor is the identity as monolithic as we may think, even in the short term. Within the same day or week, there are shifts in the sense of self as we move from one area of our life to another. A person may behave quite differently at work, at home and when out socialising with friends. In some circumstances he may feel cool and confident. In other circumstances, he may be nervous and hesitant. For example, many people find that when they go into their parents' home, they regress to earlier ways of thinking and behaving. We feel and behave differently at work and on holiday, with friends and with our families. These can all be seen as different identities, each conditioned by a different set of circumstances.

Some of these differences are intentional and obvious. People dress differently at work from how they do at home. They may be task-focused and efficient in the office but disorganised with personal papers. Other differences are more subtle. A person may express different opinions when talking with work colleagues from those he expresses over the dinner table with friends and family, but he is probably unaware that he is adopting different viewpoints on these different occasions. Whilst it is true that many of us intentionally adjust our comments to audience and circumstances, changes of tone and of the views we express also happen automatically as we move between roles and settings. We tend to think about issues and see situations differently depending on which hat we are wearing, and whilst some changes are made deliberately in order to fit into our social or work groups, many happen spontaneously because we actually think differently in different settings.

Susan is a social worker. One evening she gets into conversation with a neighbour, Jane. Jane is a friend. She is very critical of the family across the road whose garden has been neglected all summer. Susan has never particularly noticed the mess in the garden before, but after the conversation she starts to feel very irritated by it. The man who lived at the house left earlier in the year, but there is no excuse for not picking up the rubbish which is blowing around. The woman is lazy. The rest of the street should not have to look at all that litter and weeds all the time! Susan goes home and complains to her husband about the situation. She says she intends to speak to the council.

In her work, Susan sees many families who live in difficult circumstances. In fact, she probably did not notice the state of the garden opposite because it is far less messy than most of the gardens in the area where she works. At work she is often ribbed by colleagues for being too soft-hearted, but she is always quick to point out that the people she supports have had awful life experiences and that those who are better off should be more understanding.

Susan's view of the family who live opposite her seems inconsistent with her usual sympathetic style, but she is not unusual. We all have different views on different occasions and are influenced by the views of the people around us. Our opinions are conditioned by circumstances and by the particular identity which we are wearing at a particular time.

Attachment, objects, behaviour and identity

The sense of identity is closely related to our sense of the world (Brazier 2009). In Buddhist psychology the conditioned nature of perception is referred to in terms of patterns of 'attachment'. When we talk about attachment in the Buddhist sense, we are talking about the way that people are attracted to things which support their sense of self and the way that the mind tends to grasp onto these things and even, in extreme cases, become obsessed with them. Craving and clinging (or their opposites, denial and rejection) are the mechanisms by which a person engages with the world around him and thus biases his experiencing of it. My sense of who I am depends upon, and is reflected in, the mundane things with which I surround myself, like clothing, the furnishing of my home, food and drink and other aspects of my lifestyle, as much as it does on enduring character traits, although the two are closely linked. In Buddhist jargon we call these things which draw our attention *objects*. They make up a personal world or 'self-world', giving us a sense of security and continuity. Objects can be things, people, places, or ideas. We say that the sense of self is object-related because identity depends on objects.

One aspect of the process which is being described here is that our relationship to objects is based either on grasping or rejecting reactions. Our attention is drawn to objects either because we feel identified with them or because we define ourselves as being different from them. By reacting positively or negatively to objects, we create positive or negative forms of attachment to them. Attachment can also have an ambivalent or neutral form when our attention is hooked by something which we have neutral or confused feelings about. We are not sure if we like it or not, but we still cannot stop thinking about it. Ambivalence can be the strongest form of attachment. According to Buddhist psychology, the process of attachment arises out of our reactions to the world. It has three possible types: attraction, aversion and neutrality. These three ways of relating to the world are sometimes called *the three poisons*, traditionally translated as 'greed, hate and delusion'.

The particular set of attachments which a person has evolves over time, and varies from place to place, but broadly people seek out and create attachments which are similar to those which have been important to them in the past. As they react to these familiar objects, their behaviour tends to follow patterns which repeat behavioural patterns from the past. Through our behaviour, we engage with the object world. We buy things. We eat things. We think about things. We throw things away. We are drawn to certain types of people or we dislike others and avoid them, based on past acquaintances. Our behaviour is thus rooted in, and conditioning of, our sense of identity in the same way as our perceptions are. Much of it is connected one way or another to consumption or hostility. These patterns of attraction and aversion play out in human relationships but also in our relationships with the natural world and with planetary resources.

The process of attachment is cyclical. We perceive something. We react to it. The resulting action leads to the formation of identity. That leads us to experience other things in similar ways. Sense-relationships to objects, our experience in the world, our reactions and the sense of self are mutually conditioning. Attachment behaviours define the boundaries of our sense of identity, dividing experience into 'like me' and 'not like me'. For the most part these processes are unconscious, subtle and omni-present, but occasionally particular objects become so strongly identified with, or dis-identified with, that we become aware of our attachment processes.

The power of objects: *rupa* and identification

Objects which define our sense of identity have power for us. We need them to support our sense of who we are, and without some familiar objects around us we can feel lost and alienated. The Sanskrit word *rupa* describes the power in which objects have to condition our sense of identity. Sometimes translated as 'perceived form', or simply 'form', *rupa* is the colouration which we give to experience when we perceive things in a conditioned way.

Rupa qualities are linked to the process of selective perception by which our attention is drawn to one thing and not to another. *Rupa* can even result in distorted perception whereby we mistake some things for things that they are not or elaborate what we are seeing to fit our expectations. The human mind is basically lazy. Perception takes shortcuts, and, instead of looking afresh at the things in front of us, we tend to jump to conclusions about them and see what we expect to see. We construct our vision based on the blue-prints which we already have in our heads.

Recently I was walking with some friends by the River Soar. We stopped in the water meadows, looking over a barbed wire fence at the field beyond. We noticed that in the distance there was a round object, curled up on the grass beneath the tree. It was in the field where we often see rabbits, but my impression was that this animal did not have the shape of a rabbit or move in the way that one would expect a rabbit to. It was too rounded. Pointing to it, I whispered to the person who was standing next to me that I thought it must be a hedgehog. We both watched intently, keeping as quiet as we could so as not to disturb it.

As we watched, the hedgehog started to snuffle around. It seemed to be looking for food. I felt quite excited, for I had not seen a hedgehog in that field before. I am particularly fond of hedgehogs and have memories from childhood of finding them in the garden or in the long grass of the field behind the house. I was always excited if I did. I would befriend them, even if I did sometimes find their fleas crawling in my clothes afterwards. I loved picking them up and holding them, feeling the undulating rows of prickles, wriggling as I touched them, and looking at their funny little snouts and bright eyes, and their hairy underbellies. I loved the way they curled up and then gradually unwrapped themselves again. Mostly they did not seem particularly frightened of me, unlike other wild animals, and were remarkably accommodating of my interest. As an adult, I am more respectful of the hedgehog's autonomy, but as a child I assumed they were happy to be held, so long as I did it properly.

As I watched this hedgehog, however, something must have made me doubt what I saw. It was far enough away that, although I thought I could see the shape of its snout, it was difficult to really be sure what we were looking at. I wanted to get closer, so I climbed over the locked gate and crossed the field towards it. The others followed. As I got nearer, it was clear that I was right. It was not a hedgehog at all. The shape was too regular and spherical and, now that I was closer to it, it did not appear to be moving after all. I realised that what I was approaching was in fact a football. It must have been washed up in the meadow by recent floods. I smiled as I ran towards it, amused that my mind had invented an animal out of a child's ball.

As I ran, I also realised that I had a huge resistance to kicking my imaginary hedgehog. Whilst my brain told me that it was a ball, I still felt the hedgehog-ness of it and a part of me could not bear the thought of hurting it. By the time I got there, however, this feeling had largely worn off, and I finally exorcised the ghostly fantasy by sending the ball spinning drunkenly across the field towards my companions, who by now had also seen what it really was. We all laughed at the way that our imaginations had run away with the idea of the hedgehog.

Once an idea establishes itself in our minds, we start to embroider it. We build stories based on our expectations and on previous experiences. The mind receives basic information from the eyes and elaborates it, drawing on things we have seen before. It fills in the gaps between small pieces of information and creates a plausible story out of them, and usually we settle for this, unless new perceptions force us to revise our interpretations.

We see what we expect to see. When we believed that we were looking at an animal, my companions and I became sure that we saw movement. We interpreted this movement as hedgehog behaviour. Believing the hedgehog story, we looked for evidence to confirm our assumptions, using the rather ambiguous visual evidence. Despite the fact that we could not really tell what we were looking at, we needed an explanation of what we saw and became convinced by our perceptions. This sort of thing happens all the time. The mind shapes what it perceives to create plausible fictions about the world, and, in some way, those fictions support stories about who we are. For a few minutes in that field I was the hedgehog-rescuer again, just as I had been as a child. Until I was proved wrong, the imaginary hedgehog, object of my attention, confirmed my story to me. In the process it drew out a whole lot of associated memories which I never normally think about. I was the person who had loved nature since childhood. I was the one who loved the Mrs Tiggiwinkle friendliness of hedgehogs. I was bold. I was playful. I was the kind of person who would climb a gate to look for adventures.

In this way, the experience reflected aspects of my everyday sense of self, but also drew nuances from the past. We continually adjust our experience of the world around us to fit with our expectations, and also adjust our sense of self to reflect what we experience. Most of the time we have no idea that we are doing this, but, rather, carry on with our lives, projecting our personal stories onto our surroundings whilst assuming that we see the world as it is. In this case, however, I was found out.

Rupa and not seeing

When we saw the hedgehog, my companions and I saw something which was later proved not to exist. Commonly, however, the process of perception, seeing everything as *rupa*, has the opposite effect and prevents us experiencing things as they really are. The lazy mind glosses over everything which does not support the sense of identity and our perception of the world is abridged; a selective viewing, based on expectation rather than actuality. If we go to the same place time after time, we stop noticing the detail of it because we think we know what it looks like. It is only when something is altered that we might notice a difference. Even then we may only have a vague impression that something has changed, but may not be able to say what.

Memory is also unreliable. If you think about a place that you once knew well, such as your parents' garden when you were a child, you probably feel that you remember it vividly. If, however, somebody asks you about things which did not interest you at the time, like, say, the way that your father staked tomatoes or the arrangement of panes of glass in the greenhouse, unless there was a strong reason to recall it, the likelihood is that you will not be able to remember. Mostly our memories are limited impressions and sometimes we get it wrong altogether.

The other day I was visiting a friend who had recently moved into a nursing home. It was my second visit, but this time I noticed the wallpaper in her room. I had obviously not given it much attention the first time. It was a dull ochre yellow colour with a subtle pattern of flowers. I commented that I liked it and that I thought I recognised it, but could not be sure. It was only when I got home that I realised that it was actually the same design as the wallpaper in my own living room. Despite having chosen and hung the paper myself, I had forgotten its design and, although I saw it every day, did not recognise it in another context.

In other-centred therapy we take a lot of interest in the relationship between conditioned perception, *rupa*, and the reality onto which we impose this conditioned view (Brazier 2009). *Rupa* colouration is idiosyncratic, reflecting the individual mentality and the sense of self. Changing the way people see things can have a powerful psychological impact on them and on their relationships. Working outdoors, we invite people to look more closely and question their perceptions. In the succeeding chapters we will explore methods for challenging habitual and limited ways of seeing the world and bringing different things into focus. Because the cycles of nature are dynamic and unpredictable, if people are encouraged to look at them in detail, they will find a constant source of new experiences. This is personally enriching, and is also likely to influence interests and lifestyle in ways that will be positive for the environment.

Why do we distort perception?

Whilst in practice our view of the world is always coloured, we know that, at least in theory, there is a reality beyond our projections and assumptions. Our experience is limited and distorted by the processes which we have been describing, but in principle one could see the world without those limitations and distortions. So why does the mind distort our view of things? We have already seen that the process of distortion is in some way connected to the processes of identity building and that it supports our sense of self, but why is this so necessary?

According to Buddhist psychology, the drive to distort perception is strong because it creates an illusion of permanence. Our mental processes of clinging and attachment and the way we build identity on these foundations are driven by existential fears. We are frightened of losing the things we hold dear, and ultimately of our own vulnerability and mortality. Life is short and the likelihood of illness or accident happening to ourselves or to those we love within a foreseeable time scale is high. Living with this knowledge is unsettling and mostly humans push away their anxieties and live in a degree of denial. Even if we think we have accepted these things at a rational level, we are probably keeping a degree of psychological separation from them in order to get on with our everyday lives.

At a social level, existential fears lead people to distance themselves from the immediacy of nature, insulating themselves from direct encounter with an ecosystem which is based on cycles of birth, growth, death and decay. In urban lives, it is much easier to hide these realities. Living in cities, we can imagine ourselves immune to the forces of life and death and we can create artificial worlds which support a sense of continuity and reliability. We control our light and warmth, water supplies and food and we live in buildings which mitigate the worst effects of weather. We employ other people to manage our sickness and old age and thus we avoid recognising our own mortality as far as possible. At a personal level, we manage our minds by controlling the influences that our senses have on them and limiting our contact with those outside our immediate culture.

The process of identity-building previously described distorts our experience in such a way that we do not have to face the reality of impermanence on a moment by moment basis. We have a sense of personal continuity and gloss over the small changes that happen to us all the time. Whilst we cannot avoid knowing about some losses which we experience, most of the time, psychologically as well as practically, we create an illusion of security by clinging to a stable view both of ourselves and of the things around us. Identity creates the illusion that we are permanent, and though we may accept our mortality in theory, at a feeling level, our sense of personal continuity reassures us that we are in fact immutably permanent. Identity is a shield against the painful things in life. These painful things are referred to in Buddhism by the Sanskrit word, *dukkha*.

In explaining Buddhist psychology, we sometimes use Sanskrit terms so as to be precise in what we are saying. The process of self-building which we have been describing is called *bhava*. Literally this means 'becoming'. The self comes into being. We find this process described in a Buddhist teaching called The Four Noble Truths. This teaching sets out a framework of four steps, or truths (e.g. Gethin 1998, Harvey 2009), which describe the way that people can change their response to *dukkha*. In the second of these steps, the process of self-building is addressed. When we encounter something that is painful or frightening, we experience craving, and this craving leads us to cling to particular objects or experiences. The third step of the teaching is then concerned with stopping or relinquishment. Although there are some variations of interpretation of this step, in terms of Buddhist psychology, the most useful understanding of the teaching suggests that we need to relinquish craving (Brazier 2003; Batchelor 2010).

The description of the second Noble Truth includes three Sanskrit words: *kama, bhava, vibhava* and these three terms gives us the outline of the process of attachment and self-formation. Initially we respond to *dukkha* as we have already described, by craving and attachment to the object-world through one of the senses (*kama*), but gradually the repetition of these sense-attachments forms behavioural and perceptual patterns with which we identify, creating the sense of self (*bhava*). If this process breaks down and more problems arise, we then turn to non-becoming (*vibhava*), seeking oblivion and even annihilation to cope with our feelings of despair (Brazier 2003). Buddhist psychology sees the identity as constructed and delusional (Harvey 1995), but in the everyday course of things, at a mundane level, our sense of identity facilitates our involvement in the ordinary things of life. Advanced spiritual practitioners might seek to overcome attachments and desires, but for most people these forms of clinging only really cause problems when they become compulsive.

Our attachment to objects is initiated through a process of reactivity. Reaction (*vedana*) helps us dissipate the energy which arises when we are anxious, and particularly when we are in touch with our existential vulnerability. Although *vedana* only has three forms, pleasant, unpleasant or neutral, which more or less correspond to the three poisons, it leads to the full range of human responses because they initiate a chain of identification and association.

Buddhist psychology sees the way that we handle *dukkha* as central to the spiritual and psychological journey. Our fear of *dukkha* – sickness, old age, loss, disappointment and death – drives us to build psychological defences. It drives compulsive behaviours. The root fears behind these compulsive behaviours are, however, often unconscious and well below the surface of awareness because compulsive behaviours tend to be longstanding and block out anxiety. When we are enmeshed in these processes we tend to live in a deadened state of mind, operating on auto-pilot. On the other hand, facing the reality of *dukkha* creates the possibility for spiritual transformation and emancipation.

Individual and the collective attachment

The patterns of human process which Buddhist psychology suggests are true of individuals, can also be seen in groups and even society as a whole. Just as individuals create a sense of identity based on fear, so too, groups develop internal cultures in reaction to their collective anxieties. Under threat, religions fall prey to fundamentalism and countries to nationalism. Preoccupation with identity, in individuals and in wider society, drives many of the troubles in the world.

The progressive withdrawal through sense-attachment, identity-formation and non-becoming is seen in society as well as in individuals (De Silva 1990).

Greed-type behaviours manifest in consumerism, competition and the exploitation of resources (Payne 2010) whilst hate-type behaviours are seen in tightening borders, hostility towards minority groups and war. There is a rise in nationalism and factionalism as people cling to collective identities. Eventually, when such behaviours fail to address global problems, those groups which feel most threatened seek oblivion, turning to self-destruction and chaos.

As people become identified with different interest groups, it can be difficult to address global issues in a cooperative way. This is not surprising because each group is fighting for survival, trying to establish a sense of its own permanence in the face of both real and imagined threat. As the level of tension rises, whether through conflict, environmental damage or diminishing resources, the level of fear increases. In this scenario, change can only happen through some kind of spiritual shift in society, but as religion itself is often subverted by power politics (identity building under another name) and grasping at illusions of security, this is difficult to achieve.

Whilst this perspective is chilling, having insight is the first step to change. Whilst some areas of the world seem caught up in deadly patterns of mutual destruction, other areas are less embedded in the process of collective delusion and still retain the ability to step back from the brink of conflict. Understanding the roots of these human patterns of attachment can help us to approach those areas of society which we can affect, and in particular to promote the importance of connection to one another and to the environment at all levels (Macy 1990).

Grasping compulsion

The human tendency towards grasping and acquisition, characteristic of greed-type behaviours, underpins many global problems. Society has become more consumer-driven, with huge advertising industries feeding the impulse to acquire material possessions. People today expect to have more possessions than their parents or grandparents did and spend more time shopping. There seems to be an endless thirst for new things and new experiences. Such changes are in part fuelled by the predominant growth-based economic model which values productivity and sales above the conservation of resources. In the past, people bought household goods to last a lifetime, but now commodities are manufactured with limited life-spans planned in. Dissatisfaction is a requisite of this culture since it feeds the desire to have more, and this dissatisfaction is bred through deliberate manipulation of the media. People are encouraged to focus on their feelings of lack and to develop aspirations for newer and better goods in their homes and lifestyles. This focus on lack mirrors the existential anxiety which is intrinsic to our human situation (Loy 1996) and so trades on our vulnerability to fears of impermanence and mortality.

Many patterns of consumption begin in childhood. Children are placated with sweets, toys, television or treats when they are sad, angry or bored, learning to distract themselves from difficult feelings by consuming. Once established, these habits continue into adulthood. Many of us turn to consumption at times of stress and anxiety, joking about retail therapy or comfort foods. It can be difficult to break such habits because, whether the object of attachment is food, alcohol, cigarettes or drugs, the habit itself, and the desire to break it, generates anxiety which leads us to indulge even more.

At global levels, these patterns of consumption impact on the environment both directly, through the increased use of raw materials, and indirectly, because transport, energy and other resources are needed in their manufacture. These increases in consumption affect the environment, and we are already seeing the results in climate change. As this and other environmental factors lead to growing anxiety in society, there is a danger that anxiety about climate change will itself feed increasing levels of consumption, leading to a self-building cycle. This is one of the many feedback loops which could potentially escalate the global crisis.

Because consumption is endorsed by society, the media and government policies for its' apparent economic benefits, recognising the psychological origin of excessive consumption is challenging to the social order. As ecotherapists, we may find ourselves at the forefront of a social and political movement as well as offering psychological wellbeing.

Aversion and rejection

Whilst greed responses involve identification and grasping, hate responses involve rejection. Psychologically, they are concerned with the creation of identity in distinction from others. Hate-type responses assert 'I am different', creating an identity which is differentiated from the 'not me'.

Some aversion-type responses are based on anger and hatred. At a personal level this may mean rejecting family, friends or neighbours. It may mean joining a group which is hostile to others groups within society. On the global scale, aversion-type responses lead to war, alienation and the cementing of differences between social groups and nations. Other aversion-type responses are more passive, involving denial and refusal to engage with certain people or issues. These may be expressed in passive-aggressive behaviour or through withdrawal from a given situation. If there is conflict between neighbours, for example, some people who are avoidant may stop speaking to them or gossip about them behind their backs, whilst being pleasant in public, and others may get into open conflict.

Aversion-type responses often lead to feelings of alienation. Alienation from the natural environment underpins many of the social problems that humans face today, both globally and locally. Whilst modern life fosters a collective story of civilisation and improvement, people are increasingly distanced from the other-than-human world, adding to this sense of disconnection and alienation. As a result, there is only limited resistance when commercial or strategic interests make use of wild spaces and destroy natural resources. The impulse towards consumption is stronger than any concern for the long term effects of this degradation and most people are too dissociated from their environmental roots to intervene. Reconnecting people with the environment offers one way to heal the alienation which seems so deep rooted in modern life, but it is not an easy task to achieve this on a large enough scale to make a real difference.

Since aversion responses are part of the defensive system by which the sense of identity is built and maintained, letting go of these negative reactions is not easy. Many individuals and groups create their identity on a foundation of difference. Expressing hostility or ridicule of others cements relationships. Even amongst those who overtly reject this kind of behaviour, including environmentalists and Buddhists, there are often subtle and not so subtle projections of negative qualities onto those who oppose our views in the form of disapproval or distrust.

Ambivalence and confusion

Greed and hate responses are based on certainty. Confusion-type responses are based on uncertainty. They are characterised by wavering and feeling torn in different directions. This uncertainty tends to create a situation of stasis as a person dithers between options, unable to make decisions.

To get a better understanding of ambivalent processes, we can look at another Buddhist teaching which is called *the five hindrances*. This teaching describes five ways in which the processes of greed, hate and confusion manifest behaviourally. Buddhist psychology suggests that the five hindrances are the behavioural foundations upon which the sense of an enduring self is built. We find the five hindrances listed in a number of Buddhist texts immediately before another teaching[1] called the *skandhas* (Brazier 2003) which describes the way that sense of a permanent self is created through the cycle of conditioned perception and identification that we looked at earlier in this chapter. In other words, these behaviours are linked to the development of a fixed sense of self.

The teaching of the five hindrances describes different styles of clinging. The hindrances are concerned with the processes of attachment, which in turn support the sense of self. They are the processes which prevent us fully engaging with our experiential world, through which a limited and sometimes rigid world-view is created. They are: sensual desire, ill will, sloth and torpor, restlessness and remorse, and doubt. These five elements equate to the three poisons as follows:

- Sensual desire, equates with greed.
- Ill will, equates with hate.
- Doubt in this context means indecision and equates to confusion.
- Sloth and torpor combine greed and hate: the person puts things off and becomes lazy.
- Restlessness and remorse combine hate and confusion: the person becomes agitated and self-blaming.

The five hindrances are the patterns of avoidance which all of us indulge in when we are unwilling to do something or frightened at the prospect of a new experience.

Faced with the problems which arise from climate change, environmental threat and global conflict, people are likely to be caught up in one or more of the hindrances. The enormity of these global problems leads to feelings of powerlessness and indecision. Countries try to protect their own standards of living and levels of consumption. They become more concerned with guarding their borders, fostering ill will towards other nationalities. A lack of clarity about policy is exacerbated by the conflicting views of different interest groups, and those with power procrastinate or instigate enquiries into what has gone wrong in the past in an attempt to attribute guilt.

Individuals, likewise, become absorbed in bettering their own lifestyles or else fall into nihilistic hatred of others. Those who feel uncomfortable about the situation often get caught up in doubt and uncertainty, fall into passivity and do not speak out. They leave it to others to take action, dragged down by sloth and torpor, their energy sapped by the immensity of what is needed. Others become agitated and self-blaming, manifesting restlessness and remorse, trying to counter feelings of guilt by making small scale changes of life-style, whilst being ineffective in tackling anything on a larger scale.

Hope through impermanence

This chapter has focused on the theoretical base which Buddhist psychology offers for our work outdoors. The Buddhist understanding of human process is applicable both to individuals and to groups, and we have seen how it offers a way of understanding some of the pernicious cycles which feed behaviours detrimental to the individual and the environment. It suggests that humans avoid facing the realities of impermanence, loss and death through a number of different kinds of attachment and clinging. In particular, the sense of identity provides a way for people to protect themselves from thinking about these existential challenges. The sense of self provides an illusion of something enduring and reliable, defending us against the knowledge of our own contingency. This flight from reality is at the root of many human miseries.

In this way, Buddhism paints a picture of people chasing their tails in the world of delusion, imagining that reality is something even more fearsome than the pain that these cycles create. Yet the Buddhist message is a positive one. Facing our fears directly, as the Buddha did on the night of his enlightenment (MN4), leads to a shift of perception that has the power to transform our whole world-view.

Fear is often of the unknown. Facing the things which cause us most anxiety in life can often turn out to be less scary and a far richer experience than we imagined, even when those things are deeply distressing. In the darkest places, there is often a profound sense of connection at both the human and the universal level. Feeling our fears takes courage, and most of the time we run away from things that cause us anxiety. On the other hand, transcending our fears brings liberation. We are no longer limited by defensive reactions in that area of life.

Ecotherapy can help people to gain confidence in the environment and in one another. They often encounter things which are new to them and sometimes have to face up to fears as a result. It also leads to a broader kind of confidence in psychological and human processes. Confidence and trust are important to our ability to face the things that are difficult. They help us diminish the hold of the negative cycles which have been described in this chapter.

With this view, impermanence itself becomes a source of hope. When we get caught up in believing that nothing is possible and that the situation is unchanging, we can fall into profound doubt and hopelessness. We retreat into ourselves, our minds closed to possibilities. We stop trusting and disconnect. Knowing that all things are impermanent releases us. Change becomes possible. Psychological and spiritual growth flourishes in situations where we feel deeply connected to others and to our environment. If we can face our despair, and reconnect to others (Macy & Brown 2014), human and nonhuman, then there is a possibility that we can start to heal the wounds created by society at both individual and collective levels.

Note

1 For example, The Ant Hill Sutta Majjhima Nikaya 23.

References

Batchelor, S. (2010). *Confessions of a Buddhist Atheist*. New York: Spiegel and Grau.

Brazier, C. (2003). *Buddhist Psychology*. London: Constable.

Brazier, C. (2009). *Other-Centred Therapy: Buddhist Psychology in Action*. Ropley: O-Books.

De Silva, P. (1990). Buddhist Environmental Ethics. In A. Badiner (Ed.), *Dharma Gaia*. Berkeley: Parallax.

Gethin, R. (1998). *The Foundations of Buddhism*. Oxford: Oxford University Press.

Harvey, P. (1995). *The Selfless Mind*. London: Curzon.

Harvey, P. (2009). The Four Ariya-saccas as 'True Realities for the Spiritually Ennobled': The Painful, its Origin, its Cessation, and the Way Going to this Rather than 'Noble Truths' Concerning These. *Buddhist Studies Review*, 26(2), 97–227.

Loy, D. (1996). *Lack and Transcendence: The Problem of Death and Life in Psychotherapy, Existentialism, and Buddhism*. New Jersey: Humanities Press International.

Macy, J. (1990). *The Greening of the Self*. In A. Badiner (Ed.). *Dharma Gaia*. Berkeley: Parallax.

Macy, J. & Brown, M. (2014). *Coming Back to Life* (revised ed). Gabriola Island, BC: New Society Publishers.

Nyanasobhano B. (1998). *Landscapes of Wonder: Discovering Buddhist Dhamma in the World Around Us*. Boston: Wisdom.

Payne, R. (2010). *How Much is Enough: Buddhism, Consumerism and the Human Environment*. Somerville, MA: Wisdom.

Wilson, E. (1984). *Biophilia*. Harvard: Harvard University Press.

6 Triangular relationship

This chapter draws on the other-centred concept of triangular relationship (between therapist, client and the shared object of attention) showing how in ecotherapy the third element is the natural environment. Exploring relational ramifications in terms of the side-by-side relationship and changes in dynamics and boundaries, it discusses the centrality of empathy, developed both by therapist and client through resonance and attunement. The chapter shows how, working outdoors, the therapist moves in and out of close empathy, sometimes taking a more objective position. The importance of non-judgemental attitude, emphasised in both person-centred approach and mindfulness, is raised as is the consequent need for therapists to acknowledge fallibility.

The therapeutic relationship is commonly represented as a process which happens between two people, a counsellor and a client, who meet regularly in the particular situation of the therapy room to explore aspects of the client's experience. This relationship takes a particular form, defined by the therapeutic boundaries which establish limits on the length, frequency and style of sessions (e.g. Feltham & Horton 2000; Charura & Paul 2014). Within this context, which constitutes the therapeutic container, therapeutic dialogue unfolds. The therapeutic relationship is multi-layered, addressing in its complexity both conscious and unconscious material, but it is essentially represented as a dyad; two people in interaction within an agreed contract.

By contrast, the concept of therapeutic triangle is fundamental to other-centred methodology. In this model of psychotherapy, therapist and client are not seen as operating as a dyad, but rather as forming a collaborative relationship in order to engage with a third element, the world of phenomena. In the therapy room, these phenomena might be characters within the client's story, events and places which are important to him or images and ideas which inform his thinking, or they might be real objects such as photographs, artwork or figures in a sand-tray. This being the case, it is not hard to see what makes other-centred approach so appropriate to ecotherapy.

In this chapter we will explore some of these relational aspects using methodology drawn from the other-centred model, particularly as it applies to working outdoors. For a more systematic review of this approach, you may want to refer to my previous book, *Other-Centred Therapy* (Brazier 2009), which mostly, but not entirely, describes the method in terms of conventional indoor therapy. Here we will look at how conceptualising the relationship as triangular allows the contribution made by the environment to the therapeutic process to be more centrally recognised within the framework of thinking.

Since working outdoors can take many forms, we will look at basic principles which can be applied in work with individuals and groups, as well as in more open-ended community settings. The breadth of these applications means that inevitably the therapist or practitioner will need to adapt the principles to particular situations, but the core of the method will remain much the same.

The side-by-side relationship

Going for a walk with someone is probably one of the most common ways in which people experience the outdoors together. When we meet up with a friend, we might take a stroll and talk over what is happening in our lives or we might sit by the duck pond, watching the families throwing crusts to the birds and musing on how our own children are growing up. Whether we are watching birds together or standing gazing into the sunset, we do so side by side. Being alongside one another seems like the natural way to be. To face each other in such situations would feel strange. It would exclude the view and we would miss out on the shared experience of our surroundings.

Just because we cannot see the other person's face, this doesn't mean that we communicate less deeply. In fact the reverse can be true. Sometimes looking someone in the eye we have a sense of looking into their soul, but other times we get trapped by the persona, the mask, the appearance, and our intimacy is limited. Sometimes we are most guarded when we are looking someone straight in the face. It can be hard to really hear someone who fixes you with their eye, whether the gaze is hostile or seductive. Walking side by side, we do not feel any less close or less open to one another.

Often we feel freer to share intimacies. The presence of the other slips in, almost unnoticed, as we voice our musings. In the side-by-side position, the other person can be a silent companion to our solitary thoughts, like the observer-mind, watching inside our heads, or a solid presence by our sides: a henchman, a bodyguard, a protector, felt but not seen. Released from the impact of the companion's gaze, other senses are freed up. When we listen in this way, we feel the other's presence, hear their tone of voice. More importantly, we share their world-view, and in sharing experiences we tune in to their reactions. We look together at a beautiful view or a desolate industrial landscape, a dead animal or a cherry tree in blossom. We sense each other's reactions and attune ourselves to them.

Outdoor therapy often involves being alongside someone. Whether we are sitting on a bench or by a river, walking along a beach or standing on the edge of a cliff, in this work we are frequently side by side as we talk. We are together in nature, our conversation taking place against the backdrop of our surroundings, crystallising around shared points of attention. This shared experiencing invites collaboration. Participants and therapists collaborate in investigating the scene in front of them whilst therapists and environment collaborate to create the therapeutic container.

The other-centred model, in viewing the therapeutic relationship as triangular, focuses on side-by-side communication both imaginatively and literally. It frees the therapist to be alongside the people with whom she is working, looking at the world with them and sensing empathically how they perceive it. Whilst in the therapy room, the therapist achieves a shared view of the client's world, imaginatively coming alongside him and trying to envisage his experience as he describes events and relationships in his world. When we go outside, as we actually walk together or sit next to one another, we both experience the same landscape and respond to it, so we can see similarities and differences in how we perceive things.

Attention

Working outdoors, therapists and participants are presented with a wide vista of experiences. The space around them is crowded with life, be it plants, trees, animals, birds or humans. Things are near and far, above and below, constantly changing and evolving. Sometimes something appears which is so compelling it cannot be missed. This morning as we approached the pond on our morning walk, a heron flew up quite suddenly from the reeds, not far from where we stood, with a huge flapping of wings. It stopped us in our tracks. We had no choice but to look at it. Other times when we walk together, each of us looks in a different direction, our attention caught by different things, but today we all looked the same way.

There are different kinds of attention. Sometimes attention is sharp and focused, like the eye of the heron penetrating the water of the pond. Other times it is soft, giving us a broad sense of our surroundings, our eyes playing over the trees and grass and sky without alighting on anything for very long (Kaplan & Kaplan 1989). Mostly we are open to distraction. We are capable of being caught by the sight of a heron flying up.

Our attention is caught by specific things. Usually this is because we have some kind of personal interest in them. We might notice the remnants of ice on the pond, and think about how much it has thawed since yesterday because we are hoping the weather will warm up, or spot broken branches under the trees because it might be good to take some home for the fire. Such ordinary observations are personal and idiosyncratic. They reflect aspects of our lives which we carry in our thoughts and the stories which we are living out.

Outdoors, with so many things going on, there are always many different things to look at or think about. As we become conscious of our mind-process, we can be interested in our own flow of attention. What catches my eye? Do I watch people or wildlife or trees? Where is my interest focused and what do I react to? Is my attention on the surroundings or am I preoccupied by thoughts? What are the stories behind these changes of attention? Besides reflecting on our own experiences, we may also be interested in what catches our companions' attention. Therapists are interested in how their clients pay attention to the world. Sometimes this is observable by watching the direction of someone's gaze or by listening to what they comment on. Other times we are surprised when participants comment on things which they saw or heard which we missed completely.

Different dynamics and side-by-side relationship

Walking side by side feels friendly. It can seem quite informal compared to the more structured situation of the therapy room where the therapist and client are mostly seated in their two chairs. Changing our ways of working from face-to-face to side by side has implications not only in terms of a shift of attention, but also in the dynamics of the therapeutic relationship itself.

In face-to-face therapy, the therapist is almost inevitably a strong presence for the client. The client can watch the therapist's face and may interpret expressions and voice tone as affirmative or discouraging. An involuntary flicker of the eyebrow or a slight hesitation before responding may be understood immediately in terms of approval or disapproval. Some clients are very good at knowing what the therapist really thinks, even if the therapist thinks she is simply responding in a reflective style.

Other clients do not necessarily see the therapist as a real person at all. Clients often project roles and responses onto their therapists, making them into transference objects: substitute parents, lovers or friends. The therapist becomes the screen on which the client's habitual world-view is played. Habitual roles are acted out with her. The therapist may become skilled at separating projections from reality and, in imagination, standing alongside the client and seeing herself, the therapist, through his world-viewing eyes. She also, incidentally, notices the reactions which the client's behaviour evokes in her, viewing them with similar curiosity and dispassion. These reactions, sometimes referred to as counter-transference responses, reflect counterpart roles to his habitual ways of being. Thus all these fields reflect aspects of the client's world.

Projective phenomena are not eliminated from the therapeutic relationship in the side-by-side model, but they are diminished. This is because, to a large degree, in other-centred therapy the intention is to explore projections and transferences as they manifest in the relationship with the world rather than in relationship to the therapist. In the side-by-side model, whether in the consulting room or outdoors, the therapeutic relationship is primarily focused on exploration of the participant's experience of others and of the world. Whether he is talking about life events, thoughts and feelings or directly experiencing the moment, the therapeutic interaction focuses predominantly on the world that is being described – a world of other people, places and events. The therapist deliberately steps out of the limelight of attention, using a variety of responses which are all basically concerned with shifting the main attention, and the transferential projections, away from herself, so that she can stand alongside the participant in a process of shared enquiry, imaginatively looking at the things which he is exploring, and hearing what he sees in them (Brazier 2009).

As therapy moves outdoors this kind of shift tends to occur naturally. Whether walking or sitting, in one-to-one therapy relationships the side-by-side relationship becomes the practical way of interacting. The therapist easily takes a back seat and becomes less visible in the process as she and her client look together at the things around them.

Empathy

Empathy is foundational to the therapeutic relationship (Rogers 1951; Mearns & Thorne 1988). Most models of psychotherapy, at least implicitly, see the ability to listen and understand at depth as fundamental to whatever other activities they use. In order to be empathic, we need to be able to listen deeply with all our senses – sight and feeling as well as hearing – and to ground our understanding in an appreciation of human process (Rogers 1980). This understanding often comes from our own experience, but needs to recognise the particularity of the other person's way of being.

In order to empathise, we need to set aside our own agendas and listen. Because we have all experienced pain and pleasure, wonder and boredom, we have the basic building blocks with which to understand the other's emotions, but we need to be able to draw on these experiences without imposing interpretations on the other person. Sometimes listening in this way can put us in touch with painful, embarrassing or unpleasant memories of our own, and these can be a block to empathy. This is why trainee therapists undergo their own therapy. Other times, though, listening empathically can restore our faith in human processes.

Empathy arises out of the experience of standing alongside another, seeing his situation 'as if' through his eyes (Rogers 1961a: p. 29). In this, the relationship is essentially triangular. We stand beside the other and share his view of an object world, real or imagined. In establishing an empathic relationship, we do not identify with him, but, rather, attempt to feel his responses 'as if' with his heart. Empathy involves understanding how it is to walk in his shoes and eat at his table. It does not include judgement. It does not need sympathy or problem solving. Rather it respects the other's autonomy and lets him make his own decisions whilst trying to imaginatively accompany him and appreciate the depth of the dilemmas involved in his life choices.

Empathy is about listening. It is about hearing the words which are used and not the ones we think have been said. It is about hearing the complex layers which lie beneath the surface and the things which are being implied or not voiced at all. It is about reading between the lines without guessing. It is about noticing the subtle changes of tone in the voice, the twitch of the eye or the slight welling of tears.

Developing empathy with someone is always a process of negotiation and checking. In this it is a humble process. Gradually we inch our way towards the real meaning of what is being said rather than giving wise pronouncements. Typically, empathy is established through reflective listening. The therapist listens and echoes what she thinks she has heard the client say, paraphrasing, summarising or sometimes repeating his actual words. The question which lies behind every empathic reflection is 'Is this how it really is?' When we are seeking empathy, we should be willing to hear that, no, it is not. We should be willing to listen again. Voicing our tentative understanding is important. It allows the other person to disabuse us of our misconceptions.

In therapeutic dialogue, whether in conventional settings or outdoors, there is always some ebb and flow in the process. Therapist and client move in and out of close connection. The therapist feels her way into the story which the client is telling and into her own reactions to it. This is sometimes described using the metaphor of 'entering the river'. Then periodically the therapist steps back and takes a more objective viewpoint, checking her perceptions for accuracy and usefulness. This is sometimes described as 'keeping one foot on the river bank'. In this way, the therapist does not simply respond from her stream of consciousness, which would inevitably impose inappropriate interpretations and personal agendas onto the client's experience, but, rather, filters what she says appropriately.

In describing empathic process, the metaphor of 'having one foot in the river and one foot on the bank' illustrates the balance which has to be maintained between the felt-sense and the intellect. Two feet in the river lacks objectivity and runs the risk of becoming identification. Two feet on the bank is over-distanced and lacks compassionate understanding.

Resonance and attunement

Achieving empathy relies upon our ability to imaginatively enter the world of another person and see things as he does. We listen and, as we do so, we allow their story to play in the imagination like a film. As we listen, we watch, gradually tuning in to the detail of nuance and imagery until we reach a point of resonance. When we have got alongside the other in this way, an unconscious process unfolds which means that our bodies start to mirror and resonate with the felt-sense of the other person. When in empathy with another person, we feel something of their joy or their fear, their anger or their grief in our body-sense. This kind of resonance is often experienced at a low or subliminal level that we are not consciously aware of, but it still affects our understanding. It can be particularly strong when we are closely related to the other person or emotionally involved with them. The mother feels the pain of the son. The lover feels the pain of their partner. Friends share elation or disappointment, frustration or anxiety with one another.

Empathy is thus an embodied process. It relies upon the body's ability to feel and attune to another's embodied experience. Attunement goes both ways. On the one hand, the therapist is grounded and, by being so, transmits groundedness to the client. The therapist's groundedness provides safety and support, which in turn invites the client to relax and become more grounded. At the same time, through awareness of the body-sense, the therapist experiences resonance with the client's moods and reactions and may pick up aspects of the client's story through feelings which are not being overtly talked about, and are perhaps not even known to the client himself. The therapist may thus respond not only to what is being said, but also to what is not being said (Truax & Carkhuff 1967).

Attunement is not just something which happens between people. When we go into nature, we may feel body-resonance with the land around us. In a dark wood we may feel gloomy and fearful. On a hill top we may feel exuberant and free. By a river we may feel calm. By the sea we may feel energised. We may feel deeply affected by the weather or the time of day. Most people feel different on a sunny morning from the way they feel when it is overcast. The body-sense responds to cues from the environment with a feeling-based set of reactions and associations.

Such emotional resonances would not generally be described as empathy, but they do seem to involve similar processes to those of imaginative accompaniment. Perhaps such experiences raise questions about the real nature of empathy and about our relationship to our environment. Can we feel empathy for the fox pursued by hounds or the badger that is being gassed in its set? Can we empathise with the exuberance of a bird singing in the early morning? Can we develop empathy for trees which are being destroyed or vegetables which are being harvested? It is easy to think that, in feeling such resonances, we are projecting our own emotional responses onto animals, succumbing to anthropocentric thinking and irrational flights of imagination; yet do such feelings have validity? Even though we can never enter the mind of an animal or plant, perhaps such thoughts are important in cultivating sensitivity to the non-human just as they do in human relationships.

Empathy and observation

Working outdoors can be freeing. No longer constrained by the formalities of the therapy room, as we walk alongside another person we can move between conversation and silence in ways which feel natural. As we have seen, this can help us achieve a deep empathy for their world-view. Other ways of working outdoors, however, can make establishing an empathic connection difficult. Whilst it can be easy to tune in to the other person's feelings and feel a deep empathic connection whilst side by side, in some activities it is difficult to achieve a depth of contact.

It can, for example, be difficult to maintain consistent empathy in situations when participants are scattered over a wide area and we are not party to their minute-by-minute process. We do not know what they are thinking or even, sometimes, what they are doing, and lack the physical closeness needed to feel body resonance. Working outdoors in this way gives people space to explore the environment on their own without the therapist intruding on their process, but for them to maintain connection with the therapist, they also need check-in time before an exercise and to be able to debrief afterwards. Thus the group and the facilitators move in and out of empathic engagement.

In these alternating phases of engagement and separation, facilitators tend to alternate their styles of operating. When the participants come together to share, the facilitators attune empathically to their process. During the periods when participants are engaged in activity, however, the facilitators' role becomes to act as more objective observers. This means that they relate to the participants in more than one way: in dialogue and through observation.

Whilst the group is engaged in activity, the facilitators observe, watching how participants respond to one another and to their surroundings when left to their own devices. Sometimes this allows therapists to spot anomalies between participants' behaviour and the way they talk about their experiences. For example, if a participant tells the group in a sharing session that he is timid and never takes risks, but later the facilitator observes this same person taking the lead in an activity where other participants are anxious and holding back, the therapist can comment on this anomaly. Indoors, the therapist might have listened empathically to this person's sense of their own timidity, and invited him to share examples of times when he felt unable to join in with collective activities. In the consulting room the person would be likely to recall instances where he was indeed overcome by shyness and the therapist might well have responded in ways that reinforced his sense of himself as a nervous person, failing to realise that, in other circumstances that he was not reporting, he actually had much more courage than he believed. Thus in indoor therapy, with its emphasis on reportage, the negative self-story can be inadvertently reinforced.

Outdoors the facilitator can use the two vantage points, empathic resonance and objective observation, to see the incongruence between a person's story and his actions and can give direct feedback, challenging his 'out of date' self-image or inviting him to explore in more detail why he sees himself in a particular way. It is not impossible to achieve contrasting viewpoints indoors, and, indeed, other-centred approach advocates this, but the immediacy of the outdoor environment makes it easier. Finding two vantage points reveals layers within the self-story which the participant is presenting, and helps to challenge fixity in it by exposing its inconsistencies.

Other-centred empathy

Empathic connection is a skill that comes naturally to some people, but it is also something which can be learned. Being able to empathise with others is a life skill and not just something which is useful in the therapy room. It provides a foundation for all kinds of relating, helping us to get on better with people in all areas of our lives, and particularly in intimate relationships. It helps us to connect with others and appreciate why they respond to us in particular ways. It also helps us to recognise their needs and respond to them, as well as enabling us to communicate our own feelings more appropriately. Empathy is therefore good for mental health.

Other-centred approach is concerned with understanding the way that the world-view is biased and orientated towards personal agendas. It follows that encouraging people to develop empathy for the people who are significant in their life-world is important to other-centred methodology, because by doing this people become open to other perspectives and bring into question the orthodoxy of their personal view (Brazier 2009). Having empathy for others helps people to think systemically and explore situations from the viewpoints of all the people involved rather than simply from their own habitual position. Developing better empathy skills like this also encourages people to relate more directly to those around them. This does not necessarily mean sympathising with them, but, rather, involves appreciating the wider context of influences and conditions which are creating their situation so that it becomes possible to respond more skilfully. In empathising with someone else, we start to appreciate their personal logic and the emotional pressures behind their actions.

In other-centred approach, the therapist works in empathic resonance with the client, collaborating with him to build up an empathic picture of the significant people in his life. As figures emerge in his world, the therapist asks questions about them, inviting the client to reflect on, and sometimes question, the way that he sees and relates to them. The therapist asks about these people's probable motivations and enthusiasms, and, together, client and therapist develop a picture of the conditions which are significant in these third parties' lives, which may in turn have relevance to the client's situation. The process of enquiry which begins in the therapy context does not stop when the session finishes either, for, if these significant people are still part of the client's life, it is likely that the therapy will evoke his curiosity about them and their situations and he will start to relate to them in different ways when he meets them between sessions. As this happens, his relationships with them will change and this in itself may have a therapeutic effect.

Helping clients to develop empathy for others can also help to free them from inappropriate feelings of responsibility and from feeling stuck in impossible situations. Recognising that others act as they do for their own reasons, a client may realise that he cannot do anything to change the situation, or, conversely, that, if he acts differently, the other person may, of their own accord, change their behaviour. The therapist not only develops resonance and empathy for the client's way of seeing things, but also encourages him to pay more attention to the way in which he is interpreting things. The focal enquiry is on the facts of the situation, and particularly the different perspectives at play. As Carl Rogers believed, 'the facts are always friendly' (1961b: p. 26).

Attention, mindfulness and awareness

Therapy involves deep curiosity about human process. Often a dance with nuance and implication, it also involves investigating truth and exploring facts through experiential enquiry. It is thus both rigorous and fluid. Therapy can involve feeling our way into the subtlety of situations and reactions as the people we work with experience them, but it also involves observing the detail of things and not operating on assumptions. It is in the detail that we sometimes discover the roots of particular mind-states in past or present circumstances. Buddhism also teaches awareness and observation. In particular, we find these skills explained in terms of the practice of mindfulness. Mindfulness involves bringing focused attention to the things that we connect with, engaging directly and without judgement (Hanh 1975; Kabat-Zinn 1990).

When we walk outdoors, our attention is caught by many different things. Mostly, we are not aware of this process. We are distracted or absorbed in what we are doing. We may be on one thought track, and then someone or something catches our attention, shifting our mind onto something new before we have even noticed, so that our thoughts flit from object to object. We are unmindful. Unless we have reason to concentrate, attention follows the patterns of distraction which are already structured into the mentality as mental formations. The ordinary mind tends to run along habitual tracks and go around in circles.

Mindfulness provides a way of observing the mind process. It offers a method for objective enquiry into what is happening both internally and externally.[1] What is the eye seeking out? How is it looking? How wide or narrow is its focus? In the Buddhist texts on mindfulness, one image which is used to describe the practice is that of climbing to the top of an elevated platform or tower (Analayo 2003). This image suggests that, according to this understanding of mindfulness, the quality of attention which is being sought is primarily objective and somewhat distanced. The practitioner reviews the field of experience as if from a great height. Other images from the Buddhist texts suggest that the attention which is given when practising mindfulness is soft and relaxed rather than being narrow and focused (Analayo 2003).

When we are mindful, we engage with things gently. We observe the whole picture in a precise but easy-going, non-reactive way, without grasping at one particular aspect of it. Mindfulness is often reflexive. The mind watches itself. It watches the action of the senses and the arising of reactions. It is calm but enquiring. We monitor our experience and no longer identify with it so strongly. We step back from our reactivity. The fickle behaviour of the ordinary, wandering mind becomes something to smile at.

Not all attention has this distanced, objective quality, however. The process of observing mind-actions can itself seem to separate us from our experience and this is not always what we want. If I am watching my senses be caught by the song of the skylark, I am not fully listening to the bird. My attention is on the process of listening. On the other hand, if I am lost in the glorious sound, I may not even be aware that I am listening until the song finishes and the bird descends. Sometimes our attention can be so caught up in immediate experience that we become completely absorbed in the experiencing in a single pointed way. This kind of immersive absorption is similar to that which is characteristic of meditative states arising from mindfulness practice. It is the next step.

Outdoors there are many stimulating experiences. The senses can feel very alive as we become caught up in the things that are going on around us. Our attention is drawn by beautiful, exciting or ugly sights, smells, sounds and sensations. We can feel very energised and present. Other times we may be caught up in life concerns and not even notice our surroundings. Many people use walking as a time for thinking, either in order to work through problems, or for indulging in daydreams and chilling out. So, the focus of attention can vary greatly. We might be very much in the present moment as we walk, enjoying the experience of being in the countryside or a city park, or we might be so caught up in thoughts that we don't even notice what's going on around us until something happens to interrupt our reflections.

When we facilitate therapeutic work outdoors, by working alongside them, we may encourage people to give more attention to their surroundings, to look more closely and to experience things through all their senses. This sort of awareness enables people to see things around them more intensely and more precisely. It is about enquiry. Sometimes, however, we want to invite people to use their imagination and allow their attention to be less focused, letting go of the need to be in control of their experience, exploring associations and personal stories as they emerge and are reflected in the surroundings. This sort of attention is about flowing with a process which is often partly unconscious. Therapy is not always about bringing things to full consciousness. Things which are held in peripheral attention can be very influential on our mind-states and structures of thinking. This material is also important to therapeutic work. Making everything conscious, and thus verbal and rational, is not always the best route to therapeutic change. Psychological growth and influence often occur through processes which go on at the edge of awareness.

When we work outdoors, there are many things in the natural environment which impact upon the senses and affect the mood which may not be consciously recognised. In some ways, these aspects of environmentally-based therapy work can be the most important. Many approaches to therapy in the outdoors involve taking people outside for activities such as sports, arts events or walking. These approaches rely on the influence of the natural environment as a therapeutic condition, often without ever making this explicit to participants at all.

Fallibility and fellow feeling

We have already reflected upon the fact that the relationship between therapist and client may involve different power dynamics from those found in the therapy room. Outdoors, the therapist shares the environment with participants in ways that she doesn't in the therapy room. She is less able to hide behind a professional persona and often becomes more personally visible to those with whom she works. Therapist and participants become people in a landscape, experiencing phenomena together and subject to a great range of influences.

In groupwork, the therapist is probably even more visible than when offering individual therapy. She cannot always, for example, disguise the fact that sometimes she feels uncomfortable or physically taxed by the activities. Things may go wrong and there may be practical problems. She may feel stupid and embarrassed or ashamed if she feels that she has made mistakes. There may be a sudden ill-timed downpour, or the group may lose the path. She may even feel deeply negative, experiencing fear, anger, depression or anxiety about what is going on, and these feelings may sometimes become apparent to those around her.

Even when she manages to keep a professional manner, the therapist knows that she can experience the range of human emotions. While she is working she may be so focused on the individuals with whom she is engaged that she is not particularly conscious of her own reactions, and, if she does experience emotions, she may attribute them to others, interpreting them as counter-transference or contagion from the group. At other times, however, she may be all too aware that the difficult feelings that have been triggered in her are her own.

Recognising our capacity for negative feelings like shame and despair is vital to our work as therapists. We can get it wrong and make mistakes and sometimes we feel like giving up. Usually we need to moderate our reactions and deal with the things which cause us to react emotionally in our own therapy or in other settings, safeguarding the therapeutic container for our groups or clients, but if we deny to ourselves that we have such feelings, we may project them onto others and set ourselves apart from those with whom we work, making false assumptions about our own infallibility. It is our fallibility which helps us to empathise with people and which forms the basis for real connection with them. We do not necessarily need to reveal the details of our difficulties, but if we are aware of them, it will show in the manner of our responses to others because we will come from a place of mutuality. We will be more compassionate. Our fallibility, referred to as our *bombu nature* in Japanese Buddhism (Brazier 2007), is what makes us human.

In seeing our own negativity, we cannot cling on to any sense of superiority, but, rather, we meet others from a position of deep equality. Being aware of our own vulnerability helps us to develop 'fellow feeling' for those with whom we work (Brazier 2009: p. 278). This quality is the basis of the empathic accompaniment which we have been describing. It is only when we can recognise our own low points that we can really let ourselves be with others who are feeling low. Otherwise subtle levels of superiority tend to creep into our relating, debasing empathy into sympathy. The recognition which the therapist feels when sensing the client's feelings of vulnerability is communicated subliminally. When we are in touch with our ordinariness, the client not only feels heard, but also knows intuitively that his anxieties are recognised. He is not alone in his fear and shame. This recognition is not cognitive, but visceral.

Working outdoors, things are unpredictable. The therapist may suddenly feel outside her comfort zone. There are so many things that can go wrong: a change of weather, getting lost, encountering a bull whilst crossing a field, meeting a friend whilst in the middle of an activity, feeling an emotional reaction to something unexpected, getting physically tired. In such situations the therapist ideally makes a judgement about how much of her reactions to share. There are times when showing fallibility can be risky if it undermines the confidence of the group, and therapists need to deal with their emotions in supervision or personal therapy. On the other hand, there are times when being seen to be human is no bad thing and can be deeply empowering for others.

Triangular relationships in groups

In this chapter we have explored the way that principles of triangularity pervade therapeutic relationships outdoors. At its simplest, the triangular relationship is described in terms of the triad between therapist, client and the environment, but when we work with groups, other relationship triads emerge that are important to the therapy process. These include relationships between group members, the facilitators, the environment, specific objects and the stories that are being explored.

When group members are engaged in an activity together, they may be primarily focused on the task in hand. Relationships become predominantly functional and people are often not consciously reflecting on them. If a project is running smoothly, people are not necessarily aware of how they are relating, but if relationships become more strained, they may become much more aware of one another and of differences within the group. One reason for this is that in this kind of situation, each person tends to assume that other people think like him and not take into account that they may have other ways of doing things. Being in a functional relationship works so long as the task is accomplished effectively, but the relationship breaks down when things go wrong or interpersonal dynamics become conflicted. Sharing practical tasks together can create opportunities to explore interpersonal dynamics more consciously and bring awareness to the way that personal patterns of behaviour emerge in work groups. These inter-personal dynamics are often based on personal history and habitual reactions rather than on the real relations between people present. Here-and-now dynamics in a group tend to reflect longstanding behavioural patterns, and these often become more obvious when people are engaged in activities together than they are in the therapy room. Discussing the process afterwards allows participants to get feedback from other participants on roles they have taken.

Because working outdoors often faces people with new situations, it can create anxieties. These tend to lead people to revert to old patterns of reaction. If debriefing sessions are facilitated sympathetically, this can help people find new ways of relating, changing these unhelpful ways of being. In the next section we will look in more detail at the ways that personal stories and behavioural patterns can be explored and worked with outdoors.

Whilst we can gain understanding from looking at inter-personal process in this way, some ways of being together in nature are valuable in themselves and do not need reflection. When two people are in nature together, the process can feel natural and ordinary. Conversation flows easily without an obvious division of roles. It can, in many ways, feel like the sort of relationship one might have with a friend or relative, undemanding and not overtly therapeutic. For people with serious mental health problems or other long-term difficulties, modelling good relating can be important in itself. Clean, straightforward relationships are fundamental to good mental health, and the experience of relating in a more mutual way may be what the person needs. Whether the relationship is with another participant or with a support worker or facilitator, inasmuch as it reflects simple friendliness, it is likely to be helpful.

Engaging with others outdoors is therapeutic on many levels. The facilitator's primary role is to foster conditions in which change can happen. The principal of triangularity is fundamental to this. The shared experience of being outdoors provides a rich therapeutic space in part because the therapist experiences the environmental conditions alongside participants. In addition, the therapist and the environmental conditions together form the therapeutic container. Other-centred methodology focuses on relationship. In the context of the outdoors, the shared encounter with nature is transformative, but so too are the relationships which emerge between participants and those who work with them. People learn from one another, discovering new skills and new facets of themselves. They gain confidence in facing new situations, and broaden their thinking and ways of seeing the world. Working together, people have the experience of becoming part of a healthy system or community, often redressing earlier negative experiences of home, school or work communities where things have gone wrong.

Note

1 This phrase, *internally and externally*, is repeated many times in the *Satipatthana Sutta*, the Buddhist text on the Foundations of Mindfulness.

References

Analayo (2003). *Satipatthana: The Direct Path to Realisation*. Cambridge: Windhorse.

Brazier, C. (2007). *The Other Buddhism*. Ropley: O-Books.

Brazier, C. (2009). *Other-Centred Therapy: Buddhist Psychology in Action*. Ropley: O-Books.

Charura, D. & Paul, S. (Eds.). (2014). *The Therapeutic Relationship Handbook: Theory and Practice*. Maidenhead: Open University Press.

Feltham, C. & Horton, I. (Eds.). (2000). *Handbook of Counselling and Psychotherapy*. London: Sage.

Hanh, N. (1975). *The Miracle of Mindfulness*. Boston: Beacon Press.

Kabat-Zinn, J. (1990). *Full Catastrophe Living: Using the Wisdom of Your Body and Mind to Face Stress, Pain, and Illness*. USA: Delacorte.

Kaplan, R. & Kaplan, S. (1989). *The Experience of Nature: A Psychological Perspective*. Cambridge: Cambridge University Press.

Mearns, D. & Thorne, B. (1988). *Person-Centred Counselling in Action*. London: Sage.

Rogers, C. (1951). *Client-Centred Therapy*. London: Constable.

Rogers, C. (1961a). *On Becoming a Person*. London: Constable.

Rogers, C. (1961b). This is Me. In H. Kirschenbaum & V. Henderson (Eds.), *The Carl Rogers Reader*. New York: Houghton & Mifflin.

Rogers, C. (1980). *A Way of Being*. Boston: Houghton & Mifflin.

Truax, C. & Carkhuff, R. (1967). *Towards Effective Counseling and Psychotherapy*. Chicago: Aldine.

Part 3

Personal process

7 The personal frame

Personal experience and history impact on the relationship to the environment. The colouration of perception introduced through association and language particularly draws on childhood influences. Through these we tend to appropriate our surroundings, reinforcing the sense of identity. This chapter explores the Buddhist theory of the *skandhas*, showing how clinging is established. It then refers to particular modes of conditioning, as presented in the seventh book of the Pali Abhidhamma, looking at *root conditions*, *object conditions*, *predominance*, *proximity*, *contiguity*, *co-nascence*, *mutuality*, *repetition* and *karma* as they manifest in real situations. The chapter concludes by showing how mindfulness provides ways of working with these.

The mind is conditioned. Our senses are conditioned. Our view of the world is conditioned. All our experience is distorted and what we perceive through our senses is based upon mental processes and habits, as well as on the things themselves. We interpret and embellish what we see and, without even realising it, ignore things which do not seem relevant to our world-view. The distortions which our minds create prevent us seeing clearly. They add colouration, based on our own interests and anxieties, to everything that is perceived.

When we go out into the woods or fields or moorland, we see these places in ways which are particular to our own frames of experience. There is no such thing as a neutral viewpoint. Each person gives attention to some things and fails to notice other things. As we look at our surroundings, we automatically create stories about them. Some stories are enabling, curious and open ended. Others are uninterested, dismissive and closed.

When we take people out into nature, one aspect of what we are doing is to help them to create new stories. By exposing them to experiences which they might not normally have, we hope that they will expand their field of interests and move beyond the automatic reactions of boredom, dislike or fear which have inhibited them in the past. We invite them to engage and let the wild spaces and vegetation speak to them, awakening in them aspects of their personalities which have been dormant or undeveloped. We invite them to encounter.

Story and association

The stories which we build are usually not conscious, and nor are we aware of their influence on our perception. Sometimes a story is so strong that it becomes synonymous with the location: the place we met, the house where I grew up, my grandmother's grave. Other times it hovers behind the words, a vague feeling of something forgotten, yet still colouring the felt-sense of being there. Associations can be both personal and collective. Sometimes they are directly based on memories. We visit somewhere we lived in the past and remember what we did there. Other times they are idiosyncratic, based on the kind of tenuous connections that minds are good at conjuring up. Sometimes they are collective, part of a shared history or particular culture. Some places carry such strong collective stories that everyone's perception is influenced by them. Everybody has a story about the Twin Towers in Manhattan or about Auschwitz.

Collective stories are strong, but generally even the compelling associations they evoke are interwoven with personal ones. For example, for many people, the Scottish town of Lockerbie is inevitably linked to the story of a plane brought down from the sky in December 1988. When I hear the story of those events, however, I am immediately taken back to the trans-Pennine motorway on a winter's evening. News of the event came in over the car radio whilst I was driving with my family on our way to visit relatives for Christmas. Today, if I hear references to the bombing, images of the high Pennines come into my mind, and the great bulk of Saddleworth Moor has somehow become mixed with images of the plane's wreckage from news broadcasts which I viewed later. The story and the location where I heard it have become intimately connected in my imagination, even though their coincidence was arbitrary and personal. Each person similarly has their own story and their own set of associations.

Significant events commonly link to personal memories like this. For example, it is said that most people remember exactly where they were and what they were doing at the time when they heard the news of the deaths of John F. Kennedy or Princess Diana. Unconnected phenomena, pulled together by quirks of timing, take us vividly back to the places where we heard the stories. Stories evoke memories of places. Places remind us of stories. Public events become anchored in our memories by personal details; ordinary moments frozen into history.

For me, Princess Diana's death is associated with stopping at a petrol station in Northern France; French motorists remarking on our English number plates and asking us if we had heard the news about the accident in Paris. I recall the journey back to England, bizarrely mirroring the repatriation of Diana's body, listening to news updates relayed on the World Service. Without those public events, those memories would no doubt have long faded into obscurity, but as it is, they stand fresh for recall, like stray photos in the family album, linked to an occasion which has become iconic in our collective history.

Humans are pattern-making beings, seeking order in things around them, trying to shape and understand so as to feel less adrift in an unpredictable world. The patterns we create give us blueprints for the future. We see family and community, relationships, the turning seasons, the phases of life and the divisions of day and night, love and hate, good and bad. We all have stories. Some are old, repeated many times. Others are new and evolving, creating new associations and new imagery. These stories which we tell ourselves affect our personal relationship to the world.

Language and perception

The process of interpretation and distortion begins at the simple level of language. We name things when we speak and in our thought processes. We use words to describe phenomena and, in doing so, build links of sorts. By naming things, we connect the world to ourselves, and, in some senses, assert ownership of it. We package it into the conceptual boxes with which we manage, commodify and tame our experiencing.

Experiencing is an inner dialogue between direct perception and words. As we observe things, we name the objects and processes that we see using nouns and verbs, colouring them with adjectives and adverbs. This is part of our cognitive functioning. The labels that we use have been collected over a lifetime. We compare information arriving through our senses with stories, experiences and words already present in our storehouse of concepts. As we call the object 'a tree', or 'an oak', we add layers of association to the raw data derived through the eye. The object before us awakens memories of trees we climbed as children or reminds us of stories that we heard. We think of druids or wood nymphs, Charles Darwin or Charles the Second.

Describing a landscape, different people use different names. Each reveals a different set of associations. Looking at a windswept hilltop, we might refer to it as 'moorland', 'sheep country', 'common land' or 'peat bog'. The name we choose reveals our preconceptions and, in naming it, we start to ascribe it characteristics. We then embroider our perception with further language. Adjectives attach themselves to nouns. We do not just think of moorland, commons or bogs, we think of 'desolate' or 'open', 'majestic' or 'dull', 'depressing' or 'enlivening'. At the edge of awareness, we start to build stories about landscape.

In creating the story, we draw on many conditions that operate in the mind, some based on past experiences and others on current influences. The process of naming is influenced by context. We draw on different repertoires of meaning and different styles of expression. The words used when talking to a child are different from those used at work or with a lover. In part this is because people tailor speech to audience, but it is also because the other person's presence conditions mental associations. The fact that a person is participating in an ecotherapy group will itself condition their perception and may lead them to talk about their experience in particular ways using particular language that they might not use elsewhere.

Language is so fundamental to human thought that it is impossible to imagine how we would experience the world without it. Our conscious experience is almost universally framed in words. Through language we express our thoughts and communicate with others. At the same time, some experiencing is so subtle that cannot be put into language. The direct experience of our senses is often difficult to verbalise. If we try to describe birdsong or the colour of a flower, we soon realise how clumsy words are and how much of what we experience is actually beyond language. Words provide a framework for communicating, for disentangling our thought processes and for making sense of our experience, but they are just another kind of map, and like any map only give part of the picture.

In Buddhist psychology, naming objects is the first step in the process of mental conditioning. As we have already seen, the process by which we perceive things in a conditioned way, *rupa*, is based on the labelling of things. This labelling is called *nama-rupa*. Naming something reflects the way we see it. In labelling an object, we pin it down. We fit it into a particular category and link it to personal stories in our heads.

Childhood roots

Small children make sense of the world by recognising the patterns within it. This recognition is linked to the acquisition of language. Language is complicated. Even simple words demonstrate the conceptual complexity involved in the child's learning process. The piece of furniture on which we place things is called a table. Tables, however, take many forms. The term is largely, but not entirely, defined by function. If we say that tables have four legs, we exclude tables which stand on a single central pillar, on the other hand, if we define tables as pieces of furniture for working at or eating from, we include a variety of non-table objects, such as breakfast bars or desks. The limits of verbal categories are largely defined by precedent and common usage. As adults we can play with the paradoxes this creates, but children have to learn definitions through a process of trial and error, which gradually inducts them into a shared language and the world of those who use it.

Early associations can be very powerful. They are often tinged with half remembered feelings of nostalgia, sadness or loss. Just as famous events link to personal memories, memories from infancy are commonly interwoven with stories which were heard and reheard at that time. The margins between real experience and personal mythology are blurred. Traditional fairy tales and modern picture books provide imagery and concepts for the developing mind. They deal with universal themes such as good and evil, safety and danger, and become building materials for an ethical compass and an emotional paint-box. Giving shape to fear and passion, love and rejection, and naming the darker recesses of human experience, traditional stories help children make sense of everyday anxieties and specific traumas. They give form to feelings and embryonic understanding by offering a language of images and characters through which events and their associated emotions can be interpreted and processed. These images are frequently based in nature, featuring realistic or mythical animals and birds, forests and oceans. They help children conceptualise and create a world-view that may incorporate nature imagery.

Our childhood stories also affect our practical relationship to the environment. Perhaps we carry stories which tell of our love of nature, illustrated by memories of playing outdoors or caring for animals. Or perhaps we carry stories about danger and bad experiences, illustrated by things which happened to us or to others. These stories originate from many different sources, some personal, others derived from shared culture. They can liberate us to enjoy the outdoors or make us seek the urban and the tamed.

Appropriating the landscape

The stories that interweave themselves with our experiencing reflect our sense of identity and belonging. We put a personal stamp on the world as we name and label things. Behind this process is the unconscious desire to tame our experience because the wildness of life is full of dangers and unpredictability. We are driven by fear. We are frightened by the uncertainty of life, by our own vulnerability and mortality, and by our lack of control over things. Consequently, we strive psychologically to regain the upper hand and take control.

The human impulse to stamp our mark on nature is deeply embedded. Even when we court danger, our adventures are often driven by identity-making impulses and an unconscious desire to conquer and possess. We cast ourselves as pioneer, risk taker or even the heroic dead. Although the impulse is often rationalised as scientific enquiry or through a conservationist ideology, adventuring is frequently driven by more turbulent emotions which are repressed from awareness. Our relationship with nature is based on our own terms, be they cavalier or liberal, exploitative or conservationist.

The natural world can wake us to the wonderful things in life, but it can also put us in touch with things which are frightening. When we are outdoors, the effects of impermanence are all around us. Going outdoors can bring us face-to-face with life at its most raw and challenging as well as at its most beautiful. As humans, however, we tend to see what we want to see. We filter experience to make it comfortable.

The Tibetan Buddhist teacher, Chogyam Trungpa, gave a series of talks in the early 1970s which were later published as *Cutting Through Spiritual Materialism* (Trungpa 1973). This book explores how the human mind subverts experience, making it into a possession rather than allowing it to happen in its own way. This process is universal, and even spiritual experiences, according to Trungpa, are often grasped and debased into chattels. They become building blocks for the mind-set, often fostering feelings of self-importance and superiority. In our relationship to the environment we can get sucked into a similar kind of spiritual materialism. We subtly shape our experiencing of nature, grasping at some aspects of it or rejecting others to suit our sense of self.

The human psyche is multi-dimensional. As fast as we extricate ourselves from one pattern of attachment, another arises. We have usually only known personal viewpoints and only listened to human-centric perspectives, so it is hard to step out of the sense of entitlement which these create. Even when we judge ourselves, we create yet more layers of identity, adding negative self-concepts to the positive and holding these battered selves at the centre of our attention rather than giving that attention to our surroundings.

The cycles of attachment

Buddhist psychology suggests that identity is conditioned by the world-view. We saw in Chapter 5 how conditioned perception, *rupa*, is the foundation of the process of building identity. We identify with things that we experience or we reject them, using projection and selective attention. These habits of perception, as we have already seen, are self-reinforcing.

The process of attachment is described in a number of Buddhist teachings. Notably two of these, the *skandhas* and the *Twelve Links of Dependent Origination*, describe the process as a cycle of perception, reaction and becoming (Brazier 2009). They are central to the study of Buddhist psychology. The teaching of the *skandhas* sets out five elements, or, as they are often translated, aggregates. These are the components which make up the person. Although they are often understood to simply be five constituents, with no particular order or connection (e.g. Gethin 1998), the *skandhas* can, as I have argued elsewhere (Brazier 2003), perhaps more usefully be understood as steps in the cycle of self-creation. According to this understanding, the cycle of self-creation starts with *rupa*, the first of the *skandhas*. We look for confirmation of identity in our surroundings and engage with the objects which hold *rupa*-power for us. The attention of our senses is caught by objects which have the power to reflect our sense of identity.

The second of the *skandhas* is *vedana*. We have already discussed *vedana* in Chapter 5. *Vedana* is the immediate felt response which we have to the object of perception. As something catches the attention, we react to it in an attractive, aversive or neutral way. We want it or reject it. This is not rational or cognitive, but a spontaneous, embodied response that wells up from our conditioned mentality, rather like an amoeba engulfing its prey or shrinking away from danger. Recognising this reaction in the body can be helpful. It is said that *vedana* is the point at which the cycle of the *skandhas* can most easily be interrupted. As we tune into the body-sense we feel the rush of energy which accompanies *vedana*. We can therefore learn to recognise when we have been hooked and let go.

The third of the *skandhas* is *samjna*. Following on from *vedana*, the mind makes sense of its reactions by fitting perceptions into life scripts in ways similar to those described earlier in this chapter. We create associations, finding stories and memories to explain our perceptions and reactions to ourselves. In this way the mind reinforces the world-view and continues to build the sense of identity. These processes are unconscious, but they are powerful in shaping our patterns of thinking and perception. *Samskara* is the fourth *skandha. Samskara* means mental fabrication. As the mind repeats old stories to itself, it builds up new layers of conditioning. The *samskaras* are mental track-ways which provide the conditions for future actions. They are created by repeating stories and actions over time. This process leads to the establishment of the fifth *skandha, vijnana. Vijnana* is the ordinary conditioned mentality. It arises, based on the other four *skandhas. Vijnana* is the ordinary mind-state which keeps us trapped in the limited world-view which defines experience in terms of identity, personal associations and usefulness.

Vijnana in turn leads us to experience the world as *rupa*, creating the cycle by which the sense of a permanent self is established. We are trapped in a conditioned mind-set. *Rupa* leads to *vedana*, which leads to *samjna*, which leads to *samskara*, which creates *vijnana*, which in turn leads back to *rupa*. Perception creates reaction, which leads us to draw on pre-existing stories. These reinforce mental formations and the common mentality, which in turn condition perception. We are locked into this mutually conditioning relationship between the sense of self and the world-view. Both identity and the world-view are conditioned and each conditions the other.

Working at the personal level

In the Ten Directions model, working at the personal level involves exploring the way that individual histories affect people's relationships with the environment. Everyone imposes interpretation and colouration on their view of the world, but as we work with particular people, we explore with them the particular details of how they see things and what this means. Because the world-view mirrors the identity, exploring perception is an important facet of the other-centred model. By exploring associations and patterns of thinking we find windows to a person's past and insight into influences in their current life. This can help us to understand the roots of present issues in their history and circumstances and to recognise those patterns which may be amenable to change.

The landscape offers metaphors which can be used to explore personal issues. For example, on a recent Ten Directions course, students were invited to choose two trees, an oak and a hawthorn, and to spend time sitting with each of them. They were to use word association and creative writing to explore the different images associated with each tree that came to them. Among the responses, one of the students was very surprised to discover when she reread her work that she had perceived one tree as her father and the other as her mother. She continued exploring the associations which she had recorded for each tree, identifying characteristics which were relevant to her relationship to each of her parents. She felt very touched by this process. In particular, the exercise left her with a warm feeling towards her mother, whom she identified with the hawthorn. This tree was covered in beautiful blossom but also had fierce thorns which she saw as being there to protect the tree's children, the berries, from animals which might steal them. It was this protective aspect which moved her. She had not previously thought of her mother as being protective, but contemplating the hawthorn had made her realise that it was indeed there and that her mother had protected her in many ways.

Other-centred working is also concerned with moving beyond our projections and encountering others in a fresher way. In working at the personal level, we can explore the way that our relationship with nature is affected by projections and use metaphor to look at personal issues, but this level of working can also involve exploring the outdoors more directly in order to challenge habitual perceptions. Places exist in their own right, beyond the projections and stories. We can investigate the soil, plants, trees, animals, rocks and so on, appreciating the rock-ness of rocks, the tree-ness of trees and the bird-ness of birds. We should not imagine, however, that we can eradicate personal associations completely.

Nor indeed would it be desirable to free ourselves from the richness of these associations. It is often through analogy and metaphor that we come to most deeply appreciate the world. These elaborations of perception also help us to communicate our experience to others. Poetry and other arts incorporate layers of imagery and meaning which come from the personal and cultural legacies that we all share. So too, our experience of life allows us to see more depth in the landscape, illustrating our perception of the immediate environment with nuances from our personal and collective pasts. To see the world in a grain of sand is to invite the imagination to dance.

Modes of conditioning

Conditioned reactions affect people's experience of the outdoors. Some of these reactions are positive, whilst others are negative. Other-centred therapy is concerned with understanding the conditioned mind and how it affects and limits our way of relating to the world. It is also concerned with moving beyond these mental limits and discovering things which surprise us.

The teachings of the *skandhas* and *dependent origination* are based on the Buddhist concept of conditionality which proposes that everything comes into existence in the presence of conditions and that nothing arises without some kind of appropriate conditions being in place. The concept of conditionality is central to Buddhist thought (Thomas 2011). It relates both to the dependent nature of all phenomena and particularly to the conditioned nature of mind-states. Problematic mind-states arise, dependant on certain conditions. If you change these conditions, different mind-states come into being. The teaching of conditionality is not deterministic. It implies likelihoods and possibilities and does not suggest that because one thing is present, particular outcomes will inevitably follow. The theory of conditionality allows for unexpected outcomes and gives space for change. It is about multiple factors and complexity rather than simple this-leads-to-that analyses.

The teachings on conditionality are quite organic. Just as a seed, landing in the soil, is likely to grow into a plant if given the right conditions, so too, if the right psychological conditions are in place, then positive mental states are likely to follow. Things are not predictable however. As in the case of the seed, even when people appear to have grown up in a good psychological climate, they may not flourish and mature as expected. Conversely, people can grow up in difficult situations and emerge apparently unscathed from the experience. Mostly, though, as in the case of Rogers' potatoes (see Chapter 1), we are affected by our conditions.

There is a collection of Buddhist texts called the Pali Abhidhamma which summarises and distils the theoretical essence of the Buddha's teachings. In these rather obscure texts, we find descriptions of the processes of mental conditioning which are put together in a different way from in the suttas, which we have looked at earlier. The seventh book of the Abhidhamma explores the nature of conditionality (Brazier, D. 1995). In it we find the categorisation of different modes of conditioning which affect mental process. These are useful to our understanding of psychological process. In all, twenty four modes of conditioning (known as the *paccayas*) are listed. Unlike the process models offered by the teachings of the *skandhas* or *dependent origination*, this list offers categorisation of particular conditional relationships between phenomena and mental states, addressing the detail of moment by moment experience, as well as providing some broad principles by which to understand conditionality.

Of the twenty four modes of conditional relationship listed in the text, some are easier to identify than others. Here we will discuss the first seven: *root conditions*, *object conditions*, *predominance*, *proximity*, *contiguity*, *co-nascence* and *mutuality*. We will also look at two other conditional relations included in the list, numbers twelve and thirteen, which are *repetition* and *karma*. Although these terms might seem rather obscure, and the lists formulaic, in fact they refer to common psychological phenomena that we can observe in ourselves and others.

Root conditions

The three poisons, described in Chapter 5, influence our experience of the world and the way in which we behave towards it. The six root conditions of the Abhidhamma, are the bitter roots, which are the three poisons, greed, hate, and confusion, and their opposites, the sweet roots, non-greed, non-hate and non-confusion. If we think about it logically, this list covers all possible responses to a situation or object. We almost always respond to things that we encounter based on one or more of these six states. For example, if things are experienced by someone in a 'greed' mind-state, they want them or identify with them, thinking of them as 'like me' or 'mine'. In a hate mind-state, things are rejected as different, alien or unpleasant. Root conditions tend to pervade the mentality, making us acquisitive, negative or ambivalent, positive or hostile at a particular time. As they do, we are likely to see things differently and tell ourselves different stories about them. If a person is in a negative, hate-based mood, they tend to dwell on all the things which are wrong, noticing the muddy pavement or the tree that needs pruning. On the other hand, if they are in a greed-based mood, they might be more preoccupied with getting a cup of tea or what colour roses they plan to plant in their garden.

Object-relation conditions

The theory of *object-relation* proposes that the mind is conditioned by the object of attention. What we give attention to conditions our reactions and mind-set. If we change the object of attention, then our mental states will respond to the new focus and also change. Different stimuli evoke different responses. When we read the newspapers, we will feel differently when reading about an international disaster, from the way we do when reading celebrity gossip. It follows that, by deliberately shifting attention, people can shift their mood and their view of the world. This in turn shifts the way they see things in general. Working outdoors brings people into contact with new experiences. Changing the environment like this is likely to change their mental states. *Object-relation* theory in itself therefore provides a rationale for taking people outdoors.

It is worth noting here that the categories of conditional relations listed in the Abhidhamma are not exclusive of one another. Rather, the different types of condition often work together. If the root condition is of the greed-type, a person's attention will probably be constantly drawn to the things which they desire. The objects of their attention will then be things for which they feel greed, so *object-relation* conditions will support the development of more greed conditions.

Predominance

The theory of *predominance* proposes that the things which are foremost in our minds tend to affect the way that we see everything. For example, if a person has just heard that he has got a new job, he is likely to go about all day with a happy, confident feeling predominating. This will make him more positive and aware of the good things in his life. Also, because the job is on his mind, he will probably notice things associated with the new job, and this in turn will tend to increase the influence of the 'new job' mind-set as he keeps seeing things which reinforce the predominating condition.

Predominance is experienced on an individual level, but it also affects larger social groups. For many people these days, the predominant preoccupation is economic. People tend to be preoccupied with work, income and lifestyle and become ambitious for increasing levels of comfort and wellbeing. Happiness and success become equated with material wealth and people become focused on generating more money so as to live in ways that they believe will make them happy. This kind of mentality is supported by the advertising industry and society at large, which tend to reinforce feelings of deprivation, encouraging people to aspire to more possessions. This in turn impacts on the environment. Shifting out of this kind of predominant mind-set is not easy because the conditions which support it are all around us. On the other hand, if individuals make lifestyle changes which bring them under the influence of different ideas, different mind-states may come to *predominance*. Taking people outdoors is one way in which we can encourage a shift of culture and facilitate change. The theory of *predominance* suggests that, once enough people adopt a new way of being, a tipping point may be reached and new values may come to predominate.

Proximity and contiguity

The sequence in which things happen is important. According to the theories of *proximity* and *contiguity*, our reactions to particular things are often affected by the things which occur just before we encounter them. These conditioning factors may occur close in time to the affected reaction (*proximate*) or immediately before it (*contiguous*). If I come home from a dental appointment and find a box of chocolates in my living room, I might see it as a source of potential pain. If I am watching a romantic film, I might view the same chocolates as a pleasant distraction. Things are seen in context, and the context is created in part by previous events.

We can use the principles of *proximity* and *contiguity* to influence our mind-states by introducing fulfilling activities into the sequence of our days. Creating regular positive experiences, like time in nature, improves mental wellbeing. For example, if we make space to be outdoors for a short period every day, this can bring about a significant shift in the mentality. By interspersing regular reminders of the natural world with time on the computer screen affects energy levels and thinking processes throughout the rest of the day, so taking time to go for a short walk in the park during the lunch hour will tend to lift the mood and improve the ability to concentrate. Even small inputs of nature-exposure make a difference if they are regular. In Chapter 9 we will look at how an exercise using daily recording of 'three good things in nature' has been shown to be effective in lifting mood (Richardson, Hallam & Lumber 2015).

Co-nascence

The conditional relationship of *co-nascence* arises when several conditions come into being at the same time. For example, when a child is born, his life starts and at the same time his mother becomes a mother and his father becomes a father. In this way baby, mother and father are all co-nascent conditions for one another. Psychological processes are commonly based on co-nascent conditions. If visiting the country as a child was associated with picnics, going on holiday and having fun, then this set of experiences will be mutually conditioning. The thought of going outdoors evokes thoughts of holidays, picnics and fun. On the other hand if early experiences of being in the country were associated with long walks in the rain, feeling tired and hungry, wearing uncomfortable walking boots and carrying a heavy rucksack, a person is likely to have a different set of *co-nascent* associations for being outdoors.

Mutuality

The conditional relationship of *mutuality* describes a situation in which a number of conditions mutually support one another. This condition is described as being like the three legs of a tripod. If one leg is not present, the tripod will fall over. It is a particular version of the fundamental Buddhist theory of interdependence. Interdependence has become an important concept for environmentalists. Many ecological systems are interdependent. Disrupting one part of them causes disruption to the whole. As we become conscious of the complexity of the different environments on the planet, the delicate balance between species becomes apparent. Changes in the health of one species can have dramatic effects on the whole ecosystem of an area. For example, the recent reintroduction of wolves into certain areas of North America had dramatic effects upon whole habitats (Eisenberg 2010). As major predators, the wolves reduced the populations of deer and other grazing animals which had previously been degrading shrubs and trees. A regrowth of vegetation followed, which in turn supported the return of many species of smaller animals and an increase in bio-diversity.

The deep ecology movement has frequently embraced the idea that all living things, including the human species, are interconnected, either through the pragmatics of scientific argument (Lovelock 2000) or using more mythological imagery. In her environmentally-based approach, Joanna Macy draws on the Mahayana Buddhist theory of interdependent co-arising (Macy 1991) which suggests that all things come into being in dependence on one another. She also uses the story of Indra's Net (Macy 1983), a mythical image which represents the fundamental interconnected nature of existence, to describe our interdependence. Vietnamese Buddhist teacher, Thich Nhat Hanh, coined the term *interbeing* (Hanh 1987) to describe a similar understanding of the inseparability of people, animals and habitats on the planet. Humans are not disconnected from other animals. We are not a special case to be absolved of responsibilities in the ecosystem. Rather, we are deeply connected with the planet's destiny, even though we may be in a state of alienation. Understanding *mutuality* challenges us to face our responsibility to the whole and take a humbler stance towards the planet.

Repetition

The conditional relationship theory of *repetition* proposes that repeating an activity makes its influence stronger. Whenever something is repeated, it becomes easier to do. This increases the likelihood of it happening again. Habits become established. These, as we know, can be positive or negative. If we establish positive habits, as this theory suggests, we will gradually create a predisposition for those positive activities to continue. Things get easier. For this reason, meditators establish a daily practice. Even if the meditation is only short, say ten minutes, the discipline of daily practice becomes a habit which, once established, is easy to repeat.

In recent years we have seen changes in the way that people live in Britain. With increasing awareness of environmental issues, recycling and energy conservation measures have become part of daily life for much of society. These changes have been incorporated into local services, and whilst practices are by no means perfect, it is evident that mainstream consciousness in Britain and other countries is no longer ignoring the environmental agenda. Changing lifestyle habits is a matter of persistence, but it can happen quickly when led by legislation. Smokers have become used to congregating on pavements, and many people now sort their rubbish for recycling and buy eco-friendly lightbulbs without thinking that they are doing anything out of the ordinary. We have learned new ways and created new habits.

Karma

Karma is created through action of the will. When we act intentionally, the action leaves a trace in the mentality. This supports the likelihood that the same thing will be done again in the future when similar conditions arise. Acting with intention means that it not only gets easier to repeat one's previous action, but also it becomes more likely that one will. Intentionality adds energy to the impulse to repeat. In acting intentionally, we create an impulse which becomes a condition for future action.

The subject of *karma* is complex and because the concept is common to other Indian religions as well as Buddhism, differences of interpretation can be confusing (Watts 2009). In Buddhist thought *karma* is not deterministic, and is often described in terms of sowing seeds. When we plant seeds, we do not know if they will all grow, but if we sow enough of them, something is likely to come up.

The analogy of seeds is useful to our understanding of *karma*. Think of a dandelion clock. If we do something intentionally, it is like blowing on the dandelion head and sending the seeds floating out into the field of our minds. On future occasions when conditions are right, some of those seeds will grow. Whilst seeds are in the ground we are not aware of them, but when conditions change and seeds germinate, new dandelion plants will appear. At this point we have a choice. We can dig up the new plants and eradicate them, or we can let them continue growing until they flower and create more seeds. Each dandelion clock produces many seeds, and each of these in turn produces more dandelions. To get rid of dandelions, we need to be vigilant, catching each one before it flowers. Getting rid of karmic habits is equally difficult sometimes. *Karma* is about predispositions which lie dormant in the psyche. Mostly, we are not aware of what *karma* we are carrying, but when the seeds are triggered, old patterns surface, and we are likely to respond to the situation as we did in the past. Sometimes this happens after a long time. Old reactions can catch us by surprise.

At the point when karmic seeds are triggered we have a choice. The impulse to act out an old pattern of behaviour may be strong, but we do not have to do the same as we did before. We can decide whether or not we want to respond in the habitual way. If the impulse no longer feels appropriate, instead of acting on it without thinking, we can pause and observe the feelings arising in us and then watch them pass away. Then we will eliminate that particular seed. Interrupting the impulse to act is rather like digging up one of the dandelion plants and getting rid of it, roots and all. It will not stop the impulse arising again since there are always more seeds to be triggered when the conditions arise, but gradually we will eradicate particular karmic seeds, diminishing our tendencies to respond in particular ways. Whilst we are doing this, we are planting seeds of other responses, making it more likely that we will act wisely in the future.

Mindfulness and mental process

The patterns of conditionality which we have been discussing influence our thinking and shape our actions more than we might imagine. Most of the time, we are completely unaware of how much we are driven by habits and circumstances. Although we might think we make free choices about what we do, in fact we live much of our lives on auto-pilot, following tracks that we have established over years or decades. Changing unhelpful patterns requires awareness.

Mindfulness is concerned with developing awareness and making choices about where we place our attention. Whilst mindfulness can be focused on physical sensations, breathing and the body-sense, other important aspects of mindfulness practice focus on observing mental processes. In the *Satipatthana Sutta*, the core text on mindfulness referred to in Chapter 2, the second and third sections of the text focus on *vedana* and mind-states (*citta*) respectively. They describe the practitioner observing reactivity (*vedana*) as the arising of the six root conditions. It also describes observing these conditions and other mental qualities in the underlying mind-state.

Bringing mindfulness to our work outdoors, we can become more aware of reactions and associations linked to particular places and things. We can also notice any mental phenomena like depression or excitement which follow them. We can notice the physical qualities of our responses and whether they basically involve positive or negative impulses. We can also recognise any associations which these responses relate to. Mindfulness gives us space to experience our reactions so that we can observe them without getting caught in responding to them or acting them out. Through mindfulness we can watch the dandelion seed floating through the air and landing on bare soil, then pick it up and remove it from the garden before it starts to grow.

Mindfulness helps us develop our capacity to observe thought processes without judging them as right or wrong. It helps us transform the compulsive elements which drive us to act on the impulses created by past events or other mental conditioning, and in so doing, diminishes the proliferation of the karmic seeds which cement the traces of past actions into the psyche.

References

Brazier, C. (2003). *Buddhist Psychology*. London: Constable.
Brazier, C. (2009). *Other-Centred Therapy: Buddhist Psychology in Action*. Ropley: O-Books.
Brazier, D. (1995). *Zen Therapy*. London: Constable Robinson.
Eisenberg, C. (2010). *The Wolf's Tooth: Keystone Predators, Trophic Cascades, and Biodiversity*. Washington, DC: Island Press.
Gethin, R. (1998). *The Foundations of Buddhism*. Oxford: Oxford University Press.
Hanh, N. (1987). *Being Peace*. Berkeley: Parallax.
Lovelock J. (2000). *Gaia: a New Look at Life on Earth*. Oxford: Oxford University Press.
Macy, J. (1983). *Despair and Power in the Nuclear Age*. Philadelphia: New Society Publishers.
Macy, J. (1991). *World as Lover, World as Self*. Berkeley: Parallax.
Richardson, M., Hallam, J. & Lumber, R. (2015). One Thousand Good Things in Nature: The Aspects of Nature that Lead to Increased Nature Connectedness. *Environmental Values*, 24(5): 603–619.
Thomas, D. (2011). *This Being, That Becomes: The Buddha's Teaching on Conditionality*. Cambridge: Windhorse Publications.
Trungpa, C. (1973). *Cutting Through Spiritual Materialism*. Boulder: Shambala.
Watts, J. (Ed.). (2009). *Rethinking Karma: The Dharma of Social Justice*. Thailand: Silkworm Books.

8 Conditioned view

This chapter continues exploration of conditioned view by investigating the role of childhood influences in shaping adult psychology. In particular it explores relationships to place, animals and people. The chapter then explores methodology for working with childhood themes, particularly with regard to groupwork, giving examples of practical exercises which can be used. The areas addressed are: introductions and warms ups; projective work; sculpts; dialogue methods; letter writing. The chapter concludes with reflections on how influences also occur in adulthood and on how patterns can be changed through methods such as Thich Nhat Hanh's Buddhist practice of 'nourishing healthy seeds'.

When I was eight years old I received the only school prize which I have ever won. It was a copy of Robert Louis Stevenson's *A Child's Garden of Verse*, and in the front of the book was inscribed 'for keenness in nature and poetry'. I like to think that things have not changed much over the years. Nature and poetry were important to me from a very young age and still influence my work today. They were part of my life long before I received the prize, but undoubtedly receiving this acknowledgment cemented my identification with them. Where did this identification come from? Did these subjects represent something innate in me, or were they subjects which I learned to identify with through chance and circumstances? How were the foundations laid for this life-long interest?

Things experienced when young shape our adult lives in surprising ways. When I reflect back, all of my interests as an adult have roots in experiences which I had whilst growing up. From earliest childhood, I learned to name birds, trees and plants, encouraged by my mother. I created notebooks full of pressed flowers before I even went to school, the names written beside each specimen in almost illegible characters, laboriously copied from my mother's original. I watched the birds in the back garden, looking them up in my bird-books. I can still picture the green woodpecker which once appeared on the lawn among the blackbirds and sparrows, shuffling about, incongruous as an owl in daylight.

Poetry also featured in my early childhood. My mother read to me a great deal, and particularly introduced me to poems. I loved listening, especially to verses about nature. I think even then I recognised how poetry could take ordinary things and make them special, and how rhythm and the sounds of the words paint pictures that reflect and amplify their meaning. I began to write my own verses and stories, scrawling them untidily in hard-backed exercise books which I bought from Woolworths, and illustrating them with line drawings. A love of language and metre has stayed with me in my adult writing and even when I am writing factual or academic pieces, I still find myself reading the sentences in my head, noticing and adjusting their pacing so that they sound right as well as conveying meaning.

The experiences of childhood establish precedents for adult mind-states. They create patterns which repeat throughout our lives, sowing seeds which can re-emerge many years later in straightforward or subtle ways. Some people carry on doing things which they did with their families when they were young, like going for Sunday walks, visiting galleries or bird watching. They make similar lifestyle choices and hold similar attitudes, values and political views to their parents. Other people react against their parents, choosing adventures instead of being stay-at-home-dull, or becoming couch potatoes because the parents always wanted to be out doing something exciting or useful. Mostly, though, we are confused mixtures of our pasts and presents, inconsistent and contradictory. We conform to the patterns we have learned, even whilst rebelling against them. *Karma* is powerful.

Exploring childhood influences

Childhood experience has long been considered important in shaping adult psychology. Freud and his contemporaries saw many adult problems as rooted in early experience, but they were not first to make this connection. Since the sixteenth century, for example, the Jesuits held the view that the first seven years of life shaped the man. Early influences condition our relationship to being outdoors. It is not surprising, therefore, that in environmentally-based work we often talk about childhood experiences, in relation both to general life issues and to nature. Being in nature often evokes associations with play and other childhood experiences. We can deliberately use exercises to explore these, or we can allow memories to emerge spontaneously through the process of being outdoors.

Some associations that we have with childhood are linked to personal history, but other associations are more generalised. Most people associate childhood with playfulness, vulnerability, creativity or naughtiness for example. Both types of association can influence our work both consciously and unconsciously: a beach becomes a place for running about and splashing in the tide, a children's park, for playing on the swings. Participants can roll down grassy banks or clamber over rocks, hide in a tree, or jump a ditch, re-enacting things they did in childhood, or things, they dared not do then, but can now find courage for. Outdoors, people sometimes access child-like aspects of themselves which they do not usually express.

Because memories can be so potent, it can sometimes be useful to know something about participants' personal and family histories before starting work. This is particularly the case where we suspect abuse or trauma. Many therapists take a history in some shape or form at the outset of therapy. If you do this, this can not only warn you of potentially difficult areas, but may also tell you about a person's early experience of being in nature.

Places

Our roots in the land shape our identities. Throughout life people are influenced by their surroundings, but the places where we grow up particularly affect our sense of self. People often feel an emotional connection to their birthplace and places recalled in earliest memories. Some people live all their lives in one place, maybe even the same house, but generally people nowadays are more mobile than in the past. So, throughout life, layers of associations are added as different places leave particular sets of memories and associations.

I recently returned to Canterbury, which was the nearest town to the village where I lived as a small child. Walking the narrow lanes near the cathedral, there were new developments and places that I did not recognise, but some things still seemed familiar despite the passage of more than half a century. In particular, the cathedral itself impacted on me strongly. At the centre of the city, it dominated everything else. Looking up at the great towers with their fine gothic tracery, I experienced them as deeply and almost inter-changeably infused with a felt-sense of my father. My father loved architecture, and as a small child, he often took me to the cathedral, pointing out details in the carvings and telling me about its history, about Saint Augustine and Thomas-a-Becket. He was chaplain at a Methodist boarding school in the city at the time, and his religious role seemed melded with the cathedral. More than this, though, the building itself, standing so tall and magnificent, seemed to echo the power of his paternal presence in my life at that young age.

Some buildings were familiar, but many left no mark on my memory, even though they must have been there when I was a child. Children, as adults, are selective in what they recall. There were places that could not have been there in my childhood. I walked past trendy bistros and boutiques, enjoying the cosmopolitan atmosphere of a small university city, but every so often I would see something that I remembered. Then a strange, wistful feeling would surface, coming out of the shadows of the past like a ghostly miasma. It felt like a homecoming.

The places of our earliest memories are often redolent with feelings which, though tantalisingly familiar, hover on the edge of remembering. These delicate, somewhat nostalgic feelings were appreciated by the Japanese, who described them as *yugen*. *Yugen* is experienced in the shadowy view of distant hills layered range on range in the twilight or in the flight of geese into the autumn mist. Translated as 'dim, deep, distant and mysterious', the term suggests the presence of things beyond the apparent, the spiritual within the ordinary and the bitter-sweetness of death within life. Childhood memories are often of this kind; hazy and fragmented, focused on the small details which adults overlook, but which were significant to the small child: red spider-mites on a wall, or weeds growing around a bus-stop.

Recalling childhood places can evoke the past; significant events or ordinary days, some happy, others less so. We remember activity, for, in inhabiting the landscape, we act within it and karmically connect ourselves to the soil. We come to know the land through walking, playing, climbing, gardening and lying on it. It is closely connected to our relationships, our friendships, our nationality and our roots. In the detail of recollection, we identify with it. These memories construct the present. They shape our sense of identity and the meaning we make of life.

Most memories are benign, but some are dark and frightening. They can haunt the places with which they are associated. Even if the actual memories recede from conscious awareness, their gloomy colouration still shapes our experiencing. Working outdoors, we may unwittingly resurrect disturbing memories. These may be different woods or a different footpath, but similarities to places from the past can bring back unpleasant, creepy or even terrifying memories, the most powerful of which may take the form of flashbacks. Working therapeutically with traumatic associations usually requires a long-term commitment, so it is wise to be cautious about triggering these kinds of experience unintentionally. Where they do occur unexpectedly, flashbacks are usually best contained using grounding methods so that they can be dealt with elsewhere, unless you are able to give time to working in depth. On the whole, it is usually best to try to pre-empt unexpected reactions of this kind by providing space for sharing feelings and associations before going into places which might arouse such responses.

Animals

Children usually love animals. Animals can be held, stroked and related to. They are friends when human friends are not around and family when human families hurt. They populate stories and cartoons, songs and television, sometimes true to life, but other times fantastic versions of reality. They can be friendly or fierce, funny or timid, bigger than the child, like a horse or an elephant, or smaller, like a gerbil. Children have pets at home or at school, and see animals in zoos or running wild in parks and gardens. The family dog may have been a special friend as long as they can remember and they may have responsibility for smaller pets. From animals children learn to care and about the realities of life and death, intimacy and love. Thus animals fill gaps left by human shortcomings.

Children watch birds in the garden and feed ducks on the pond. They visit city farms or go pond-dipping at the local nature park. They watch animals on television and learn about natural history at school. These activities are often initiated by adults but the adults' agendas may or may not shape the child's experience. Children often learn things in spite of adults and fail to learn things that adults want to teach. An adult might persuade a child to pick up a slow worm and feel how it moves on his hand, but she cannot control whether the child enjoys the experience or is terrified by it. She may not even know what impact the experience had on him.

In the past, children often played outdoors unsupervised, and in the process encountered wildlife unhindered by adult values. As a child, I spent hours catching frogs in my grandfather's garden. My brother and I used to search them out in the rockery, and, when we found one, would grab it with our bare hands and imprison it in the old greenhouse. It was exciting. Looking back, of course it was cruel to the frogs, though I do not remember injuring any, and they did get released at the end of the holiday. These frog-catching exploits left me with a lasting sense of frog-ness. I still remember the feeling of their slippery muscular bodies and their sharp, black eyes. Although there was not the same sensitivity to animal welfare then, we encountered nature more directly and perhaps became more interested in it as a result.

Animals often respond to children with their own curiosity. Some years ago I took my children and some friends to a safari park. Once inside the perimeter fence, a group of monkeys climbed onto our car bonnet. Trapped in a queue of cars, I watched helplessly as families of monkeys got to work on our vehicle, stripping the rubber windscreen wiper blades and chewing the outlets of the washer system. Whilst the children in the car were very excited about this, the smallest monkeys also got very excited, peering in through the windscreen and gesticulating to one another and at us. In a strange role reversal, we found ourselves imprisoned like zoo exhibits in our metal cage, providing entertainment to those who were destroying our resources.

People

Children are influenced by the adults around them and parents in particular. Some families go outdoors a lot, others rarely do. Some families expect children to get muddy and are not worried about torn clothes or grazed knees. Other families keep their children clean and tidy or worry about them getting hurt. Some parents send their children to organisations like scouts or guides or woodcraft folk which take them out into nature. Others leave them to their own devices. These patterns can be passed down the generations. If parents were keen walkers, children may well go walking with their children when they grow up. Sometimes though, people react against family traditions. They might avoid doing things outdoors because they hated family walks. Family patterns inevitably influence us, however, and, even when we intend to do things differently, we can find ourselves repeating our parents' patterns when we become parents ourselves.

Despite this, society changes and people come to question things which they previously accepted as normal. It can be a shock to realise that things which we did as children are now considered inappropriate and harmful to the environment, especially when we learned to do them from people we loved. Fifty years ago it was considered educational to catch butterflies or collect birds' eggs. There were plenty of books aimed at children, full of instructions on how to do it. The headmaster at my primary school used to teach the boys (for it was usually boys who had such hobbies) how to kill butterflies and moths in old tobacco tins using some sort of poison. He then showed them how to stretch the wings out, using pins to hold them in place before they 'set' in a closed position. At the time, this seemed quite normal, but now I find it sad to think that someone I liked and respected was teaching such cruelty. Times have changed. We no longer encourage children to kill butterflies, but I still value some of the inspiration which my headmaster provided because he fostered my interest in nature and the environment in many ways. This interest continues, albeit in different ways, and I feel gratitude, even though I do not agree with everything he taught me.

Relationships with peers also shape our attitudes. In the modern world, most children have less opportunity to play outside unsupervised than children did in the past. The current generation are probably more limited than any other in history in this respect. In the past children often spent much of their spare time playing outdoors unsupervised and learned to be self-sufficient in lots of ways. Taking people out into nature can remind them of freedom which they experienced, or wanted to experience, in childhood. Camping in the woods, climbing rocks or enacting make-believe fantasy dramas can recapture childhood excitement and memories of growing up. In reliving the past, participants may rediscover freedoms which they have lost.

Working with personal story

The remainder of this chapter is focused on practical ways of working outdoors. We will focus on exploring the influence which the past, and particularly childhood, has in shaping identity and fostering adult relationships with the environment. Taking people outdoors can put them in touch with early memories. Whilst participants may talk about childhood experiences spontaneously, we can also use structured exercises to evoke memories more intentionally. Such exercises and activities can be pre-planned or can emerge more naturalistically from the process of the group or individual. We can use exercises to help people reconnect with positive aspects of childhood or to explore unpleasant memories, anxieties and fears. Exploring these difficult memories whilst immersed in nature can be grounding, healing and positive. Sometimes it can be enough to talk and feel listened to, but other times using structured activities can help to focus the work.

It is possible to work spontaneously from the group process, introducing structured activities when a theme emerges out of a sharing session. This requires the facilitators to have skills and experience, however. Whilst this approach can make exercises particularly relevant to participants' needs, potentially leading to greater therapeutic intensity, if you are not confident in your ability to respond to group process in this way there can be benefits in pre-planning activities. Pre-planning allows you to create a satisfying sequence of exercises, building on a theme. The latter may have come out of the previous session or be something you determine. It helps you to manage time and allow for debriefing and discussion, which are important to whichever way you work.

When you are co-working pre-planning can be easier to manage, but doing so does not preclude the need, on occasions, to re-negotiate structure as a session progresses. Co-facilitators need to develop trust in one another so that one can take a lead and introduce a change of plan if necessary, as it is not always possible to discuss every decision in advance. Other times, however, discussion about how to proceed can be overt and collaborative, allowing participants to make suggestions too.

If as facilitator or therapist you intend working more spontaneously, it is good to have a few basic structures in mind. These can be infinitely adapted to specific situations. The basic structures below help to make up a tool-box of methods for groupworkers and therapists. These are:

- introductions and warm-ups
- projective work
- sculpts
- dialogue
- time-lines
- letter writing.

Introductions and warm-ups

Sessions usually start with an introductory exercise or activity. This brings participants together and introduces themes for the day. Though most important in early sessions of a group, some kind of warm up or check-in is needed every time you meet.

A warm-up can be a simple go-around in which people share something about themselves, their current situation, their hopes for the group and any concerns which they have. On subsequent sessions, they might share reflections on the previous meeting. If the group membership has changed, facilitators might acknowledge absences or bring people up to date on missed sessions. Introductions can be formal or informal, and different on different occasions. For example, they might be non-verbal, with participants using a gesture to show how they feel or finding an object to represent themselves. These non-verbal warm-ups can be particularly useful outdoors as they are more dynamic and allow people to engage with their surroundings straight away.

Warm-up exercises enable people to introduce themselves and get to know one another. They can be simple. You might ask people to talk in pairs or small groups on a particular topic and then report back. This can introduce the session theme, such as, for example, telling a story about childhood. Where personal stories are shared, however, it is important that people check with one another before talking about their partner's story with the whole group. This kind of exercise helps people get to know one another better and also elicits personal material, which can later be worked with. There are many kinds of warm-up exercise that are commonly used, some of which are suggested below. You will also find many groupwork manuals available which have ideas for this kind of activity (e.g. Brandes & Philips 1979; Ernst & Goodison 1981).

Warm-up exercises

- Talk in pairs about a place where you played as a child, then share something which you talked about with the whole group.
- Find a place in the vicinity which reminds you of a place where you played as a child and take the rest of the group there.
- Find an object which represents your mood today and bring it back to the group. Talk about what the object says about you.
- Remember a photograph from childhood which was taken outdoors. Describe the photo to the group, then choose a place which reminds you of where the photograph was taken and re-create the image using other group members to pose as figures in it.
- Choose an animal which you might hear in the countryside and make its sound. Close your eyes and try to find another participant who is making a similar animal sound to yours by following their call. When instructed, open your eyes and see who you have connected with. Were you intending to be similar animals? What other things do you have in common? (Note that this needs to be done on even ground in a contained area.)

Projective work

Projective methods involve representing groups, systems, psychological processes or abstract concepts in physical ways using a variety of media and techniques. By externalising psychological material and representing it with objects or symbols, these methods enable thoughts, feelings, memories and ideas to be discussed, explored, related to and changed in a somewhat more contained way than by simply talking about them. Drawing is one kind of projective method. It allows the person to represent personal material on paper. Other common projective methods include 'sculpting', sand-tray work or using an empty chair.

Projective methods can be used to represent real phenomena such as relationships within a family or work group. They can also be used to represent abstract phenomena such as sub-personalities or values. Projective work is always subjective. It represents the feelings and perceptions of the person who is doing the activity rather than objective reality, although these methods can allow people to achieve some objectivity about their subjective experience. Once a projected image or story is created, it can be viewed more critically and in different ways. We can have imaginative dialogues with elements in the picture or sculpt, explore the viewpoints of different parties, experiment with multiple perspectives and achieve a comfortable working distance from emotive material (Leissen 1993).

Family sculpts

Sculpting is a projective method commonly used in therapy. It involves using objects such as stones, coins or small toys to represent members of a social group. It can sometimes be used to explore more abstract groupings such as a set of concepts or ideas. This method is often used to represent families, either now, or at some point in the past.

To create a sculpt, pebbles or other small objects are chosen to represent each person in the family. These are arranged (on the ground or some other flat surface) to show relationships between family members. They can show closeness and distance between different people, and reveal sub-groups or alliances within the family as a whole. Creating sculpts involves both conscious and unconscious processes. Objects are ideally placed intuitively, as this often reveals dynamics between people which were not previously recognised. Though objects may be selected to symbolise aspects of the person or relationship and deliberately placed in particular positions, it often turns out that there is other significance in the choice of objects and their positions. These unintentional factors can reveal previously unrecognised connections and associations.

Groups can use sculpting to explore their own dynamics. Such sculpts may be created collectively, with each person placing an object representing himself in a position to reflect how he feels himself to be aligned in the group. This will involve some negotiation between group members. Sculpts can also be made by participants, each placing themselves within a given space in relation to others. Alternatively, a series of sculpts can be made by different participants, each showing how they see alliances and connections within the group. Multiple sculpts like this can reveal different aspects of group experience and show a variety of ways of viewing the same process. No sculpt should be seen as an absolute representation of 'how things are'.

Working outdoors, natural materials can be used to create sculpts. Because space is not limited as it is indoors, sculpts can be made big enough for people to walk around within them, which can itself reveal new facets of relationships. Other times, however, sculpts can be tiny, made using small objects on a flat surface. In either case, working directly in the landscape grounds the work in the physical. Existing features such as trees or rocks can be incorporated. Participants can even find naturally occurring groups of objects, like the hawthorn and the oak described in the last chapter, which function as 'ready-made' sculpts.

Facilitating sculpts

When working with sculpts, it is useful for the facilitator to give broad instructions and then let people interpret these in their own way. Sometimes people will complete sculpts before discussing them. Other times it is possible to facilitate the process as it unfolds, exploring the different elements as they are placed. In either case, the facilitator may observe:

- Is the sculpt based on current or historic material? Does it represent a fixed time or is it more generalised?
- What objects are chosen? Look at shape, colour, weight, size and material of objects chosen and see if they spark associations.
- How are objects handled? Are they treated with care or distain? How are they placed?
- In what order are objects placed? Is anything missed out?
- How are objects placed in relation to one another? Are there groupings or pairs?

Having created a sculpt, the work can be developed in a number of ways:

- Experiment with making changes. Try 'before' and 'after' sculpts; e.g. the family when the children were young and then after they had grown up; before and after a death or marriage break-up.
- View the sculpt from the different positions within it. What does the family look like from father's position or from mother's?
- Explore different perceptions within the group by asking different members of a group to sculpt the same subject in turn; e.g. the group in last week's session.

Dialogues

Relationships can be explored using pairs of objects to represent two positions and conducting a dialogue between them. Typical of this might be the use of the 'empty chair' developed in Gestalt therapy (Meier & Boivin 2010). In this method two chairs are commonly used to represent two people. The client can then experiment with sitting on each in turn, talking from each about how it feels to be in relationship with the other and also speaking to the other directly. By moving between the two chairs, an imagined conversation can be enacted. This kind of two chair method can be used to explore real relationship dynamics, or to dialogue between different viewpoints or even different sides of a dilemma.

The sculpting methods seen above can be extended through this kind of dialogue. Different pairings within the sculpt can be explored, or the author of the sculpt can dialogue with an object (person) within it. This creates a number of possible dialogues:

- Talk about the sculpt, describing how it was created, what it represents and about elements within it.
- Talk to individuals represented in the sculpt and explore what you would like to say to them.
- Stand in the place of one or more individuals and explore what they would like to say to you and to others represented in the sculpt.

This kind of work requires a level of immediacy, which is achieved by a shift to present tense questioning. The therapist indicates an object, asking: 'What are you seeing?' or 'What would you like to say to this person?' Use of the present tense invites the participant to speak as if to the real person who is represented. The use of present tense amplifies the imaginative intensity of the work.

As the third option above suggests, participants may also literally or imaginatively step into the sculpt, experiencing other people's perspectives. This technique, known as 'role reversal', is drawn from psychodrama, a therapeutic method devised by Jacob Moreno (Karp 1998). Through it, a participant can temporarily experience the role of his mother, father, friend or child and explore their viewpoint, speaking in their voices in the first person. He can then return to his own position to reply or reflect on the process. The facilitator might say: 'So, if you are John (pointing to one of the other stones), what are you thinking at the moment?'

The following suggestions can be used to develop these dialogue methods outdoors.

Dialogue method

- Choose a tree to represent someone important in your life, for example a parent or partner.
- Think of three adjectives which describe the tree. What do these tell you about the way you see the person you have chosen?
- Stand facing the tree and imagine the person it represents standing in front of you. What would you like to say to them? If nothing immediately comes to mind, let yourself talk freely. (If you feel self-conscious talking outdoors you can write things down instead of speaking them, though this is less powerful.)
- Place an object such as an item of your clothing (perhaps your coat) where you were standing. This represents you. Stand in front of the tree and imaginatively become the other person. Imagine receiving the words that were just spoken to you. How do you feel when you hear

them? Speak in the voice of the other person and say whatever comes to mind.

- Return to your own place. Imagine hearing the words of the other. How does it feel to receive them?
- Move in dialogue between the two positions, exploring how it feels to be on each 'side' of the relationship.
- When you have finished, touch the bark of the tree and recognise that it is a tree rather than a person.

Time-lines

Sculpts represent relationships at one point in time. Time-line methods, however, represent events over a period of time. Typically a time-line is drawn across a sheet of paper from left to right. This represents the person's life from birth to the present, and is commonly marked off in decades. Significant events are added along its length, together with other details such as relationships, places, employment or predominant feelings. Time-lines offer an overview of major life phases, traumatic incidents, successes and changes. They reveal sequences and patterns occurring over time, showing factual details and psychological process.

Time-lines can be created outdoors in a number of ways. At its simplest, a line can be marked out on the ground and natural objects used to represent events along it. Working in nature also allows us to make bigger scale representations of passing time, so a time-line could be mapped out along a path or track. Working on a large scale introduces new possibilities. We can walk up and down the line, retracing our steps as necessary to explore the past.

Different scales introduce different possibilities to the work. The time-line drawn on paper or represented in a small-scale linear sculpt gives an overview of the life process, reduced to a size that can be seen as one entity. Whilst 'seeing the whole' can be lost if the work is spread over a distance, large scale time-lines bring other insights. For example, a walk can be used as a time-line, adding scale to the work. The arduousness, length and unpredictability of the journey may reflect real life experiences and the whole exercise may become a kind of personal pilgrimage like the one in France which I described in Chapter 3.

Time-lines do not need to be personal, however. They can represent the course of history, either on a global scale or more locally. Using time-lines in this way can be emotive, linking personal stories to world events and discovering connections. We can create time-lines which include our grandparents' and grandchildren's lives as well as our own, or which incorporate the whole of history. We can create lines that show the lives of other species and of the ecosystem.

Time-line exercises

Here are some examples of time-lines that might be created outdoors.

Working alone:

- Invite participants to choose a section of a footpath to work on. This might be long or short, depending on the theme of the exercise.
- Let one end represent birth and the other the present (or even the future). Mark out significant life events or phases using found objects or by identifying particular features along the path.
- Walk up and down the path, reflecting on embodied feelings and associations that arise.

Working together as a group:

- Agree a time-line location, perhaps along a path or across an open space.
- Designate areas along it as 'childhood', 'adolescence', 'young adulthood' etc.
- Invite participants to add objects to the different areas and to share associations, building a collective representation of each life stage.
- Walk up and down the line, noticing associations, working either alone, or in pairs.
- Explore commonalities and differences between different people's experiences and associations.

Exploring historic and geological time spans, you might create a time-line representing:

- the history of the area in which you are working, perhaps through industrial and post-industrial changes
- the life span of a particular tree
- geological time in this area (and the role of humans)
- the past and future of the planet.

Writing, letters and letterboxes

Therapeutic writing can be used outdoors in many different ways. Journaling and creative writing provide a medium for inner dialogue, useful in solitary work, but also in groups. The journal allows participants to record thoughts and perceptions, particularly in situations when the therapist is not immediately present. It mirrors their process, allowing them to re-read and reflect on what has been written, gaining new perspectives on the issues they explore.

Another writing method involves writing imaginative letters. These might be addressed to people, current and historic, with whom there are unresolved issues, offering an extension of dialogue methods discussed above. Letter writing differs from other dialogue work in creating an artefact which is composed rather than being spoken spontaneously. This can be read and re-read later on. It can also be delivered, usually in symbolic ways. It is rarely wise to deliver therapeutic letters to real people, since they generally contain complex mixes of past and present feelings, but symbolic delivery can provide psychological completion.

Whilst one would not wish to encourage littering the countryside with letters to deceased or estranged loved ones, because paper is generally bio-degradable, it can be left in places where it will not become unsightly whilst decomposing. Letters can be pushed into a hollow tree, left in a crevice, buried in the ground or burned. If written on thin, soluble paper, they can be thrown into a river or lake (care should, of course, be taken not to contaminate water sources). Leaving a physical token of therapeutic work can be very powerful and these activities often mark the culmination of a longer piece of work. We can draw on traditional rituals for ideas. For example, practices used at funerals and memorials, floating paper boats with candles in them onto a lake, or burning messages for the spirits in a ritual fire, can be adapted for therapeutic work, particularly around grief.

Not all letters need to be written. In Yôjirô Takita's film, *Departures*,[1] returning to his childhood home, Daigo, the central character, remembers how, as a child, his father once gave him a 'stone letter'. The memory is poignant, for Daigo's father left shortly after the incident, abandoning the family, and Diago never saw him alive again.

In one scene in the film, Daigo gives his wife, Mika, a stone. She is perplexed by this gesture, but he explains, 'Long ago, before writing, you'd send someone a stone that suited how you were feeling. From its weight and touch, they'd know how you felt. From a smooth stone, they might get that you were happy. Or from a rough one, that you were worried about them.'

We can take the idea of stone letters and develop it. Group participants might be invited to find a stone letter which either reflects their own feelings, or something which they want to say to another participant. Stone letters can then be exchanged. They might be used for silent sharing in pairs, or be passed around the whole group. They could simply be given to a chosen recipient without any verbal exchange at all.

Other influences on conditioned view

The past has a significant impact on our current lives, but present conditions are also influential. Immediate circumstances influence the way that people see the things around them, and the way they react to them. For example, if other participants are talking about environmental politics, a person who has brought a canned drink for her lunchtime break may suddenly become self-conscious.

This self-consciousness may be temporary, and the person may revert to her usual behaviour when she gets home, or it may influence her to think about what she buys when she next visits the supermarket.

Adult relationships have a big influence on our habits. A new partner may introduce new interests that may include being in nature. Conversely, they may not share enthusiasm for the countryside and this may lead both partners to go out less. Life circumstances change. People have families or travel, change jobs and make different friends, experience changes of health and get older. All of these create changes in lifestyle which in turn affect attitudes and interests.

Life changes also affect the way that we look back on the past. Childhood experiences look different when we think about them at the age of twenty from the way we recall them at thirty or forty or fifty. Becoming parents or grandparents ourselves, we often develop more understanding for our own parents and grandparents and the ways they acted towards us. This may affect the stories that we tell ourselves about them. For this reason the past is constantly being rewritten and is, at least in part, a mirror to the present.

Whilst many of our attitudes and behaviours are influenced by patterns established early in life, there are also gradual and sudden changes of circumstance throughout life which feed into a person's world-view, sometimes supporting radical shifts of interest, activity and psychology. This flexibility in the human process is something that therapy draws on. People change. At the same time, the depth patterns of early experience tend to remain and reassert themselves throughout life in different guises. This paradox is at the root of the Buddhist understanding of working with the ordinary mentality.

Watering good seeds

Karma is one of the forms of mental conditioning described in the seventh book of the Abhidhamma. Like many of the forms of conditioning which we have been exploring, *karma* operates as a cycle. Intentional action leaves traces (Tsering 2006). These have been likened to seeds (*bija*), planted in the fertile soil of the psyche. They lie dormant, ready to be activated when similar circumstances occur to those which created them originally. Then karmic seeds are triggered, making us likely to repeat the action which gave rise to them in the first place. If we do not restrain ourselves when the impulse to action arises, it is as if the seeds grow and come to fruition and, in repeating the action, we sow more seeds, adding to the store in the psyche and influencing future actions.

According to this understanding, action creates conditions for future action. The theory also suggests that we always carry many seeds from past activity which are dormant, ready to spring into life if circumstances arise. The more times we have done something, the more seeds are waiting to be triggered. This is why childhood patterns are very difficult to eradicate. They have been revisited many times. The theory also suggests that if we stop acting on habitual impulses and do things differently we will plant different seeds, eventually changing the predominance in the psyche; but this takes time and requires deliberate choices, which may feel unnatural at first.

Based on this appreciation of *karma*, Vietnamese Zen teacher, Thich Nhat Hanh, advocates a practice called 'nourishing healthy seeds' (Hanh 1991). This involves deliberately doing things conducive to healthy mind-states so as to create a predominance of good karmic seeds in the psyche. He suggests increasing slow, mindful activity and decreasing anxiety-ridden busyness, thus becoming more peaceful in our ways of thinking and more appreciative of the world around us.

This theory is also relevant to therapeutic work. It is important to be aware of what karmic seeds we are watering in our clients. Working with historic pain and trauma often evokes feelings of anger and alienation. To be ultimately useful, however, the person needs to re-engage with positive experiencing of the world as it is now, watering good seeds as well as angry ones. Working in nature creates balance, allowing the exploration of past hurt to coexist with present awareness of the everyday processes of the natural world. Being outdoors, we water good seeds in the psyche, and, as we have seen in much currently emerging research, this is good for mental health.

Note

1 Yôjirô Takita (director) 2008 film, *Departures*.

References

Brandes, D. & Philips, H. (1979). *The New Gamesters Handbook*. Cheltenham: Nelson Thornes.

Ernst, S. & Goodison, L. (1981). *In Our Own Hands: Book of Self-help Therapy*. London: Women's Press.

Hanh, N. (1991). *Peace is Every Step: The Path of Mindfulness in Everyday Life*. New York: Bantam.

Karp, M. (Ed.). (1998). *The Handbook of Psychodrama*. London: Routledge.

Leissen, M. (1993). Creating a Working Distance to Overwhelming Images: Comments on a Session Transcript. In D. Brazier (Ed.), *Beyond Carl Rogers* (pp. 129–147). London: Constable.

Meier, A. & Boivin, M. (2010). *Counselling and Therapy Techniques: Theory, and Practice*. London: Sage.

Tsering, T. (2006). *Buddhist Psychology*. Massachusetts: Wisdom.

9 Encounter

Having explored conditioned view, this chapter investigates the role of encounter in enabling people to change their conditioned experiencing of the world. Offering methods which encourage observation, it suggests use of photography, writing, solitary retreat and gardening, and describes Miles Richardson's practice of recording 'three good things in nature'. The chapter offers practical guidance for these activities, including advice on safety considerations. It also provides exercises which can be used with individuals or groups to facilitate encounter. The chapter concludes by reflecting on the role of healthy encounter with impermanence and death in nature as a route to psychological wellbeing.

Despite what has already been said regarding conditioned perception, selective attention can be functional. When we go for a walk, we notice signposts and stiles. When we go outdoors to paint, we choose a pleasant view. When we go blackberrying, we look for accessible brambles. This selectivity is not driven by the grasping mind which is basically concerned with psychological protection, building defensive structures through selective attention. It is about practicality, yet even in practicalities, attention is partially driven by unconscious searching for safety and stability. We relate to the object-world through perceptive processes such as naming and categorisation which give us a sense of 'power over' our surroundings, and make nature useful to us.

Fear haunts us, making us wary and self-protective. Modern peoples, susceptible to scare stories, often see wild spaces as infiltrated by disease and danger. Such fears lead people to fence off or destroy areas of threat both literally and psychologically. Swamps are drained and jungles turned into farm land. Nature is appropriated for human use and in the process loses its wildness.

Environmentally-based therapies cannot avoid the problem of appropriation. The natural world provides resources for our work as therapists and facilitators. We may think that our approach is collaborative and respectful, but it is a one-sided agreement to which nature has not necessarily signed up. It is therefore our responsibility to reflect on our work and try to ensure that, by taking people into the outdoors, we help them to reconnect and live more responsibly. We cannot heal the person whilst neglecting the whole. The interconnection of individual and global ecosystems renders mental health a function of collective ecological wellbeing.

Nor are all ecotherapies of one mind. Different approaches take different philosophical vantage points, fostering different kinds of relationship between humans and nature. For some, ecotherapy provides a tool-box of green resources for psychological wellbeing. For others, humans are wild children of nature, inseparable from other life-forms, who need to find harmony with the other-than-human. Both these stances, however, shape nature to the human eye. Whether by expressing exotic, chaotic shadows or well-manicured personae, the nature they evoke is as much a mirror or a chimera as a reality. Only inasmuch as we transcend personal motivations do we really engage with that which is not projected self-interest and so encounter our world.

Encounter is vital to the planet and vital to our mental wellbeing. So far we have reflected on factors that shape our experiencing. Exploring these factors is the substance of most therapies. In addition, we have seen that encountering others, human or non-human, helps people change habitual patterns of thought and perception and view things freshly. In the therapy room, it is easy to become self-absorbed in the contained constancy of the therapeutic frame, but when we go outdoors, we are suddenly plunged into a cacophony of unpredictable and sometimes insistent others. Plants, trees, weather, birds, animals and the Earth itself constantly interrupt the flow of personal process, potentially waking us up to the reality of the present moment. Despite our tendency to appropriation, we are likely to be touched by others in the park or woodland in a way that we will not be indoors. Thus we return to ecological sanity.

When we step over the threshold of the therapy room into the outdoors, we find ourselves in relationship with environmental forces. Even in city landscapes, wind touches our skin and the air quality feels different. We cannot help but be conscious of changing weather systems and light levels. We hear sounds, coming from all directions: humans and animal life, mechanical processes, wind and water. We sense the spaciousness of land and sky and the boundaries of buildings and structures.

Being outdoors changes us. We become more embodied. Movement becomes imperative and walking the norm. If we sit, it is not on a cushioned sofa, but, rather, on a bench or tree trunk which demands we sit with awareness. If the sun shines, we take off coats and relax. If it rains, we put up umbrellas and don waterproofs or run for shelter. Outdoors we are forced into awareness of things beyond the human world. Nature is hard to ignore. Though many people push past its inconveniences, returning to the urban shelters of precincts and shopping centres, even in the city, outdoor life invades.

Urban observation

The object of attention and the way it is viewed conditions our mental states. We can use a variety of exercises and methods to encourage people to look more carefully at nature and encounter it in new ways. The intent of these activities is to challenge preconception and look more closely at real phenomena. Observation requires us to ask questions. Whilst conditioned view is based on assumption, encounter is based on not knowing. We become curious and open our mental space to discoveries. In this section we will look at two examples. Photography and writing exercises bring attention to details of the natural world. People can use these exercises to connect with nature in urban localities on a regular basis. Both methods have a number of common factors:

- focus on specific experience which might otherwise be overlooked
- using new ways of engaging to sharpen the attention
- creating a product (a photograph or piece of writing) which can be seen by others
- creating a product which can be related to and evaluated by the author.

Such methods are particularly appropriate to urban locations and for people who want to work alone. I have, for example, facilitated online courses in which participants were sent daily instructions for exercises of this kind. Photography exercises especially proved both popular and therapeutic.

Photography

Some years ago I visited the Baltic Art Gallery on the quayside in Newcastle-upon-Tyne. Perhaps the displays inspired me to look at my surroundings in a new way because, having finished looking at the exhibitions, I found my camera in my bag and, as I had some spare time before meeting my daughter who worked nearby, I set out into the city to take some photographs.

At first I began photographing buildings. The modern architecture of the quayside was exciting and I enjoyed capturing the play of light and dark on walls and the linear juxtapositioning of windows and railings. The lens drew unexpected detail from its context, creating abstract shapes on the rectangular camera screen, making me look more carefully at my surroundings. I became interested by contrasts of new and old; recent developments in concrete and glass set against decaying wooden frames of partly dismantled wharfs.

Standing on the Swing Bridge which crosses the Tyne, I looked down at partially refurbished shells of mooring platforms. The ledges of decaying timbers, infiltrated by plants, had gashes of white down their sides, marking the roosting sites of seabirds. I continued photographing. Wooden posts and cross-hatched decking continued the linear theme of the architecture, but encroaching buddleia and ferns blended the crumbling edges of the beams, creating impromptu gardens above the water line. I became fascinated by the complementarity of human artefacts and self-sown plants. Looking around for other subjects, I noticed that, even where I stood, on a smaller scale, nature was invading the edges of the pavement. Small plants grew in the cracks between tarmac and kerbstones and even along the rusting iron girders of the bridge. As I walked back up into the city, I continued to photograph, now focused on the cracks between the paving stones and the flotsam which they contained. There were small mossy gardens, grasses, miniature plants and fragments of broken glass or paper. All afternoon I walked the streets, photographing these examples of nature in places which we usually overlook.

This experience showed me how photography can be creative and therapeutic, bringing attention to commonplace things which are not ordinarily noticed. The camera introduces objectivity, and, by highlighting small areas of the visual field, focuses attention on detail. Since my experience in Newcastle, I have used photography on a number of occasions to help people explore their surroundings in a different and intense way.

Photographing nature in the city

One way to develop a fresh visual perspective is to look for and photograph images of nature in unexpected places.

Plant and animal life creeps into even the most sterile spaces of modern developments. Nature is remarkably inventive and resilient. Plants grow on walls and roofs, guttering and wastepipes, as well as in gaps between paving slabs, and anywhere that soil collects will host seeds. Moss grows on algae and grass on moss. These tiny spaces create ecosystems with micro-animals and insects.

Take a camera and, if possible, using a macro setting, photograph instances of nature in the human environment. Look for details. Try photographing from different angles. Notice how your eye tunes into different perspectives as a result.

Reflect on the images. Are they aesthetically pleasing? Are they informative? Are they interpretations of what you saw? Have they changed your view?

Writing

Therapeutic writing can take many forms. It can be creative, introspective or imaginative. It can also be used to record details of nature, whether in the countryside or in cities. Recording urban experiences can bring nature-therapy right into people's everyday life and create new habits of attention which can positively affect people's day-to-day experience.

In a recent study, Miles Richardson, Jenny Hallam and Ryan Lumber (2015) invited sixty-five participants to keep journals recording 'three good things in nature' every day for five days. The material thus generated was analysed to identify significant themes and values. Participants completed questionnaires immediately before and after the exercise and at a two month follow-up and were assessed in terms of their perceived connectedness to nature. The primary purpose of this research was to identify themes which participants experienced as important, and thus to find ways to facilitate the development of a sense of nature-connection. Richardson reported,[1] however, that, although evidence was inconclusive, it seemed people's general wellbeing improved through the activity.

There does indeed seem to be value both in regular observation exercises, and in the process of writing itself. Although the time spent in daily recording was brief, the impact of the task was more significant. This was partly because establishing a habit of recording experiences like this changes people's thinking, leading them to think about the exercise at intervals throughout the day. Recording three good things about nature probably means observing and discarding at least an equal number of nearly good things. Experiences are recalled and reflected on to make the selection, and attention gradually shifts towards the natural world as a consequence. 'Writing is not just an output of thought, but it shapes and enables our thinking' (Richardson, Hallam & Lumber 2015: p. 609).

Recording good things in nature

At the end of each day list 'three good things in nature' that you have noticed.

After a week, look back at your list. Which of the things that you recorded do you recall? Do you recall them in images or words?

Do you remember other things which you have not written down? Has writing affected your experiencing of the natural world in other ways?

What sorts of things did you record? Does this reflect your interests in nature? Were you surprised by anything?

Has your mood changed over the week?

Journaling and other writing tasks also provide valuable therapeutic tools. Recording experiences and perceptions, people tend to observe things more closely. Notably, this does not require introspective attention, and, though subjective perspectives inevitably creep in, the focus of attention is less on the self, and more on the phenomenon being described. Searching for appropriate language, particularly adjectives, to adequately reflect experience, means that the writer must search their linguistic field, making efforts to refine their description by comparing it with what is before them. This is especially true of brief writing exercises where the essence of something is distilled into a few words.

Solitary work and wild spaces

Whilst photography and writing exercises can facilitate connection to nature in ordinary life, solitary periods and wilderness experiences create intensive encounters with nature by leaving the ordinary behind. These apparently different ways of working complement one another, addressing different needs.

Daily observation exercises bring nature into the heart of people's lives, influencing day-to-day behaviour, but solitary experiences interrupt the daily routine, challenging its orthodoxy. Like a flash of lightening on a dark night, they can cut through current preoccupations, waking participants to new possibilities.

Solitary experiences vary in their purpose and intensity. They usually involve an element of personal challenge and can vary in length from a few hours to a number of days or longer. Some Buddhist traditions even support solitary retreats of several years. Solitary experiences, like initiations or vision quests, can also form part of a spiritual or shamanic practice. In the ecotherapy context, the intention of a solitary exercise is generally to encounter the forces of nature as well as to work with inner psychological processes. Whether the main focus is inwards or outwards, these experiences can be deeply transformative. People emerge changed, often with a deep sense of affinity with nature.

Solitaries can be undertaken by individuals wanting to experience solitude on their own initiative, though this is only advisable where a person has prior experience of personal work and being outdoors alone. They are commonly done within a wider group context with participants distributed over a limited geographical area, out of sight and hearing of one another during the actual solo period. In both cases, people usually have minimal equipment, perhaps using a bivy-sack rather than a tent. Solitaries are also done in remote buildings, huts or caves. These experiences allow time for reflection on what is really important in life, so provisions are generally cut to a minimum. This makes participants more aware of their attachment to particular items. It often means simplifying eating, and participants may choose to fast, as food can become a distraction. Reading materials and phones are not usually taken unless needed for safety, but journals or drawing materials may be useful if they support the process. These restrictions intensify the experience.

The provisions which are taken on a solitary vary with weather and terrain as well as therapeutic needs. People might take water, food, bedding, some form of shelter, warm clothing, sun-screen, rainwear and insect repellents as well as whistles, compasses and other safety equipment. Safety is an important consideration and a risk assessment should be done, taking into account potential for extreme weather, injury, illness, and, in some parts of the world, dangerous animals. Facilitators need to assess potential risks, taking into account participants' prior experience, and set limits accordingly. With inexperienced groups, it is wise to locate people close enough to one another and to base that they can return or shout for help if an emergency occurs. For this reason, facilitators generally remain at base throughout the exercise.

A solitary experience usually has three distinct phases, each of which has particular tasks.

Preparation

The period of preparation is important to the depth and outcome of solitary experiences. This has two focuses. Firstly, it provides participants with practical, spiritual and psychological resources. Secondly, it acts as a warm-up. Participants start to reflect on personal stories and anticipate the time alone. This practical and psychological preparation provides the foundation for the solitary experience and creates a sense of containment. As participants begin to reflect on issues in their lives, facilitators can also listen for indications of potential problems which have not already become apparent. If someone is disturbed or has a history of mental illness, or if they are in the midst of difficult emotional processes, facilitators may check further into their current mental state, making sure they are able to self-regulate and are ready for the solitary period.

During the preparatory phase, participants may learn skills like night walking, fire lighting and other bushcraft techniques and experience short periods working alone. They will receive specific guidance on safety. Preparation might also include exercises introducing themes to be explored during the solitary time. There might be an opening ritual or ceremony. The preparatory phase needs to be long enough to contextualise the solitary period and build cohesion so that the group becomes a holding space for participants. It also builds people's confidence in themselves and in the facilitators so that, even when out of sight, their presence is felt.

The solitary period

Solitary experiences vary in length. More intense ones usually involve at least one over-night stay and some may be considerably longer. Time is generally unstructured, but sometimes exercises or activities are given. Typically each participant has a designated area where they can sit or lie or walk about as they wish. This may be limited as the intention is usually that they should not accidentally meet other participants. In this space they might meditate or just be still, sometimes using writing or drawing to record thoughts and experiences. Unstructured time is part of the challenge. Most people are used to being busy, so being limited to a small area and only having essential provisions forces a mental gear change. Although 'doing nothing' might sound attractive, the period of extended solitude can be intimidating. Once eating and sleeping are done, huge expanses of uncharted time stretch out without the habitual distractions. The only possible experience is encounter. Encounter with self and with nature.

Solitary experiences can evoke fears and anxieties, particularly at night. Alone outdoors in the dark, noises are amplified and shadows become strange. The mind reverts to old patterns and childhood terrors can surface. We also experience instinctive, animal reactions, deeply buried in our DNA. In daylight we may be confident outdoors, but alone at night, irrational, visceral reactions can arise, reminding us of our vulnerability. The mind will not sleep and we watch its habitual churning. Other times, experiences are vibrant with wonder. The intense sensory connection to life, the landscape, the sun, moon, stars and sky can be deeply emotional and sometimes transformative. Treasured memories of loved ones bring tears and release. Sunrise and morning mist and crystal clear moonlight become so vivid as to be almost painful. Joy rises in the heart and the spirit sings.

Debriefing and integration

After the solitary period, participants return to base. It is a homecoming. The experience will have been profound and facilitators need to be ready to receive them with sensitivity and awareness of their heightened emotional state. A slow period of unwinding is often best initially. People may want to stay silent as they meet one another. They might engage in simple tasks, preparing food, washing, drinking tea, talking only sparsely and holding the memory of silence in their manner. Other times people return from the solo wanting to pour out stories about their experiences and reconnect with others who have been through similar processes. In this case, it may be good to slow things down so that the return is not too abrupt and the spaciousness of the solitary time is not lost. After this initial period of returning, there is usually debriefing, perhaps in a sharing circle. This allows participants to reconnect with one another in a calm, respectful way. Sometimes the return involves a ritual or celebration. This symbolic acknowledgment of what has been learned can help to consolidate the experience, preventing it from being lost in too many words.

An example

Solitaries provide a deep encounter with nature. This can be profoundly affecting and also sometimes mysterious. The following account was written by a participant in a recent Ten Directions intensive, held in woodland overlooking the Rheidol Valley near Aberystwyth in Wales. After two days of preparatory exercises, participants took part in a solitary overnight exercise, sleeping in hammocks amongst the dense trees, some distance from our main living area. Most of participants climbed the hill into the woods, finding their own pitches out of sight of the facilitators and one another. Afterwards one participant wrote:

What question is it that I need to work with?
Tasked to consider this question in preparation for the overnight solo, I'm keen to find something meaningful to focus on while I'm alone in the woods. Reading through the hastily scribbled list of my jumbled thoughts, I realise I'm pre-occupied with feeling stuck – unable to let go of the past, yet also finding it difficult to move into the future. I decide my question will be 'What do I need in order to move forward?'

I set off for my chosen spot mid-afternoon. In distance it's not very far from the main camping area but higher up on the steep terraced slopes of the wood. Scrambling up to the last terrace with the aid of a dangling rope, I inch my way over roots and brambles to my pitch. Level with the tree tops, there are far-reaching views and a persistently calling kite teases me with occasional glimpses as it crosses the sky. Gnarled oaks are dotted around me and proud rowans tightly grasp onto their few remaining red berries.

After two hours of slow, steady endeavour I've made my camp – a hammock slung between two trees and a tarpaulin suspended overhead to protect me from the threatened overnight rain. With the practicalities sorted, I sense my true encounter with nature can begin.

Just in front of me a clump of tree stumps form a moss covered seat. I relax into its coolness and my bare feet sink into the dense green. To one side of the hammock there's a small bush – bare twigs, adorned with dangling pine cones, sprout forth from lichen coated branches. I instinctively label it 'sacred'.

I sit and eat, think, meditate and observe. Studying my immediate surroundings, I spot a dandelion seed head caught in a spider's web. I start to write.

> *Held by an invisible silken thread*
> *thistledown fairy, in her gossamer finery,*
> *dances on tip-toe*
> *to the rhythms of the falling rain.*
> *Suspended in time and place, she waits.*
> *In elemental acquiescence*
> *she curtsies as raindrops tap her head*
> *and sways as the breeze whispers in her ear.*
> *She floats in time passing –*
> *part of the web, part of the whole.*

The natural world around me seems to accentuate the creative and words tumble from my mind onto paper as I keep writing. I'm torn between stillness and the desire to capture my thoughts.

As the evening moves on, I explore higher up the slope, behind my hammock, towards an area of close-knit woodland. This area is known as the hemlock wood by the land owner. My curiosity has been aroused by his tales of badgers living there. I'm tempted to explore further but my scramble up the hill is becoming increasingly difficult. The wood itself looks dark and inviting. I turn to head back. At this moment, my attention is caught by a large animal skull lying on the ground. Was it one of the badgers? I cradle it gently in my hands. Should I move it? I decide to take it with me. Back at camp, I place it at the foot of the 'sacred' bush which has now become a shrine. I sit and chant the Buddhist compassion chant – om mane padme hum.

The light's fading fast now and, back on my seat, I sit peering through fuzzy edged trees into the dim distance. I climb into my hammock and wonder how easy it will be to sleep. The atmosphere has changed and I sense I'm waiting for something.

And then in the night, the badger comes to me

Lying awake, I see him approaching through the trees, followed at some distance by a man with a gun. Instinctively I freeze. He comes right up to my hammock and, with eyes shut tight, I can hear him sniffing the air and nudging the fabric with his rough snout. I shout to scare him off, but then panic as I realise that I've alerted the man to my presence. I don't know whether to fear the man or the badger, or both or neither. A few minutes later the badger leaves my side and walks away. The man doesn't come close.

They return a while later – the badger close by again and the man further away. I wait to see what will happen this time. The same scenario plays out and I start to sense that the badger is an ally rather than hostile– a companion. As before, man and badger walk away.

The third time, the badger comes alone. I'm not afraid. There's an unspoken bond between us, a nurturing connection that keeps me safe. The badger is my protector. I sink into sleep.

Waking in the early morning, the night's events resonate strongly in my mind. Adjusting to the daylight, I re-live each scene and its emotions. Gradually, and with a hint of resistance, I start to recognise my experience as a vivid dreamscape, rather than 'real'. While the images and emotions remain vibrant and powerful, I begin to see that they exist outside of the realm of my waking life. The realisation is transforming. I start to move forward.

Gardening and land work

Whilst some encounters with nature take us into isolated, challenging settings, other ways of being with nature are, apparently, more mundane. People have grown crops and managed land since Neolithic times, and intimacy with the land has been part of life for many generations. Only since the industrial revolution have the general populations of the country become urban and cut off from these fundamental activities.

With the modern concentration of agriculture in large scale, industrial-style processes, food production has become the activity of a few, leaving the majority of the population, distanced from the earth. Despite this, gardening has remained popular and, whether or not it produces food for the table, it still enables many people to connect to the soil. The therapeutic value of gardening is becoming increasingly recognised, making therapeutic horticulture popular for people with learning difficulties and mental health problems. National organisations like Thrive[2] and Mind[3] run training programmes for those working in the field and provide services to a variety of user groups, and there are also many local projects.

Horticultural therapy works on many levels. It is often recognised primarily for its behavioural aspects, providing positive conditions in which people can gain confidence and experience increased wellbeing, but it also offers other therapeutic benefits which can be related to a Buddhist model of working:

- experiences of growth, change and conditioned existence
- increased embodied awareness through physical activity and contact with plants and tools
- discharge of anger or other emotions through physical effort
- mindful connection to the soil, helping people become more grounded
- discharging grief through recognition of impermanence and cycles of life
- increased confidence through experiences of competence and success
- informal interaction with others, with possibilities for solitude or sociability
- side-by-side interactions with therapeutic workers.

Gardening offers more than just a pleasant way to engage with others. Going outdoors and engaging in activity with the earth, people directly encounter processes of growth and change. Growing plants from seed they become aware of the preciousness and vulnerability of life forms to changes in weather, disease or insect attacks. They appreciate the need for cultivation, soil care and attention to water and nutrients, and these skills can transfer to care of self and others. Working with nature is inevitably collaborative, and even the best gardeners lose some plants. In the following account a volunteer at a community gardening project writes about her work:

Twice a week I volunteer at a community gardening project. Sandwiched between neighbourhood allotments and the local leisure centre, two acres of land provide a space in which people living with mental health issues and learning disabilities can meet, socialise and garden together.

The project offers a variety of spaces and activities. Much of the land is taken up with vegetable plots, soft fruit growing areas and raised beds. Two small poly-tunnels serve as potting sheds in the spring and a space in which to grow tomatoes and peppers in the summer. Towards the back of the plot, a cluster of fruit trees, a mature pond and several living willow structures inhabit a 'wilder' area.

Participants, who self-refer or are referred by a carer or relative, can attend for up to three mornings a week. Some people stay for whole mornings, others pop in for shorter periods or just join in with a cup of tea at break time.

Each individual session starts with a group get-together – a time for everyone to reconnect and check in – followed by a discussion of jobs to be tackled that day. The garden is cultivated using organic methods and planting, cultivating, harvesting and maintenance work are all scheduled in accordance with the 'moon calendar' (a method of agricultural astrology based on the relationship between the moon's gravitational pull on the tides and successful growing). We choose the day's tasks based, as far as possible, on the stage of the moon.

Some participants like to be allotted a task, while others opt for activities that have, in some sense, become 'theirs' over time. People work at their own pace and may simply choose an activity to suit their mood on any particular day. Collecting tools from the shed, and a wheelbarrow if necessary, people head off to start work. Some prefer solitude and happily spend time alone, pruning the roses or sowing seeds in the poly-tunnel. Others form groups and begin to dig over a weed filled vegetable plot, attack a tangled mass of unruly brambles or harvest a crop. Users and volunteers work side by side. Conversations emerge. Heads down, intent on the task, thoughts are shared, ideas discussed and people relax into the surroundings. Sometimes attention spans are short and, after a while, individuals wander off in search of a different task, a new conversation or maybe just to put the kettle on! The garden is an environment in which everyone is supported and accepted, whatever their circumstances and how they're feeling.

Much of the therapeutic nature of the project is implicit. Confidence grows as participants reap (sometimes literally) the rewards of their efforts. Taking produce home with them, and encouraged by ideas for recipes and the soup which is often made at the project, they are motivated to be more experimental in their eating and cooking. People make connections – both with each other and with their surroundings. The natural environment invites individuals to experience the changing seasons and the cycle of life and, within this, allows the routine of regular sessions, familiar tasks and friendly faces to create a stable, supportive atmosphere.

Investigation, observation and curiosity

Encounter with the natural world comes about through curiosity. As children we were almost certainly curious. Young children poke and pry into the things around them even before they have words to express them. Can you eat it? Does it come apart? What is it made of? Will it respond to me? As adults we have generally learned to silence our curiosity about the world with assumptions. We have learned to know answers rather than asking questions. Environmentally-based therapies often seek to give us back our questioning minds. Questioning leads to looking. Going into nature, people learn to look more carefully. There are many ways of doing this, but here are a few examples.

Investigate a tree

When we look at an object in the landscape such as a tree, we tend to impose meaning on it. Our impulse is to name, and in naming we limit its characteristics, making them partly what we see, and partly our interpretations. Getting beyond this everyday mind-set requires systematic observation. The following exercise offers one way of doing this.

Investigating a tree

Stand in front of a tree. Ground yourself, looking at the tree as you do so. Notice how the tree is rooted in the ground. Feel your feet connecting with the earth and imagine that you have roots going down into the ground just as the tree has. Notice the branches stretching upwards and outwards, and feel your body expanding to occupy its space. Notice the air circulating between the branches, and feel the air entering your lungs. Feel the spaciousness within your body.

Now reach out and touch the trunk of the tree, at first with your eyes open, then with your eyes closed. Feel the texture of bark and the shape of the wood beneath it. Notice irregularities and projections, observing how the bark changes colour and texture on younger wood higher up the trunk. Notice any scars on the tree and see if you can work out what they were caused by, as, for example, the horseshoe leaf-scars on a horse chestnut tree. See what you can discover of the tree's history from the marks on its bark. Having finished, close your eyes again and place your hands on the bark. Feel the tree, connecting with it as a living organism. Sense its history. Feel its presence.

Now step back and look at the whole tree. Watch it. Notice any movement of the branches. How much wind is needed to make them sway? Does the whole tree move? How flexible is it? If you can, reach a branch and test how easily different sized twigs bend. Lean against the tree and see if you can make it move, then step back and watch what happens.

Look for signs of the tree's seasonal cycle. If deciduous, which point is it at? Are there new buds, summer foliage or tinges of autumn colour? What has already been and what is to come? If evergreen, look for signs of growth and decay.

Notice what lives on your tree: insects, plants, animals, birds, moss and lichen. Make an inventory. Check the leaves and branches, bark and roots. What can you identify? Where do different creatures live? What do they eat? Do they cause the tree harm or benefit?

Stand in front of the tree and reflect on its quality of being. How have you met this tree? How have you encountered it? Acknowledge its presence as a separate living form, and notice your heart response as you finish this exercise.

This kind of investigative exercise invites people to look for detail. It does not dwell on personal reactions, although it acknowledges them. Its intention is to encourage observation of the tree as a separate entity, existing in its own right. Participants see the tree with fresh eyes rather than making stereotyped observations and in the process become less bound by pre-conceptions and more curious about their surroundings.

The dinner plate exercise

A popular exercise for raising awareness outdoors involves taking a ring that is about the size of a dinner plate (this could be made of twisted willow or could be a manufactured hoop such as an embroidery frame) and throwing it onto an area of ground where it can be left and observed over a period of time. The space which the ring encircles is small, and regular observations focus on details which would otherwise be missed.

Dinner Plate Exercise

Throw your ring onto the ground in a place where vegetation is fairly sparse and where it can be left undisturbed for a few weeks. (You may need to 'help' it land if it gets caught on something.)

Sit or kneel beside your ring, looking to see what has been enclosed by it. Use a notebook to record what you see. Draw diagrams of the space.

Firstly, look at the ground itself. What colour is the soil? Feel it. Is it sandy or stony, smooth or uneven? If there are bumps or depressions, what caused them? Is anything else noteworthy about the ground?

Now look at plants. What do you see? What sort of leaves do they have? What condition are they in? How are they arranged on the stalk? Are there flowers? Can you identify any plants from memory or using reference books?

Now look for animal life. Notice insects or other creatures. Are they still or moving, solitary or communal? Can you identify them? Draw what you see, noting details of anatomy and behaviour. What do you think they eat?

Return to your circle daily and observe any changes. Keep a record, noting weather conditions and time of day. After a week, reflect on your notes. Revisit your circle at intervals over a few months. Notice how things change over time.

Observation and identification

Many people go outdoors because they are interested in specific aspects of nature such as birds, trees, wild flowers or fungi. Although we might not associate such activities with therapeutic work, these interests can positively affect people's mental states. Besides simply spending more time outdoors, people often develop a positive sense of identity and gain access to particular social groups with other enthusiasts through their interests. They also learn to look carefully to identify species, echoing some of the observational work described above.

Besides offering access to nature, the countryside also reveals human history. We can study ruined buildings, industrial remains, archaeology and geology. The landscape has been shaped by its past, and its stories are embedded in buildings, waterways, tracks, field systems and stone piles. There can be a tendency to romanticise history, but going outdoors we are reminded of the bleak reality of lives lived working in quarries and mines or on subsistence farms on this same land that we now walk for pleasure. We can reflect on how many people in the world still live in similar conditions. Understanding human impact helps us develop new stories about places and the on-going relationship between people and the planet. The past manifests in present features, and we can imagine the impact of present activity on future landscapes. Seeing history in the landscape gives us a sense of scale and of processes of time and change.

Working outdoors, I sometimes comment on wildlife or archaeological features when I notice something interesting. I might point out fieldfares on telegraph wires or a hawthorn in flower, or the sound of a blackbird singing. Such comments interrupt our activities, acting rather like the mindfulness bell, used to bring people's attention back to the present moment on some Buddhist retreats. Sometimes, even outdoors, people become immersed in their thoughts and distanced from their surroundings. A reminder to reconnect with immediate environment prevents them getting lost in introspection.

Other times, I take bird or tree recognition books along and get people identifying wildlife. This involves comparing what is seen with pictures and descriptions in the books. It forces people to observe details more accurately to distinguish one species from another. Some people find such exercises revitalise childhood interests, while others find the task challenging, either because they dislike its formality or because they feel unconfident about their skills of recognition. We can explore these responses in subsequent process sessions. The main purpose of the activity, however, is to encourage people to look more carefully and encounter nature with interest and curiosity.

Impermanence and encounters with death

In Buddhism, the relationship with death holds particular importance (Hookham 2006). According to Buddhist psychology, it is only when we come to terms with our impermanence and recognise our dependently originated nature that we become fully alive. Teachings such as the Four Noble Truths, referred to in Chapter 5, and the Satipatthana teachings on mindfulness, discussed in Chapter 2, show how fundamental human fears about mortality and the inevitability of change and loss drive the processes of grasping. These in turn lead to the establishment of a defensive sense of self and distorted ways of perceiving and interacting with our surroundings. As we reconcile ourselves with death and other existential threats, we become more mentally stable and fully alive.

Fearing death and change, people live in flight from the world and other people, which in turn isolates them, leading to more fears. It follows that by connecting to one another and to the environment, the self-perpetuating loops of mental confusion created by this avoidant behaviour can be broken. In modern life, most people live in sanitised circumstances where disease and death are distanced. In nature, however, change, death and decay are all around us. They cannot be avoided. Since most mental distress is rooted in our fear of death and impermanence, encountering these natural processes and becoming more at ease with them will improve mental wellbeing.

When we go outdoors there are plenty of opportunities to see death. Whether in woods or fields, beaches or moorland, we come across reminders of impermanence: a dead sheep or the remains of a bird, torn apart by a fox; bleached corpses of fish and seabirds on the tide-line. We are constantly reminded that death is part of life, an interweaving dance of living and dying. As one thing dies, new life emerges. Rotting wood hosts insects and grubs. Magpies and crows live on roadside carrion. Urban foxes thrive on rubbish heaps. Ferns grow on dead tree stumps. Fallen leaves create the forest soil. Processes of predation and decomposition re-cycle everything into the web of life. Nothing is lost.

The truth of impermanence is all around us. All things are of the nature to come to an end and to decay. Life hangs in a fragile balance, dependent on conditions and subject to finitude. But between the realities of conditionality and impermanence, all the beauty and magnificence of the natural world evolves. The encounter with death is the last human challenge, and whilst observing the ubiquitous presence of death does not necessarily assuage our individual fears, being outdoors and bringing these matters to awareness, we may become less driven by them, thus becoming more alive in our moment by moment experiencing.

Notes

1 Nature Connections Conference, Derby, March 2015
2 www.thrive.org.uk
3 http://www.mind.org.uk/information-support/drugs-and-treatments/ecotherapy/#.VSAQt2d0yT8

References

Richardson, M., Hallam, J. & Lumber, R. (2015). One Thousand Good Things in Nature: The Aspects of Nature that Lead to Increased Nature Connectedness. *Environmental Values*, 24(5): 603–619.

Hookham, S. (2006). *There's More to Dying than Death: A Buddhist Perspective*. Birmingham: Windhorse.

Part 4

Collective and cultural frames

10 Collective process, myth and ritual

The influences on human psychology are not confined to individual conditions. Chapter 10 begins exploration of cultural and collective themes in human psychology, and particularly the role of myth and ritual in ecotherapy. Myth has been important in the development of Western psychology and is often nature related. The chapter suggests ways of working through story, thematic work, enactment and movement. It then looks at use of ritual in therapy, suggesting ways of structuring activities in opening and closing sessions, establishing group territory, enabling sharing, honouring the Earth and seasons, expressing grief, exploring women's experience and creating forms for initiation. Myth allows exploration at depth but also offers a distancing medium, thus regulating emotional levels.

Life themes are not individual. If they were, we could not communicate with one another, or recognise each other's joy and pain. The themes of our individual stories play out on a bigger scale through collective processes within social groups. Whilst many of our reactions and views are based on personal experience and the layers of meaning which we have internalised from our families and through our education and friendship groups, our personal views are conditioned by the greater melee of culture and society within which we and our loved ones live.

Much of the way that we see the world is coloured by wider cultural perspectives and collective ideas about the order of things. These shared views manifest in common assumptions and biases and are so deeply enmeshed with the experience of everyone within a given social group that they are taken to be objective truth rather than the product of shared history and vision. It is usually only when we meet people from completely different cultures in other parts of the world that these assumptions are challenged.

There are, of course, different levels of shared culture. Some are local to a region in which they occur. Others are national. Others belong to large regions of the world. We talk about European or Islamic culture, Western or Eastern; Asian or Afro-Caribbean, capitalist or communist. Most pervasive of all, however, are experiences and views which centre on our humanity and are probably recognisable to all peoples. We live in a human-centric system.

This deepest level of shared perspective is described by the theory of archetypes. The concept of archetypes has been recognised in European philosophy for centuries. Its authorship is attributed to Plato, but it was brought to psychology particularly by Carl Jung (Jung 1959). Jung saw archetypes as the patterning of the collective unconscious, which, rather like instincts, informs the human psyche, giving rise to images, dreams, ideas and associations, and leading all of us to interpret the world in particular ways. These archetypal blueprints are universal but the ways in which they shape conscious thought and action are particular to the person and their culture. Archetypes reflect and are reflected in the themes of mythology which we will be looking at in this section.

When we explore cultures, we become aware of both commonality and contrasts. Some themes such as motherhood or home are familiar to all human groups, but the manifestations of these themes and their associated attributes are different in different areas of the world. Exploring such similarities and differences can expand and enrich our personal associations, and make us more aware of the relativity of our views. Such exploration can take us deeply into what it means to be human. It also invites us to reflect on what lies beyond the human realm. As we watch animals, we hover between recognition and estrangement, identifying behavioural similarities between their world and ours, yet not quite knowing the emotional meaning of what we see. How close are our archetypal senses to those of a dog or hyena? Does motherhood span the species barriers, or do we simply project human values onto the animals we watch?

In this section we will explore ways in which the wider perspective of the collective culture, whose influence is often less easily recognised than that of personal stories because it is shared by most of the people around us, affects our view of nature. We will look at how collective themes, expressed in cultural artefacts such as story and myth, can enhance our therapeutic work in the outdoors, giving us metaphors and symbols to work with and drawing people together around common experiences. We will also look at how collective psychological, cultural and spiritual experience can be expressed through ritual and ceremony, and at how these shared experiences can become catalysts for creative work.

Myth

Myth and story are found in virtually all cultures. There seem to be universal human processes whereby story is used to convey the wisdom of the group from person to person across societies and down the generations. This process unfolds on big and small scales. Societies produce myths and stories which are important to their sense of identity, expressing their preoccupations in poetry and song, ceremonial and literary traditions. Families also develop private folklore and anecdotes which support their shared identity, giving family members common roots and differentiating them from other families. Families know that 'in our family women are strong like Grandma Dora', or 'We were on the picket line together in 1983'.

Myth is a living form, evolving over time and reflecting current preoccupations in society, often shifting subtly in imagery and themes as it does so. For example, folk tales recorded in the nineteenth century often seem dark and moralistic today. These same stories are given lighter, and sometimes sentimental or ironic twists when developed into modern cartoons. Despite such changes, however, central themes remain constant, reflecting concerns that are common to all human societies. For this reason, myths which are centuries old speak to us today, dealing in universal subjects of life and death, relationships and aloneness and human emotions such as love, anger, longing, jealousy or greed, as relevant now as in the past.

Stories are told. The narrative evokes the imagination. Listeners draw on a combination of personal memory and imagination to bring the story alive. Recalling familiar locations, they furnish the storyline with personal associations, placing fictional events in local settings, just as medieval craftsmen, working centuries ago, created carvings based on local people to illustrate Bible stories in churches and cathedrals. Stories are collaborative co-creations, a conversation between teller, listener and the story itself, marrying the universal to the personal through the imagination.

The forefathers of psychoanalysis drew heavily on mythology to illustrate their psychological theories. Freud based two of his best known theoretical models on the Oedipus and Narcissus myths, whilst Jung's theory of archetypes and the collective unconscious employed mythological material from many cultures, recognising the centrality of traditional stories in the formation of human culture and psychology.

Traditional stories are multi-dimensional. They convey overt messages which are often moral in tone. Good conquers evil. Persistence brings rewards. They also contain implicit messages which unravel in the unconscious, sowing seeds which are more subversive or enticing. Dark spaces are dangerously attractive. Love is embedded in a nest of thorns. Thus folk tales speak to the unconscious as much as to the conscious. The storyline message is explicit but wisdom is often buried in shades of implication. The storyteller, shaman-like, transports the listener into the drama of the tale whilst conveying other messages subtly and viscerally in the transitional space of the imagination. In that liminal space, myth shines light into the dark recesses of collective and individual psyche, mirroring our darkest thoughts and feelings and speaking to our deepest longings, explaining that which is not understood, and teaching us how to live skilfully within the values of our social groups.

Working with myth in nature

Working with mythological themes helps us to develop the imaginative dimension in outdoor therapy, bringing psychological depth to the process. It provides a medium for exploring projection and association without being linked to one person's story. This makes it particularly suitable for groups where people find it difficult to share experiences, for example in early stages of trauma work. Myths introduce powerful themes and, with their complex narratives, provide participants with a range of elements to identify and work with.

In mythology, natural phenomena commonly offer mirrors to human passions and dilemmas. Powerful elements drawn from nature, such as storms and sunshine, forests and mountains, oceans and rivers, reflect the characters' moods or thwart their intentions. They show how, as humans, we are at the mercy of greater forces than ourselves. Drawing on these themes, as therapists we can work with traditional metaphors and nature symbolism, finding places nuanced with the familiar iconography of myth in which to work, which suggest moods or echo themes of the group. Mythology is commonly embedded in the terrain of its originating culture: Greek myths among the islands of the Aegean, and Norse tales upon the oceans and fjords of Scandinavia. Place and story complement one another, helping us to penetrate the psyche of peoples who first told them, but also enriching our experiencing of the environment being portrayed. Story gives us language to depict places, enhancing our experiencing of them. Standing on the Northumberland coast, looking out to sea and thinking of the Viking sagas, we look with different eyes, seeing the dark and fearsome power of waves and clouds touched with the echoes of history.

Myth can be introduced into our work in practical ways as the following examples show.

Storytelling

Traditions of storytelling go back to pre-history. Being a storyteller is an art (Gershie 1991; Estes 1992). It uses poetic language, caricatured impersonation and dramatic phrasing to convey narrative and description. In our groups and workshops, stories can be told around a fire-pit or in the home circle. We can re-tell folk tales or embroider personal accounts of life events. Stories can emerge spontaneously within group process or be written by participants.

Exploring themes

Myths and stories speak deeply to our individual life-experiences. In groups we can discuss these tales and share insights and feeling responses, drawing out personal relevance from their universal themes. Different participants may respond to different parts of the story-line, so wide ranging discussion can allow different themes to surface. Some stories may evoke personal associations which are painful or disturbing, and might be used to seed therapeutic sessions. Others are lighter and can be explored in a more general way.

Enactment

In many cultures, stories are told through drama, dance, music and puppetry. In the next chapter we will see how a traditional folk story was used with a group as the basis for a kind of enactment using a series of group exercises, each centred on a part of the story. Other enactments might allow self-expression, creativity and exploring inter-personal dramas. Working outdoors provides a large stage for such activities and with imagination the storyline can be married with the landscape creating exciting, immersive experiences.

Movement and embodiment

The re-enactment of stories is embodied. As a student, I took part in the re-creation of a battle from the English Civil War. During this event a group of us had to walk up an isolated Pennine valley in the dark. We anticipated an attack from troops of the opposing side and as we walked we scanned the surrounding hills for lights. Although it was just a re-enactment, the atmosphere was very powerful. The attacking group in fact got lost and never found us, but I still associate those moors with the embodied sense of fear that I experienced that evening.

Ritual

Storytelling is often dramatic, formulaic and ritualised. Myth and ritual are closely connected. People are sometimes frightened by the idea of ritual, assuming it to be dangerous. Indeed, ritual can be powerful, but the definitions of ritual are broad, and mundane rituals are part of everyday life. Ritual commonly involves repetition, but not all repetitive behaviour is ritual. To be considered a ritual, repeated action needs to involve symbolic meaning as well as practicality. Something needs to be added to the ordinary and meaning invested. Making a cup of tea each morning can become a ritual if details of the process of making it and its timing take on importance and become concerned with psychological preparation for the day ahead.

Everyday ritual is often protective. This is particularly so when people are psychologically troubled. Ritual behaviour is part of a number of psychiatric diagnoses. In obsessive compulsive disorder, people repeatedly check that light switches are off and doors are locked or wash their hands many times a day, whilst with eating disorders, meals involve precise measurement of ingredients and use of particular utensils. Such behaviours, which are considered ritualised, are generally concerned with the need to create psychological safety amid overwhelming feelings of fear or anxiety.

Most rituals do not attract psychiatric diagnoses, however. Many people use rituals to induce sleep, for example. They might develop elaborate night-time routines involving milky drinks, watching particular television programmes or reading book chapters. Whilst normal behaviours in themselves, when done in order to induce sleep, these activities function ritualistically. The person who adopts them believes that they need these behaviours in order to drop off to sleep, and, because they have that belief, it becomes a self-fulfilling prophecy. Other everyday rituals are concerned with achievement. Sports people engage in rituals before competing and students take mascots into examinations to help them pass. Such everyday rituals are largely private affairs. They are ways in which humans try to psychologically moderate and control unpredictable environments.

Other everyday rituals are social, connected with maintaining order in the community. Social rituals include shaking hands, standing up when certain people enter the room or dressing appropriately to an occasion. They convey direct and subtle messages about the person performing them and about those to whom they are directed. They establish and maintain power structures, often related to status, class or role. Some social rituals facilitate change or act as rites of passage. Marriages, funerals, degree ceremonies or coronations are all social rituals of this kind. These public rituals can be secular or religious. Like personal rituals, they can be concerned with maintaining safety and mediating threat for the whole community, or with sustaining the framework of society. They might include initiations, celebrating collective successes, expressing gratitude, and performing acts of commemoration.

In rural areas, some traditional rituals survive as local festivals. These bring communities together, building a sense of local identity and allowing people to behave outside the normal rules. Local events of this kind have usually developed over time, however some are not as old as they seem since, whilst many village rituals claim to owe their origins to pagan times, many were invented, or at least revived and embellished, by the Victorians. Other traditions are genuinely old, their origins obscure. Age does not necessarily affect their purpose, however. Ritual is a living process and what matters is its expression in the present, not its pedigree.

Ritual in therapeutic settings

Ritual is constantly reinventing itself. Each generation develops its own rituals out of the old forms of previous generations. We can draw on traditional forms in our therapeutic work. Different ritual elements can be brought together to construct symbolic activity which is meaningful and transformational (Scheff 1979).

Conventional therapeutic work involves elements of ritual: the structures of the session, the time boundary, the weekly formality of sitting together in the same chairs and various conversational norms, for example. Like other rituals, these elements are protective. They guard the therapeutic space, preserving its integrity and intensifying the therapeutic process. Outdoors, similarly, the structures of the therapeutic relationship give power to the therapeutic work. It is not casual conversation, but has formality and discipline which come from its ritual aspects, and which set it apart from ordinary life.

The components of ritual can be thought of as a language. There are basic elements which occur repeatedly, forming building blocks from which ritual is constructed. These might include activities like sitting or standing in particular formations, bowing, walking slowly, using special objects or structures, passing a talking stick, wearing distinctive clothing or insignia, speaking dramatically, ringing bells, drumming, dancing, using masks and laying on hands. These, and similar elements, are found in rituals around the world.

Rituals involve use of space. We have already identified three types of sacred space which can be used for ritual in Chapter 3: the circle, the shrine and the pilgrimage. We can identify other spaces inspired by secular rituals like the forum, the throne room or the village green. Time can also be important. Some rituals take place at particular times of the day or year: at sunrise or sunset, in darkness or moonlight, at the equinox or solstice. Other rituals involve ascetic practices such as fasting or staying up all night. By familiarising ourselves with some of these forms, we develop a paint-box of resources from which to invent and improvise therapeutic work.

Most therapeutic groups employ simple rituals to mark the beginning and end of their work. They might have a check-in round or a few minutes of silence at the beginning, and a sharing circle at the end, perhaps using a talking stick or a go-around so that everyone can be heard. These structures tend to become established in particular ways for each group, sometimes by the facilitators and sometimes emerging from the group's own process. Though not generally identified as ritual forms, they nevertheless have ritual qualities and are important to the function and security of the group.

In addition to these common ritual elements, we can deliberately introduce other distinctively ritual forms into our work. This might serve a number of functions including establishing group cohesion and collective identity, marking transitions and changes, or expressing individual and collective emotions such as grief. This kind of intentional ritual might be initiated by facilitators or created collaboratively. Often it emerges naturally, the facilitators shaping ritual forms out of elements which are arising spontaneously within the session. This kind of spontaneous ritual is commonly created and enacted according to the following pattern:

Sharing phase: People share personal feelings and associations related to the group theme. From this, either one common theme emerges or else one person's material becomes so compelling that other participants want to work with it.

Planning phase: Ideas are shared about how the theme can be expressed in action. The facilitators may make suggestions and provide resources to support this process.

Transition into ritual: Participants make experiential shift and move into ritual space (both physically and psychologically). Roles are taken up.

Enactment: The ritual takes place.

Transition out of ritual: Participants move out of role and leave ritual space.

Concluding phase: The process concludes with sharing and debriefing. This phase provides integration and a full return to ordinary space.

These phases are important in creating any ritual. It is the facilitator's role to clarify the boundaries between them as each phase has its modes of being and its purpose. The facilitator acts as consultant to the group, offering practical suggestions, and providing materials and other resources.

On other occasions, groups may engage in pre-planned rituals, developed and initiated by the facilitators. These might include rites of passage, solstice celebrations, vision quests or traditional festivals. The subject of ritual is vast and there is not scope here to look at specific rituals in depth, however the remainder of this chapter will describe some possibilities, giving examples of work that can be done. These suggestions are primarily intended for use in group settings, but they can generally be adapted to individual work.

Opening and closing rituals

Group sessions commonly begin and end in ways which can be considered to be rituals. These may simply involve introductions and initial sharing as described above, but more elaborate ritual forms can also be used creatively, particularly with larger groups. The opening ritual establishes the group boundary and the space in which the work will take place so that the therapeutic work feels contained. It also sets the tone of the group and may introduce themes to be picked up later in its main activities.

At the start of a group, participants commonly share expectations. This sharing can take a ritual or dramatic form. Participants can, for example, express hopes and fears symbolically, bringing objects, gestures or words into the circle to represent them. These offerings can be revisited at the end of the group as participants review their experiences and reflect on whether hopes and fears were fulfilled. They may also reflect on what they are taking away, and what they want to leave.

There are many kinds of opening activities and rituals, but here are a few possibilities:

- invoking Nature, the elements or the four directions to witness the work of the group
- creating a group circle or working space in a ceremonial manner
- inviting group members to introduce themselves and describe or enact their journey to the group

- sharing a grounding exercise, meditation or reflection
- creating a focal point within the group space, reflecting the group's purpose.

The ending of the group is also important. It establishes closure, acknowledging and integrating the work which has been done. Beginning and ending activities provide structure to the whole session, acting like boundary walls for its other activities. The closing ritual can thus mirror the opening, drawing on similar imagery or actions. Things introduced at the outset may be picked up again at the end, giving a sense of closure and completion. There might also be expressions of gratitude, an orchestrated departure from the group space, silent reflection time and the removal of any symbolic objects which have been brought into the circle. Participants may be invited to carry the spirit of the group forth into the world. For example, if the four directions were invoked in the opening ritual, the closure of the group may include a reminder that everyone is dispersing to these same four directions, taking with them the wisdom gained through being together. Thus the group is contextualised in the wider sphere of people's lives.

Objects used in ritual are powerful and often carry potent symbolism. They need to be treated respectfully and disposed of thoughtfully when the ritual is over. This is particularly the case where objects are chosen by participants, either reflecting aspects of their own process, or representing loved ones. They may carry strong associations and can be seen as transference objects. Objects can be relinquished in a number of ways. They might be symbolically de-roled and restored to their ordinary pre-ritual state. They might be taken home. They might be left somewhere significant, burned in the fire-pit or given to a river.

Marking territory

In Chapter 3, we discussed how groups create home circles. The sense of home is archetypal, evoking a variety of qualities like safety, nurturing, intimacy, identity or ownership. The home circle is a small contained area to which participants return at various points including the start and end of sessions. Groups also usually leave their home circle and use a much wider area for working. It may therefore be useful to demarcate an outer boundary of the group's territory, limiting how far people spread out during exercises, and creating a sense of ownership and potential.

There is an old British tradition called 'beating the bounds' which goes back to Anglo-Saxon times. It involved parishioners walking the boundaries of their parishes once a year and locating the positions of boundary stones. The name of this tradition is said to come from the fact that in some areas, young boys of the church were whipped at each of these marker stones on the assumption that the pain of the beating would fix its location in their memories. Setting aside this latter practice, walking the boundary of the area in which a group will be working can be a practical way of exploring the extent of the working space and giving a sense of its possibilities.

When I worked in our previous centre in France (Brazier 2011), walking the boundary of the land was an important part of establishing groups. This was relatively easy to do because there was a clear circuit of footpaths that more or less followed the perimeter of the property. In our centre in England, however, we work in a variety of different locations on paths radiating from the house, so walking a boundary is not meaningful or even possible. In this latter case, we tend to start the group sessions in the garden in order to establish a sense of home territory, and then go out to various other locations within walking distance, taking different directions on different occasions. This process is not obviously ritualised, but it is done with the intention of familiarising people with the potential of the local environment and also establishing a sense of territory and of the extent of the working space available.

Sharing circles

The circle is a fundamental structure in most therapeutic groups. Forming a circle is a ritual act, both practical and symbolic. A circle allows everyone to be heard and also symbolises equality and inclusion. Sitting in a circle is different from sitting in a crowd. Whilst both involve closeness and even intimacy, the circle suggests intentional cohesion whereas crowds can be chaotic and even threatening.

The size and spacing of a circle affects its quality. It needs to be large enough to be spacious but small enough to feel contained. If there are gaps in it, these can feel disturbing to the group energy and people can feel disconnected from one another and easily become distracted. Setting up a meeting circle, we can respect its ritual nature, as far as possible choosing a space that is naturally circular and providing seating which is of similar heights and types. The circle's interior is symbolic of psychological space within the group, and most people instinctively choose a place where the ground is relatively clear, like an area of cut grass or a forest clearing. Any objects placed within the circle need to be relevant to the group process otherwise they feel like contaminants, detracting from the quality of the space. It is therefore best if people put back-packs or other possessions behind them when they sit down so that the interior space is kept clear. Even outstretched feet can sometimes feel intrusive.

Generally in a sharing circle there is an explicit expectation that people do not interrupt one another, and we may introduce structures to enable this. These may be simple. People may take turns to speak or just talk when they feel moved, indicating that they wish to speak by making gassho.[1] Some groups use a ritual object such as a talking stick or stone. This object represents the group's energy and attention and is passed to the person who wishes to speak. Such objects may be chosen from the locality or have other significance, such as, for example, coming from a particular place or being decorated in some way. Facilitators may guide the form and subject matter of sharing, or allow a more natural process to unfold.

Honouring the Earth

In the environmental movement, people often come together to discuss issues of global ecology. Such meetings may include ritual forms to express their sense of connection to the environment and grief at the difficulties the planet is facing. This work draws on many sources, including practices taken from pagan and other Earth-based spiritual traditions. Buddhism offers inspiration too. Joanna Macy, for example, uses ritual extensively in her 'Work that Reconnects' (Macy & Brown 2014) both to explore grief at the terrible destruction facing our planet, and also to foster the spirit of renewal and transformation which underlies what she terms *The Great Turning*.[2] In her work, Macy uses traditional Buddhist forms such as the mandala as foundations for her rituals. The mandala is a circular representation of the universe and the universal which, whilst originating from older times, was particularly developed into an object of practice in Tibetan Buddhism. In her rituals, the mandala is constructed by participants using a series of guided steps, each involving readings, reflection and symbolic action. It is then dissolved at the end of the ritual. The process of these workshops mirrors the creation and dissolution of the mandala in meditation practices. In meditation, the mandala provides a kind of map, guiding the practitioner through the meditative process. It represents both the whole universe and mental spaciousness which can be discovered in meditation.

Connecting to the seasons

People's connection with nature is often related to the seasons and expressed using rites and dramas. Celebrations and rituals like those of the solstices, equinoxes, Beltane, Halloween and Obon, ploughing and harvest times, moon phases or blossoming of cherry trees, are held at particular times of year. Interest in these old practices is growing and some ancient festivals are being revived both in spiritual and in therapeutic settings. Linked to the seasons are ancient myths such as the story of Demeter and Persephone, central to the rites in Delphi, or nature figures such as the May Queen or the Green Man. Such celebrations can be serious, connecting people to dark unconscious fears, but they can also be rowdy and exuberant, for ritual does not have to be sombre. Nature is robust and generous, and participants can enjoy her fruits with shared jollity.

Traditional sites as ritual spaces

Sacred sites carry stories and associations, and, where it will not cause offence or raise difficulties with landowners or the public, working within a stone circle or a henge can be powerful. Whether or not they are historically accurate, myths associated with these places can be used to inspire workshops and therapeutic activities. Alternatively, it is possible to take people to a site and work spontaneously, exploring their immediate reactions to the place. Stone circles and ruined buildings are often evocative and offer a canvas onto which groups can project personal stories and associations.

Expressing grief and creating memorials

Many rituals that are commonly conducted relate to grief. Some mark individual bereavements (Weinrich & Speyer 1997), others recall collective losses. The latter include commemorations of war, major accidents and natural disasters. In some contexts, rituals are held to express grief for the planet. Some expressions of grief may have political implications, such as those for refugees or victims of terrorism.

Ritual allows people to explore and express difficult emotions. Sometimes these expressions of grief are linked to creating a memorial to commemorate the loss and give a focus for the grieving process. Memorials are reminders of loved ones who have died or events which have occurred. Some are permanent monuments, like gravestones or commemorative plaques, but we can also create temporary memorials as part of therapeutic work outdoors. Memorials can be created by individuals, working alone or with the support of a group, or by the whole group working together. In Chapter 3 we discussed the process of creating shrines to work with grief. Once the decision has been taken to create a shrine, the process of building it has a number of phases.

Building a shrine

Selecting a location: The place chosen is often secluded, offering natural containment. It may reflect aspects of the person or theme being commemorated.

Dedication: The space may be dedicated before work starts using a simple ritual. For example, the chosen area could be circumambulated or offerings could be made there. A dedication can also take place after the shrine has been constructed.

Construction: The shrine is constructed in the focal point of the space. Usually this will be done using found materials such as stones, branches, pieces of wood or other materials.

Making offerings: Objects which are symbolically significant are placed on the shrine. Some of these might be offerings and others might represent the people or things being commemorated. These objects can reflect personal or collective feelings and be chosen individually or by the group as a whole. The process of placing objects is central to the ritual. People may place things in silence or can talk about their meaning before they offer them. An atmosphere of solemnity is important during this time. If objects are to be left on the shrine after the group disperses, they should be natural objects which will with time return to the environment, or made of perishable materials such as paper or card which can be left to decay. The dissolution of the memorial or shrine as it reverts to nature is important to the process of letting go, being itself a reminder of impermanence.

Sharing: The final phase of such an activity involves giving time for the group to come together for sharing and reflection. This enables integration of the work and gives space for emotional release, as well as allowing participants to find and acknowledge new insights.

Besides building shrines and memorials, there can be other ways to work with grief. We can work creatively, drawing on collective stories and using sounds, movement and drama, keening like Gaelic women or sharing stories and memories, as we might at a wake. We can light candles in the darkness, sail paper boats down a river, or write letters to the deceased. We can bury representative objects or burn them on a symbolic funeral pyre. These methods draw on rituals used in different cultures for mourning the dead. There is a rich legacy of such practices which can inspire our work.

Initiation and transformation rituals

Many traditional rituals mark life-transitions and rites of passage. These might take place at birth, puberty, coming of age, marriage, retirement or death, and celebrate transition points which occur in people's lives. They often provide time separated from society wherein people can grow into their new roles, moving from one state to another or one life-stage to the next. Transitions need space and people need time to adjust. New skills and new wisdom may be required. In nature, transformation often happens in places apart. The caterpillar creates a chrysalis. The salmon seeks the deep ocean. Plants and animals go into dormancy over winter. Bears hibernate, plants die back and trees lose their leaves before new life bursts out in spring. The moon waxes and wanes. Humans age and die and give way to the next generation.

In modern life, many of the old rites of passage are no longer part of our experience, but new rites are emerging within our society – the first date, the school prom, freshers' week, the stag night – though these rarely carry the weight of traditional ceremonies. Some people are devising new ways to offer rites of passage using nature-based practices drawn from traditional sources. In this process, many are turning to shamanic forms such as sweat lodges, vision quests or other traditional ceremonial practices. These new rites of passage often include ritual elements. These might include symbolic representations of birth, for example, by negotiating a narrow space; drumming and chanting; night walks or being in a dark or enclosed womb-like space; receiving a new name; offering symbols of renewal such as flowers or candles to nature spirits; or writing things down on a sheet of paper and then burning it.

In the previous chapter we saw how the solitary wilderness retreat or vision quest can be profoundly transformative. Such experiences are traditionally used as part of an initiation process. They may involve the initiate in undertaking frightening or dangerous feats which push him to his limits, as well as enduring an extended period alone in a natural environment. Such initiations can lead to the discovery of an object or totem which will support the initiate in his future life. These practices are often deeply embedded in a culture and belief system and when we use them we should hold an appreciation of their original purpose and respect their roots in earlier cultures. Many people are attracted by the idea of initiations or vision quests, but unless the activity is taken seriously, these rituals may just become a 'one night stand with nature' (Jordan 2015: p. 18).

As with other ritual processes, participants in these ritual activities usually need space for sharing and reflection as well as for solitary contemplation. These experiences generally include the three phases described previously: a preparatory phase in which to reflect on what lies ahead and contextualise it in terms of previous experience, hopes and anxieties; the central phase in which some kind of immersion experience or challenge takes place; and a final phase of consolidation, reflection and integration. The preparatory and consolidation phases may include ritual elements to intensify the experience as a whole.

Creating this kind of profound transformational experience in therapeutic contexts is not always easy or appropriate. In the modern world there needs to be a balance of challenge and caution. Traditional initiations often involved life and death encounters, however our work is limited by considerations of safety and good practice. At the same time, although limited by modern sensibilities, we can draw on the spirit of traditional initiation rituals and include elements from them to intensify and deepen the process.

Menstrual practices and women's rites

Nature is often equated with the feminine, and women's experience has frequently been marked by nature rituals. In particular, nature practices have been linked to menstruation, pregnancy, childbirth and menopause. These practices have not always been sympathetic. Some societies have been discriminatory, segregating menstruating women from the rest of the population and creating taboos around normal female processes. Women were often considered unclean during their menstrual period and following childbirth, and menstrual taboos are still widespread in some cultures, with women being excluded from many ordinary activities such as cooking, socialising or taking part in prayers at those times. Christianity, until recently, required women to receive a special blessing or 'churching' after giving birth. This ceremony, at least in part, had its origins in ideas of ritual cleansing. On the other hand, other practices were more ambiguous or even positive. Withdrawal to the menstrual hut away from the village has been interpreted as a practice of exclusion, but it can also be thought of as a practice which allowed women to go into a special space in order to connect with one another and with their wild feminine wisdom. The segregation of women brought together the generations. Grandmothers, mothers and daughters congregated and wisdom was passed down in the privacy of the harem and the kitchen, hidden from the rest of society and excluded from history books.

There is a growing movement of practitioners who work in positive ways with women's rituals, celebrating menarche, menstruation, birthing and menopause as personal spiritual events and rites of passage. Drawing on the tradition of the menstrual hut, they offer 'red tents'[3] and other spaces for sharing and celebrating these aspects of women's lives and honouring the power of these intimate experiences. In particular, by helping women connect to these bodily cycles, this movement helps them to develop affinity with the processes of the natural world in its fluidity and changeability (Shuttle & Redgrove 1978).

The strength of women's experience often comes from the quality of sharing and commonality deriving from creative use of this shared legacy. Women's connection with nature gives rise to a rich array of imagery which many women can relate to. The moon, night-time, mountains and seas have all been linked iconographically with female themes, and these connections are often cross-cultural, expressing sentiments which are universally felt. If we are devising rituals for women, drawing on such imagery enriches our work.

Engagement and distancing

Ritual and myth reflect collective themes. They speak deeply to our nature as humans, embedded in ecological, social and familial systems, and they can address themes of life, death and connection in our individual and collective psychologies. Working with rituals we engage with the collective level. We are no longer enmeshed in our isolating individual processes, but rather draw on our common heritage. Ritual helps us bridge the spaces between personal and shared experience, realising that we are not as separate as we might imagine. In Buddhist thinking we are inter-dependant and inter-connected and our being rests upon non-self conditions, which are greater and more ancient than any of us individually.

Awareness of mythic themes can deeply enrich our therapeutic work. They draw out commonality within a group and enhance our appreciation of shared culture, locating personal stories within a bigger picture, elaborating their details and giving expression to feelings that are sensed but remain beyond words. Myth and ritual provide jumping off points for creativity. At the same time, working with collective themes can lead to abstracted thinking and generalisations. At worst, this work can be lightweight and clichéd. If we get lost in the grand themes and arcane practices without grounding them in real personal experience we may only engage superficially, dabbling in concepts of higher personal development but never really integrating them. Without integration, the collective level can distance emotions and block psychological insight.

For some people, however, this distancing process may be what is needed. Some people get involved in environmentally-based work because they have experienced trauma and severe mental distress. They do not necessarily feel ready to face their histories directly. Working outdoors can be appealing because it doesn't require the same level of emotional interaction with the past as indoor psychotherapy would. Emotional release achieved through working with story or shamanically inspired practices may also be easier for them than traditional therapy since they provide metaphors for traumatic experience, and these offer somewhat distanced ways to explore personal material and provide projective mechanisms, making the work a safer container for emotional healing.

Notes

1 Bowing with joined hands.
2 http://www.joannamacy.net/thegreatturning.html
3 http://redtenttemplemovement.com/

References

Brazier, C. (2011). *Acorns Among the Grass: Adventures in Ecotherapy*. Ropley: Earth Books.

Estes, C. (1992). *Women Who Run With the Wolves*. London: Rider.

Gershie, A. (1991). *Story Telling in Bereavement*. London: Jessica Kingsley.

Jordan, M. (2015). *Nature and Therapy*. London: Routledge.

Jung, C. (1959). *Part One: Collected Works*, Volume Nine, *The Archetypes and the Collective Unconscious*. New York: Bollingen Foundation Inc.

Macy, J. & Brown, M. (2014). *Coming Back to Life* (revised ed). Gabriola Island, BC: New Society Publishers.

Scheff, T. (1979). *Catharsis in Healing Ritual and Drama*. US: University Of California Press.

Shuttle, P. & Redgrove, P. (1978). *The Wise Would: Menstruation and Everywoman*. UK: Littlehampton Book Services Ltd.

Weinrich, S. & Speyer, J. (Eds.). (1997). *The Natural Death Handbook* (revised ed). London: Rider.

11 Working with myth and story

This chapter describes at length a piece of work, taking place over several hours, involving exploration of a myth through a series of exercises within the context of an on-going training group. It includes discussion of the themes from the myth, the traditional folk tale of Vasalisa and Baba Yaga, as told by Carissa Estes in her book, *Women Who Run With the Wolves*, and of the activities which were derived from them. There are also reflections on co-working, division of roles, use of space in two locations and handling an incident when the group was interrupted by two community support officers.

In the previous chapter we looked at the role of myth, story and ritual in inspiring work outdoors. This chapter will look at an extended example of working with a folk tale. In doing this, I hope to demonstrate how some of the principles and ideas outlined in the previous chapter can be applied in a practical setting. This chapter describes how a traditional story was used as a basis for personal and collective work. The example is taken from a training group run as part of our Ten Directions programme in the UK. Although the group was not specifically therapeutic, the example illustrates work which might equally have been carried out in a group with a therapeutic agenda.

The story of Vasalisa – an example

The work described in this chapter was based on a traditional folk story from Eastern Europe. The sequence of exercises took place over a half-day period, although, since the story was complex and addressed many archetypal themes, the material could have been used over a much longer period. The group was relatively small, with four participants and two facilitators, and activities took place on the first morning of a training weekend.

Planning and preparation

Since group members already knew one another from previous weekends together and had met over breakfast for informal greetings, we decided to have a relatively short round of introductions at the start of the formal session, which gave us maximum time to work with the myth. Since the group was small, as facilitators, we decided to focus largely on individual work rather than entering into a whole group drama. We therefore asked participants to bring notebooks in which they could write. We explained that we would be taking the myth in sections, using exercises to explore themes that these evoked, and that they would be using journaling to explore personal associations. The process was going to be continuous so they should be prepared to work for about two and a half hours without a break and should bring any drinks or snacks that they needed.

We chose to work with the story of Vasalisa and Baba Yaga. This story is common to cultures of Russia, Poland, Romania, Yugoslavia and the Balkan area. In her seminal book, *Women Who Run with the Wolves*, Carissa Pinkola Estes (1992) uses this story to explore the feminine journey to psychological maturity through the development of intuition. We decided to use this version of the story as we particularly liked Estes' prose, which is beautifully poetic, but we did not follow her interpretation. In the account below, I have summarised important points from the tale, but have not attempted to bring the same literary quality to it as Estes does.

We chose to read the story aloud. On another occasion, it might have seemed fitting to tell it in our own words, but on this occasion we wanted to use the version from Estes' book. We felt that reading it as written was important in conveying the powerful and rather brooding atmosphere of the folk tale. At the same time, rather than following Estes' analysis, we created our own sequence of stages, breaking the story into ten parts and using each as a basis for personal work. This identification of stages was inspired partly by reading the text itself and partly by identifying themes in it which seemed relevant to our understanding of Buddhist psychology and to the group. On another occasion, we might have presented the whole story to the group and allowed them to identify themes in a more open way. We were aware that on this occasion, by choosing the sections and introducing exercises we were imposing our own interpretation on the material, but doing this allowed us to structure the morning whilst still giving plenty of space for individual reactions to the themes.

When we presented the story, we decided that one facilitator should read the text, taking it section by section. The other facilitator should draw out the main themes in that section, shaping her summary to reflect areas which seemed most relevant to the group at the time. She then formulated an exercise for each stage to be carried out by participants, working on their own and recording thoughts in their journals. Throughout this process, group members were told not to interact with one another, but that space would be left for sharing at the end of the morning. The ten stages which we, as facilitators, identified were typed out in advance and were given to the participants at the end of the morning as a summary of the process for teaching purposes. In this way the overall structure was pre-planned, but some improvisation remained possible in setting the exercises.

The activities started in the garden where the course was being held. It was a familiar place to participants and we met in the sitting circle where we have worked many times. This is a circle of benches and garden chairs at the lower end of the garden, surrounded by large trees and shrubs. We began as usual with a simple grounding exercise to bring ourselves present and to honour our return to the space and then had a brief check-in round before starting to work on the story.

Stage one

The story begins with the scene at the deathbed of Vasalisa's young mother. As in many folk tales, the good mother is dying, leaving her young daughter alone in the world with a father who, throughout the story, remains shadowy and ineffectual. Before she dies, the young mother passes her daughter a secret gift. From under her blankets she pulls a doll, dressed in the same clothes as Vasalisa herself, which she gives to the girl. She tells Vasalisa to hide the doll in her clothing and protect it. She must always remember to feed it. The doll will guide Vasalisa, and she must take it with her at all times.

Our first exercise of the morning focused on the gift of the doll. We chose this aspect of the story because the doll plays such an important part in the subsequent story. The death of the good mother, which Estes emphasises in her commentary, might also have provided a focus for working had we had more time available, but, in the context, we felt that the doll was a more appropriate element to explore explicitly. As we will see, however, the good mother was, in any case, implicitly present in the element of the garden itself.

Initially, we instructed participants to walk around the garden, which was already familiar to them from previous training weekends, allowing the space to offer them the gift of a 'doll'. We specified that the 'doll' which they received needed to be a real item, as opposed to an experience or something imagined or abstract, and also needed to be small enough that they could carry it with them throughout the rest of the morning. We were aware that, in suggesting this, we were creating an implicit connection between the garden and the good mother as the giver of the doll.

We emphasised that the doll must be given to the student rather than being something that they chose. In the story, the doll is not taken, but rather is an unexpected gift. Buddhist approaches to therapy often emphasise the adventitious nature of things which happen to us. We do not earn most of what we receive in life, and nor are we entitled to favours from the universe. Such expectations are part of the ego-driven delusion. Much of life – the air that we breathe, the food that we eat, the ecosystem that we inhabit – comes to us as a gift. Nature is generous in ways that we often fail to notice.

The doll is given to Vasalisa by her mother before she dies. In this way, it becomes a kind of transitional object, symbolic of the lost mother. By guarding it, Vasalisa maintains her connection to her mother as things become increasingly difficult. The mother's love does not die. Matriarchal wisdom is passed down the generations. Meanwhile, the doll, dressed in identical clothes, is a mirror to Vasalisa. A child learns to see her own worth reflected in her mother's eyes, and likewise, the doll by proxy reflects her identity, offering a mother's love and approval.

The process of finding the doll offered an opportunity for the group to walk around the garden. At a functional level, this enabled the students to reconnect with their familiar working space. At the start of weekend workshops we usually include an activity which allows this to happen. Having previously worked there several times, participants would have had memories of particular objects and spaces, and we wanted to honour their associations and provide an opportunity to reconnect with the space as well as with other participants, recalling past activities and noticing changes.

Stage two

With time, Vasalisa's father remarries, and his new wife brings her two daughters to live in the house. The stepmother and stepsisters, as in many fairy-tales, are cruel and wicked. They reduce Vasalisa's life to miserable servitude. She complies, yet they are still vindictive towards her. Eventually the three other women devise a plan to get rid of Vasalisa. They put out the fire, which Vasalisa has been charged to tend, and send her off to fetch new fire from Baba Yaga, the witch, who lives deep in the forest. This task is intended to be impossible. They expect that Baba Yaga will eat Vasalisa and that thus they will be rid of her.

Vasalisa's childhood home becomes hostile and she finds herself in exile from it. We picked this latter theme for our second exercise. The theme of exile is a recurring motif in myth and legend, and in their online studies prior to the weekend, the students had already been exploring personal feelings and associations with this topic, as well as reflecting on wider social implications of exile and the plight of the many displaced peoples in the world today. We therefore knew that they would already be attuned to the subject and to the inter-connection between personal experiences and global themes.

The students were invited to connect with the themes of alienation and exile as they walked around the garden, reflecting on the prospect of leaving it and allowing memories to surface of any personal experiences which resonated with the themes. We asked them to gravitate to a place where they could sit and explore these associations, particularly reflecting on experiences of feeling alienated in a place that is supposed to be home. The place where they chose to sit should not be comfortable, but, rather, somewhere which spoke to them of hostility and rejection. They were to write freely in their journals, recording whatever came to mind.

Stage three

Vasalisa sets out on her journey to find Baba Yaga and bring back fire to her home. On her way, Vasalisa has three strange encounters. First she meets a horseman dressed all in white. Secondly she meets a second horseman who is dressed in red. Finally she meets another horseman who is dressed in black. The journey takes her to Baba Yaga's house.

The theme of the journey, like that of exile, is a common motif in folk tales. It is also a theme which we often draw on in environmentally-based therapy work since it reflects important aspects of the relationship between people and places. We journey through landscapes and, in doing so, we engage dynamically and intimately with their changing characteristics.

Journeys take many forms. We have already discussed how pilgrimage and the spiritual journey can be introduced as themes into therapeutic work, but there are other types of journey which can inspire our work. Journeys can involve acquiring necessities like food and shelter or transporting luxury goods on camel trains across deserts or with merchants following the Silk Road. They can pursue love and fortune, adventure and learning. They connect places and weave together peoples and resources. They can lead to conquest or export imperialist or religious values. They can be a quest for rare or precious things. Vasalisa journeys in search of fire. She is sent away on the pretext that her household needs her to find it so as to carry on cooking and sustain themselves.

The concept of journeying is both real and symbolic. Space can be a metaphor for time, and in therapeutic work, the life path can be equated to a journey. The process is experienced as linear; a series of events, meetings and changes, one thing leading to another. Everything has its roots somewhere in the past and its consequences in the future. Perhaps it is easier for us as humans to conceptualise things in this way, unfolding sequentially in a neat order. We want to believe that there is purpose and continuity in our experience, a beginning and a destination. We talk of the journey through adolescence, a train of thought or a career track. We live our lives journeying along our habitual scripts.

Other journeys take us into unfamiliar places which feel frightening or threatening. Vasalisa's journey takes her deep into the forest on an unmapped path. Like many mythic journeys, it leads her into an underworld of hidden places and dark forces. Therapeutic journeys frequently take us into difficult places in the depths of the unconscious which we may have spent decades avoiding. They bring to light painful memories and raw impulses. Such journeys are lonely and we are grateful for any companionship.

After reading this third section of the story and giving instructions for the exercise, we left the garden and walked through the village where our centre is situated, heading towards the water meadows where we planned to continue our work. This walk was on pavement, passing shops and other buildings. The road crosses the railway by a level crossing and then, almost immediately, crosses the river too. On the far bank, we turned off the pavement through a metal kissing gate, following a narrow gravel path, running alongside the river. This path is flanked by brambles on one side and thorn trees and thicket on the other, separating it from the water. We followed this path for about a hundred yards to where it opens into a small triangular patch of long meadow grass, enclosed on two sides by hedges and trees, with open spaces where the river can be seen more clearly.

The students were instructed to make this walk in silence, reflecting on the theme of journeying as they did so. In particular we asked them to be aware of the 'doll' that each of them carried in their pocket and think about how they might feed it. Recalling the meetings with the three horsemen, they were also invited to notice any encounters which they had along the way. In the village there are always people and cars around, as well as animals, signs, shop windows and street furniture, any of which might have symbolic significance for individuals.

Working outdoors, we often move from one place to another, creating transitional spaces between departure and destination. This kind of space can easily be overlooked as in-between time in the anticipation of the next activity. Drawing attention to the experience of journeying can have several functions in the therapeutic process.

Firstly, the transition provides space in which unconscious material can surface. In unprogrammed time, the guard of consciousness can be let down and personal defences diminish. This provides space for psychological insight. Reflecting back afterwards and noticing chance thoughts and casual observations, participants may become aware of aspects of their experiencing which they had not been consciously aware of. People they encountered are, at one level, inhabitants of a Leicestershire village going about their Saturday morning business, but at another level, they become ghostly figures, half registered in awareness, sought out by idling minds as repositories for projections. They can symbolise personal themes or issues which need addressing, and hover in memories of the walk because they hold keys to questions which are hardly formulated, but yet need answers.

Of course, such insights are fleeting. As soon as we turn the light of attention onto unconscious process, it shrinks back into the shadows like the shy creature that it is. Liminal spaces are dream spaces, held in the dark corners of the mind and glimpsed only sideways through veils of imagery and association. The insights which come are like visitations from another world, the world of the unconscious space, neither personal nor collective, but perhaps both at the same time.

Secondly, besides allowing unconscious material to arise, the walk also affects the group energy and intensity. Walking can intensify the process or dissipate it. In this instance we walked in silence, one behind the other. This ritualised walking intensified the atmosphere, focusing participants' attention on the task and encouraging introspectiveness. As facilitators, we wanted to keep continuity in the work, building on what had preceded it, so we were keen to prevent the group chatting and losing focus. Walking through a street of shops, we would encounter passers-by and this was potentially disruptive of the group process, so it felt important to walk in a disciplined way, creating a bubble of silence around ourselves.

This is not the way we always handle walking from place to place. Sometimes it is good to use a walk for people to chat and relax a bit. When this happens, energy tends to dissipate, but this is not necessarily a bad thing. Groups need periods of intensity and periods of release, and when we get to the new working space we can use grounding exercises to help the group to refocus. In this case, however, keeping continuity in the psychological process was important in holding the overall structure of the morning, so we chose to preserve a reflective silence.

On arrival in the meadow, the group took time to write about the journey. They were told to record figures they had encountered on the way, how they had fed the doll, and what symbolic connections they had recognised in the experience. This reflection process created a small shift of energy as participants had to draw back from their experience in order to reflect on it and to write about it. In this, they moved from being psychologically immersed in the process of walking to a more objective mind-state from which they could reflect upon it.

Moving between immersion and the observer-mind is a skill which we exercise continually in our work as therapists, so, as this was a training group, there was useful learning in shifting between the two modes. The skill is useful for anyone, however. The ability to attain objectivity and be reflexive about one's own process is the bedrock of mindfulness. We have a thought and we see that the thought has arisen. We have an impulse and we recognise that the body has leapt towards action. In our therapeutic work we draw on this skill ourselves and support its development in others.

Stage four

Baba Yaga is a fearsome figure, and her house is both strange and frightening, surrounded by a fence of skulls and bones which glow with inner fire. The story describes in some detail the ghoulish qualities of the witch's hut in the forest as Vasalisa arrives in front of it.

Standing in the open ground by the river bank, we read the description of the witch's hut. Whilst doing this, we asked the group to turn and look into a thicket of bramble and old man's beard behind a barbed wire fence. Behind the brambles were trees. These were crack willows, growing along the course of the old riverbed, abandoned since the 1960s when the River Soar was re-routed, canalised and straightened in a misguided flood prevention measure. They were tall, big limbed trees. Half fallen branches made strange angles amongst the uprights, having broken off and re-rooted themselves in the ground. The whole area felt wild and chaotic compared to the path along the river bank, and the barbed wire was reminiscent of the fence around Baba Yaga's hut.

We continued walking through a gap in the fence, between the trees. The ground here was bare clay, with just a thin cover of leaf mold in places. Following the old river course, a reed filled depression between thicket and trees, we came to an untidy, overgrown area where local youngsters build dens. There we found a space, roughly square and completely surrounded by the fallen trunks of huge, broken willows which had new saplings growing out of them. This space seemed a perfect location for the witch's house.

Journeying into the forest, Vasalisa encounters wildness, and in finding Baba Yaga's hut, enters into the wildest space of all. Baba Yaga's hut is surrounded by skulls and bones and infused with a strange other-worldly fire. It is the fearful place from which all human nightmares emanate. Entering the hut is therefore symbolic of meeting our deepest terrors and the raw, unmediated experience of impermanence and death. This encounter is both existential and personal.

As Vasalisa arrives at the witch's house, Baba Yaga appears. This meeting is a dance with darkness. We encounter our wildness and our shadow and all that we fear in the world and beyond it. Many myths explore the encounter between humans and the forces of darkness. There are many versions of the story. Sometimes it depicts the ultimate battle between good and evil. Other times, the hero outwits hoards of demons, or an abandoned child becomes lost in deserted woods. The mythic world is deeply infused with shadow aspects of the psyche and of life. Taking human anxiety, it paints it large.

Encountering dragons, however, makes us stronger and through the trials of the mythic world the hero or heroine emerges wiser. The darkest places become crucibles of transformation. This is how it is for Vasalisa. In Buddhist psychology the encounter with impermanence, sickness, old age and death is central to the spiritual path. The Buddha's spiritual quest began when he left his comfortable home and met with The Four Sights: a sick person, an old person, a corpse and a holy man. These encounters raised questions for him, setting him on his journey. Spiritual fire is to be found in such experiences. Indeed, it was through an encounter with fear that he reached his spiritual breakthrough. In the text called the *Sutta on Fear and Dread*[1] we read about how the Buddha, prior to his enlightenment, went into forest shrines where evil spirits lurked to test his resolve and develop fortitude. Those shrines were terrifying places, filled with bones and skulls and somewhat reminiscent of Baba Yaga's hut. Avoided by ordinary people, restless ghosts were believed to haunt them, particularly on certain nights of the year.

There, deep in the forest, at those darkest times, the Buddha meditated. He sat, and if, as he sat, fear arose in him, he carried on sitting until it dissipated. He walked, and if, as he walked, fear arose in him, he carried on walking until it dissipated. He lay down, and if, as he lay, fear arose in him, he carried on lying down until it dissipated. In this way, he faced out his fear, going deeply into its roots and not allowing it to distract him from his purpose. Despite any impulse to flee, he remained steadfast. It was through this practice that he became Buddha and reached his enlightenment. Wild, dark places are not simply dangers to be avoided. Rather, they have the potential to transform us if their wild energy can be embraced and harnessed.

In the depths of the crack willow thicket, we invited the students to explore their experience of wildness. We sent them out into the scrubby woodland around the square of trees that we had designated as Baba Yaga's hut to explore and to reflect on images and themes from the story. In particular we invited them to find words to describe their felt experience of the space. Rather than trying to make sentences, they were to collect words in an uncensored way, allowing them to be disjointed and raw.

The invitation to write freely was intended to release wilder aspects of the unconscious. Usually when we write, we censor ourselves and deliberately shape our prose, polishing the images that we want to present to the world. We are careful and guarded, making the content of our writing respectable so it communicates the right impressions to ourselves and to others. In the process, however, we may stifle the wild energy that is there initially. This writing exercise was intended to invite the uncensored to break through. Baba Yaga is the personification of wildness. She is the hag; not controlled, not civilised, not limited. It is from Baba Yaga that Vasalisa must take the fire, the wild energy that is both dangerous and potent.

At this point, by a strange synchronicity, two young community support officers appeared in the woods. Seeing the two uniformed men walking towards us, I realised that, as facilitator I needed to intervene to protect the group from an intrusion. Participants were standing around in the space, writing in their journals, so I decided to take charge of the situation. Clambering over the fallen branches, I approached the two men.

As I walked towards them, I was thinking fast about how to describe what we were doing in order to minimise any questions and protect the process of the group. I therefore explained that we had come from the Buddhist House and that I was leading a creative writing exercise. This seemed to me at the time to be a more plausible explanation of what we were doing than a complicated description of the training or of ecotherapy. I hoped that the reference the Buddhist House would give an, albeit alternative, respectability to our group. The two young men seemed happy enough with my explanation and departed with a cheerful wave.

This sort of interruption is something that one can anticipate from time to time when working outdoors. It is worth thinking through such eventualities in advance. Handling the situation assertively and briefly is important in protecting the integrity of the work. I do not know why the two officers came to investigate us. They said they were looking for something, and had seen a group of people among the trees, so had come over to investigate, but it was also possible that somebody had seen us going into the woods and tipped them off that something strange was going on. On the other hand, maybe they had seen us from the road and were simply curious about who we were, and why a group of adults were clambering about among the fallen trees. Whatever the reason for their arrival at that point, the coincidence of its timing alongside Baba Yaga's appearance roused some wry smiles in the group.

Stage five

Vasalisa asks Baba Yaga for fire, but before she gives it, Baba Yaga sets Vasalisa tasks to do. Before she receives the fire, Vasalisa must wash Baba Yaga's clothes, clean the house, prepare food and sort the mildewed corn from the good.

The motif of 'setting tasks' is common in mythology. In many stories protagonists undergo trials requiring intelligence, courage and wit. As in many traditional tales, the tasks set for Vasalisa appear to be impossible. They are riddles and tricks. It seems, indeed, that Baba Yaga's intends her to fail. Baba

Yaga is looking for her next dinner. In folk tales, however, good generally triumphs over bad, and we sense that, despite the near impossibility of doing so, Vasalisa will succeed in completing the tasks, and will eventually take the fire home. She will find her power. As is often the case, it turns out that Vasalisa has the necessary resources with her already. She has the doll which will save her in her pocket. The doll instructs Vasalisa to go to sleep, and, whilst she is asleep, it completes all Baba Yaga's tasks.

This story shows us the power of the unconscious. It is not usually through our conscious efforts that deep psychological change happens. Real transformation comes by way of shifts in the hidden tectonic plates of the unconscious. Whilst Vasalisa sleeps, the doll, her intuitive, wise aspect, works on the tasks. Our everyday minds are caught in defensive patterns which confine and control our thinking and our actions. As we cling to illusions of security, we restrict our options and limit ourselves to the narrow parameters of our habit-patterns. When everyday consciousness sleeps, however, those other aspects of the psyche which are generally locked into the repressed shadow-consciousness do their work. Buddhist practice also provides methods within which the mind can be freed of its controlling impulses. Through the discipline of meditation and other practices, the ego is invited to sleep and space is created whereby wiser aspects of the psyche can emerge.

Vasalisa seeks fire. Fire is powerful and transforming. We see this repeatedly in nature. Some forests rely on wildfires to regenerate themselves. When detritus and undergrowth burns, clear space is left for new plants to grow amongst the remaining trees. Nutrients return to the land as ash and sun floods into dark areas where nothing previously grew. Wildfires are even necessary for some tree seeds to germinate. Only in such heat are their thick shells broken open for the shoots to emerge. Fire turns wood into ash and draws gold out of raw rocks.

Penetrating the dulling effects of habit energies, spiritual energy ignites. Vasalisa seeks fire. To find it she must first immerse herself in repetitive tasks, rather as regular meditation performs housekeeping for the psyche. Then she must persuade her ego-driven consciousness to let go and sleep so her wild self can discover the fire-energy of the spirit that is deep within her.

The final task, given on this first night, involves sorting mildewed grains from wholesome ones. This seems to echo the practice of 'nourishing healthy seeds', advocated by Thich Nhat Hanh (1991), referred to in Chapter 8. This practice involves supporting positive thoughts and behaviours so that they grow at the expense of negative patterns. In order to do this, however, we first need to determine which patterns are wholesome and which not. We need to develop objectivity and the capacity to discriminate between that which is alive and vibrant and that which is deadened and stale. We need to identify the good seeds and reject the bad.

At this stage of the exercise, we also talked about the way that repetition can provide a protective shield for the psyche and introduced the idea of the mantra. A mantra is a traditional phrase which is repeated many times. Practitioners commonly use strings of beads called malas to count repetitions. The mantra occupies thought processes and is said to guard the mind. By holding conscious attention on the process of chanting, the mind is not distracted by unhealthy thoughts. The mantra also infuses the mind with positive energy, linked to a particular image or deity that it invokes.

We compared the repetition of tasks in the story with the repetition used in practising with a mantra, and used these ideas to dramatise this part of the story. The students went back into the wild space around our circle, repeating the list of tasks to themselves in a similar way to practising with a mantra: 'cleaning, feeding, sorting, cleaning, feeding, sorting, cleaning, feeding, sorting'. We invited them to observe how the words affected their experience. What did they notice as they walked and chanted? What effect did chanting have?

Stage six

On the second day, Baba Yaga once more sets tasks for Vasalisa. Once again she asks Vasalisa to wash her clothes, clean the house and cook her food. This time she is also asked to sort poppy seeds from a pile of dirt. Once again the doll tells Vasalisa to go to sleep whilst it completes the tasks.

Poppy seeds are opiates. They dull the mind into lethargy and slumber. Buddhism, conversely, is about awakening ourselves from self-preoccupation. We can understand the motif of sorting of poppy seeds from dirt as symbolic of the process of sifting self-deluding patterns of thinking from clearer mind-states. According to this understanding, the true mind-state which emerges when the poppy seeds have been removed is the dirt. Although this sounds implausible, the meaning makes sense if we recall that real self-knowledge involves recognising our dark aspects and realising how enmeshed we are in karmic residues of unskilful actions. Seeing these aspects of ourselves requires profound honesty. It brings us closer to the true heart of the psyche and is healthier than putting on a positive face for the world. Recognising our unconscious dirt brings us down to earth, connecting us metaphorically to the soil, to fertility and to our potential for growth.

Both Vasalisa's tasks involve sorting clear mind-states from dulled and irrational ones. Poppy seeds are opiates and mildewed corn is associated with the hallucinations and wild behaviour known as ergotism or St Anthony's Fire, which is caused by fungal growth on rye and other grains. In the past there have been occasions when whole populations have behaved as if possessed as a result of eating contaminated grain. So, on the first night, Vasalisa is charged with sorting the deluded from the wholesome. On the second night she is required to transcend the sleep of delusion and find uncomfortable truths.

So, in this exercise, we sent the group out into the wild space again, reciting the mantra: 'cleaning, feeding, sorting, cleaning, feeding, sorting, cleaning, feeding, sorting'. This time, however, we asked them to focus on the question: 'What is true?' This invitation was to encounter the world with fresh eyes, trying to see it without the seeds of delusion.

Stage seven

Having completed the tasks with the help of the doll, Vasalisa asks Baba Yaga if she may ask some questions. Baba Yaga agrees, but she warns Vasalisa that too much knowledge can make a person old too soon. Vasalisa reflects on this, and asks Baba Yaga about her encounters on the road into the forest. She is also tempted to ask about some of her experiences in the hut, but the doll in her pocket jumps up and down and restrains her.

Knowing which questions to ask and what to leave unasked requires wisdom. The Buddha saw certain questions as not conducive to spiritual practice. He used the analogy of a person shot by an arrow. Do not try to find out who shot the arrow or who made it or of what material it was made, but rather pull the arrow out of your flesh before you die of the wound, he said. We might assume that our clients need to investigate every aspect of their past in order to cauterise the wounds which it has left, but sometimes it is better to simply work with the things that give trouble in everyday life, trusting that by addressing these, unconscious, long-buried trauma will heal in its own time.

In therapeutic work, there are things that we need to know but sometimes there are things better left undiscovered. Issues can be worked through by proxy using everyday examples or metaphors without ever needing to be stripped back to their bones. Working in nature can offer psychological healing without delving too far or too often into memories which are raw and hard to bear. Connecting with the environment, we do not need to re-live past pains in every detail. Walking in the woods in a soft rain, our tears may flow, and yet we do not need to know what we weep for. Watching the new leaves appearing on the trees in spring, we may feel the possibility for renewal and growth, even when we despair of ever shaking off our sadness.

At this point, the participants went back into the wild for a fourth time, with instructions to find a space that seemed to represent the heart of wildness for them. Even within the wild, there is a wilder wildness. Sitting there, they were to find the questions that were powerful for them at the moment, and, having done so, to identify which questions should be asked and which should not. These questions were written in their books. No answers, just questions.

Stage eight

Baba Yaga sends Vasalisa back into the world. The wild witch of the forest takes from her fence of bones a skull, glowing with fire in the depths of its eyes. Baba Yaga impales this skull upon a stick and gives it to Vasalisa so that she can carry it home.

Before we returned to the garden, we invited the students to write about their sense of their own spiritual fire. Where did they store their life energy? Where was their passion? What power did they need to free their lives? They were then invited to find an object to take back with them. This object was to represent the skull, a container for the fire, the psychic energy.

The story of Vasalisa conveys a pattern of ebb and flow, exile and return, journeying into the wild unconscious and back to consciousness. In the process,

Vasalisa is accompanied by two objects: the doll and the skull. The doll is the gift of the conscious world. It is a transitional object, carrying the voice of the birth-mother to be integrated into the psyche, a moderating influence on Vasalisa's adult self. The skull, on the other hand, addresses the wild, free psyche, drawing untamed transformational energy from the depths of the unconscious.

Stage nine

Vasalisa is about to thank Baba Yaga but the doll prevents her from doing so, urging her to leave the witch's hut without looking back. Vasalisa takes the skull with its inner fire glowing out of the eye holes and starts on her journey back to the house. On the way back, the fire is so bright and frightening that suddenly she becomes alarmed and ready to throw it away. The skull itself, however, prevents her from doing so, urging her to continue her journey. The doll in her pocket meanwhile guides her, telling her which path to take. In this way, the two objects guide her back to her home.

We returned to the garden, retracing our route in silence. Each student carried two objects: the doll and the fiery skull. We also collected wood as we walked back so that we could light a fire in the home circle. The return journey had a sense of purposefulness. We asked the students to reflect as they walked, noticing how it differed from the journey into the forest. How did it feel to be bringing the skull back? Did they notice any fear in bringing the wild energy back into their lives?

The walk to the woods intensified the process, but the walk home provided time for consolidation. Walking creates an energetic break, allowing emotions to settle and learning to be integrated at many levels. The return journey mirrored the earlier walk, so participants experienced the contrast between the two journeys. At the same time, the similarities between the journeys created psychological bookends around the process in the woods, bringing balance and facilitating closure.

Structuring a piece of work outdoors, the rhythms of repetition and flow often follow the natural patterns of music and verse. Repeating patterns create chorus lines, strengthening and reinforcing the predominant melodies. Our work with the story of Vasalisa had a number of threads running through it, some of which were constant: the doll, the search, the encounter with wildness, whilst others introduced contrasts: the journey into the wild and back again, the contrasts of light and dark, conscious and unconscious.

Stage ten

Vasalisa brings the skull with its fiery contents back to the house. Her step mother and sisters greet her eagerly, for they have been without fire since she left. Once in the house, the skull is placed beside the hearth. All night, however, the skull watches the three wicked women. It does so so intently that by morning they are all three burned to a cinder, leaving Vasalisa and her father to live on in their home alone.

Back in the garden, the students were invited to explore their home space once more. They were asked to find a place to sit and reflect on what they had done and the journey that they had been on and write final notes about the experience. They then returned to the circle. During this last exercise, the facilitators brought a metal brazier into the centre of this circle and participants were invited to put the wood which they had brought back on the ground beside it. The fire-bin was already filled with kindling and newspaper and, as the participants stood around it, the fire was lit. The bin was quickly filled with flames.

Fire is the cleansing element. Standing round the flames, participants were invited to reflect on their journey and how it might have involved elements of cleansing or letting go. Some chose to symbolically throw their 'skulls' into the flames, whilst others decided to keep them to work with later. We concluded the morning with a short period of sharing, sitting around the fire. Participants were invited to talk about what they felt was most immediate for them from the activities. Most of the experiences, however, were left without discussion at this point. We took a lunch break, after which we were able to talk in more depth about the process of the morning.

Note

1 Majjhima Nikaya 4.

References

Estes, C. (1992). *Women Who Run With the Wolves*. London: Rider.

Hanh, N. (1991). *Peace is Every Step: The Path of Mindfulness in Everyday Life*. New York: Bantam.

12 Creativity

Creativity can be rooted in myth, but also in direct encounter with nature. Culturally embedded, it draws directly on the senses. This chapter presents creativity in terms of process; a natural ability often lost in childhood through an emphasis on outcomes. Enabling creativity often involves reducing self-judgement and developing empathy for the materials being worked with. After addressing some practicalities – use of resources outdoors, protecting the environment and managing public exposure – this chapter includes three practice examples: large scale sculptures, weaving and writing poetry. The chapter concludes by reflecting on the value of multi-media sequences as previously described by the author and as proposed by Natalie Rogers.

The cultural legacy enshrined in myth and legend provides rich soil from which creativity grows. Just as fallen leaves become compost in which new trees take root, so too, our creative imaginations take nourishment from what has gone before. The stories of the past spawn imagery and paintings, songs and literature. They inspire dance and theatre, sculpture and poetry. When old stories are re-told they spark modern imaginations into action, giving birth to new expressions of perennial themes. Creative process is hungry for material and expansive in its development of it.

Art is culturally embedded. Artists work within the context of their times. Schools of art influence one another in a slow evolutionary journey of image and form. Nobody escapes the influence of others and even in challenging established norms, the artist remains in relationship with them, pitting new works against those of predecessors.

Other creative inspiration comes through encountering the world and the forces of life within it. Encountering nature releases creative energy. Faced with life and death, growth and decay in all its rawness, words become inadequate and we look to the arts to find other forms of expression to capture the emotional and intellectual complexity of our experience. Contact with the elements profoundly affects the person. In their beauty and ferocity, the natural forces of weather and landscape inspire different emotions. We feel awe, contentment, fear and joy. Sunset and storm, the dawn dew and the wild winds of autumn offer the artist or writer an ever changing palate of experience. This otherness of the natural world is sometimes depicted in its complexity and mystery, but it also provides metaphors for human experience. Such metaphors offer receptacles for feelings otherwise too powerful to be contained in words, and mirrors which reflect humanity in extremis more completely than common human imagery allows.

Art involves interaction. It builds dialogues between nature and culture, myth and representation, becoming a catalyst which invites the viewer into conversation, and, in the process, changes the way he views ordinary things around him. It translates the world, presenting it to a diverse audience which in turn debates what it sees. The artist, like the storyteller, is a shaman, prompting people to experience things differently. Midwife of new perspectives, standing a little apart from the mainstream, yet always conversant with it.

Art and culture

Artists exist within the movements of their times, interpreting and representing what they see through the media of their generation. These media are material, whether brush pens and parchment or oils and pastel, and intellectual, both in the immediacy of poetic form, iconography and symbolism, and in the broader cultural preoccupations of philosophy, politics and the viewpoints that arise from them.

Thus the artist draws on her culture, but at the same time creates and transmits it; sometimes the gadfly, stirring up reactions to the status quo, and other times the commentator and holder of tradition. Sometimes, ahead of her time, she languishes in obscurity, only to be discovered and validated years after her death. Other times she is patronised by royalty and power, an advocate of the system which feeds her, but disappears from history when the regime changes. Totalitarian regimes sponsor the arts as propaganda. Dissident movements maintain the last strongholds of intellectual freedom through art that is subversive and impassioned. Thus, moving between different sympathies, the artist is both held within society and set apart from it, mediating ideas and representing its collective identities.

The artefacts of each age, inherited by future generations, are material representations of cultures which created them, but they are not sacrosanct. They are open to re-interpretation, conveying new meaning. To understand a piece of art in its creator's terms, requires insight into the mind-set of its times, yet great works of art speak in new ways to people of different generations. Art is not possessed by its authors, but, rather, as a free entity, exists in the present, observed, related to and projected upon by people of the culture of the time. Nothing is original. Nothing exists in isolation from the environment in which it grows. We are all products of combining conditions and so are the things which we create.

Art is also conditioned by nature. Ever since people first sketched bison and deer on the walls of caves, nature and art have been powerfully inter-linked. Indeed, nature is a connecting thread weaving through the whole of art history, emerging at certain times as a central organising principle, for example, in the Minoan vase painters, the nature poets and artists of medieval Japan or the Romantic Movement of eighteenth- and nineteenth-century Europe. In all these cases, and others, nature was a central inspiration, but as these examples show, the results have been very different in different cultural contexts.

Nor is this art limited to earthly themes. Nature provides language to mediate experiences of the spirit. Throughout history, painters, writers and sculptors have created representations of the divine and these were often grounded in nature imagery as the human, other-than-human and other-than-form have all been portrayed in religious art.

Art and the senses

We encounter the world through our senses. We filter experience through sight, hearing, taste, smell, touch and the imagination. Our senses are doors by which we admit stimuli, feeding our conditioned reactions. The senses show us the world, introducing us to new experiences and helping us encounter others, but paradoxically, the senses are conditioned, grasping at anything which is interesting or familiar. They fit the world into pre-formed structures of understanding, bringing together cultural and personal idiom and reinforcing and developing personal agendas.

As I write this, I turn and see in the corner of my window the golden light of the setting sun illuminating the sky behind the autumnal leaves of a huge horse chestnut tree. Almost involuntarily, I find myself breathing out more deeply and smiling. Why do I do this? Why does this radiant sky touch me so much that I involuntarily relax and smile? Why is this quality of light so different from the amber glow of a sodium street lamp? Why does it have the power to affect me in ways that other lights do not? There are no words, no meaning, just a heart-opening moment of connection.

But yet, almost certainly, my reaction is conditioned. The setting sun has so many associations that it is hard to know where to start in understanding my smile. Perhaps it is embedded in my sense of the mythic. Perhaps my feeling of joy, of relaxation, of fulfilment, echoes stories which I imbibed in childhood. Does it speak of romantic sunsets, tropical beaches and end of the day contentment? Or is the feeling more wistful, like stories of peoples travelling west in waggon trains with hope as their only companion? Does it echo religious imagery; Amida Buddha welcoming us from his Pure Land in the West at the moment of death? Or am I touched by the fading light and the mysterious turning of hours and seasons? Or maybe it is a simpler, more animal reaction. Perhaps I am instinctively programmed to grow towards the light. Perhaps my animal-self is a sun-worshipping creature who revels in warmth and light. Or maybe I simply smile because the colour, so golden and glowing, fills me with joy devoid of meaning at all.

The senses catch an object, in this case the sun, and propel us into connections and possibilities. We draw on what we know, stories and past experiencing, and simultaneously reach out towards the object of our perception, seeing it both in its immediacy and in the layers of interpretation which rest upon it. Colour, raw colour, touches me; drawing out stories and helping me to paint pictures in my mind. The light fades and the delicate tapestry of leaves shimmers on the chestnut in the evening breeze. The smile on my face remains as a shadow of softness. I am changed.

Our creativity is of the senses. The life-energy of the mind, it arises through the spark of connection, and, catching an impulse triggered by sense-contact, it responds in vocabulary drawn from our mind-scripts. It twists our experiencing, finding new angles through other senses, and particularly the imagination. It dances with colours and sounds and sensations, expanding raw moments of contact into new ideas and artefacts.

In Buddhism there are six senses. Each is conditioned and programmed to grasp experience in its own way, attaching itself to thing after thing. Those things, encountered through the infinite series of particular circumstances, support the process of experiencing. They are known as sense-objects. Buddhist practice is often concerned with taming and ordering the senses so that we are not carried away by desire and aversion so frequently or so completely. Curbing these impulses and freeing themselves from compulsion, practitioners transform their passions with mindful attention, watching as impulse after impulse arises, then, if not enacted, falls away in a gentle ebb and flow of thought moments. Mastery of the senses is of course never perfect, but outdoors it becomes easier to observe the flow of attention. There is less craving for possession of its objects. No longer bombarded by the anxieties of urban consumption, we are freer to experience our surroundings. We are caught by sunsets and flaming leaves, but do not crave or fear them in the same way. Our senses draw on colour and texture, sounds and silence, scents and sensations and we are enriched.

Creativity as process

Many adults say 'I can't draw'. Three year olds at nursery do not worry about whether they can draw or not. Everyone does painting. Sheets of sugar paper are embellished with lines and dots and splodges. Paint is layered colour on colour until the muddy surface becomes indeterminate grey and the paper starts to disintegrate. Aprons, hands and faces get covered and brushes drip dirty paint-water onto the floor but nobody is bothered. It is all mopped up later. At home-time, pictures are hung on the wall or taken home, and no-one is concerned about how good they are. Mothers smile and proudly pin them on their fridges. It is the process of painting that matters rather than the outcome. Painting is a verb and not a noun.

Too soon, however, somebody starts to look for results. Painting is no longer an experience but becomes an artefact. It is 'my painting' or 'his painting' or 'hers', closely identified with its executor, a representation of their identity. It is ascribed status and a mark. It is good, bad or mediocre. Feelings are hurt. Mess is no longer tolerated. There are hidden rules for success or failure. Why is her painting always on the wall while mine never gets displayed?

The same is true in all the arts. Children discover that they are flawed. They cannot draw, cannot sing, cannot write poetry or stories, they have no imagination. Critical comments from teachers or parents or other children sting deeply into the forming identity, leaving impressions which last far longer than any counterbalancing praise. This is because art is always personal. Expressive arts involve self-revelation and baring the soul. Creating something meaningful is an intimate act, and often this is not respected, so many children learn that to expose ideas in paint or words or movement leads to humiliation and, in their embarrassment, they become shy and sometimes learn to tease others.

This is not always so, however. Some children learn to succeed. Their paintings go on the wall and their poetry is read in assembly. They get the praise and encouragement and develop pride. This too can be a dead end, however. Praise breeds the desire for more praise and the child who is 'good at art' or 'musical' soon learns how to gain more favour. Focused on success, this child learns techniques, passes exams, creates a portfolio, and, in tune with social custom, becomes conformist. He or she learns to ride the tide of success.

In our society, product is foremost. This has often been so. In the past much art was functional. Pots were used for cooking. Sculptures embellished buildings. Illuminated manuscripts recorded history. Then, however, artists were anonymous. Today, in our celebrity culture, anonymity is out of favour. Successful artists are courted and, driven by money and the mentality of commerce, as with other areas of life, the arts have become fields of production. We view the artefacts and not the process. Along the way, the value of journeying is lost.

The process and the artefact

In therapeutic work we refocus on the journey. Like the children in nursery who have not yet learned self-consciousness, in therapy settings we can explore simple experiencing and not worry about outcomes. We can interact with materials, investigate their possibilities and rediscover the expressive qualities of colour and texture. Therapy is about process. It is about being. Working outdoors, creative work offers ways to loosen rigid conceptualisations and interpretations, allowing people to hold back judgement and assumptions and play once more. We do not need products, but, rather, can enjoy being in the flow of imaginative interaction. As Natalie Rogers suggests in her book, *The Creative Connection* (Rogers 1993), in therapeutic work the process of creativity, and not the product, is the primary concern.

> When using art as an expressive mode for self-healing or therapeutic purposes, we are not concerned about the beauty of the visual art, the grammar and style of the writing, or the harmonic flow of the song. We use the arts to let go, to express, and to release. Also, we gain insight by studying the symbolic and metaphoric messages. Our art speaks back to us if we take the time to let in those messages.
>
> (Rogers 1993: p. 2)

Working outdoors makes possible things which are difficult indoors. People are often willing to experiment creatively with natural objects in ways which they might not if given commercial art materials in an art room. Pine cones and leaves do not carry the same associations as paint-boxes and crayons do. They are not contaminated by the kind of painful history which comes from failure in the classroom and mockery at home. When people create artefacts from natural materials, these are not subjected to the same critical evaluation. The work is understood within the therapeutic context, apart from any assessment of aesthetics.

The object which is created in this kind of therapeutic work is as an expression of the personal. It reflects the creator's identity and their personal issues, but it is also something new and separate from the creator's self. Birthed by its creator, it has become separate enough to be viewed, reflected on and encountered as something 'other'. In her book *The Revealing Image* (Schaverien 1992), Joy Schaverien suggests that the picture produced in art therapy can be viewed as a transference object, holding powerful projections of both the client himself and other significant people in his life. Through the creation of this transitional entity, the client can relate to the image as something separate rather than as a part of himself. He can talk to it, look at it, distance it or discard it. It can be destroyed or disposed of, or treated with care.

Thus, when a piece of art like a poem, sculpture or painting is created, it may become associated with self-elements, but also distanced from the person, a projected, disembodied object. Then it becomes possible to explore one's relationship with it at various levels. We can walk away and become more objective about it. We can engage with it as something fresh, as if we had no previous connection. We can identify with it and inhabit its energy. We can move between these states of being and explore different aspects of relating with it, and with whatever it represents, whether it is a self-representation or a representation of something or someone else.

In this process, therapist and participant stand together and examine the artefact, making the object into a third element in the therapeutic triangle as they observe it and relate to it together. Other times, the participant will identify with the object whilst the therapist maintains a more containing role. These ways of relating evolve and change as the work progresses. Creative work goes through different stages.

As facilitators we may sometimes encourage raw creativity and exploration. Other times we may explore the associations which artefacts hold. Sometimes these are too frightening or too immense to be explored directly and creativity will help people find a comfortable working distance with difficult material by moving between metaphor and direct expression of painful and shameful stories. Sometimes nothing need be said at all, the objects speaking for themselves without discussion or verbalisation.

Empathy for materials

How does a piece of charcoal make marks on paper? Can a strand of ivy be twisted into a spiral? Can seven river stones balance one upon another? Can a willow branch be bent into a ring to make a base for a basket? How do we draw interconnecting circles on the sand without leaving footprints? What sort of paper will make a boat that will float downstream as far as we can see on the river? What sort will be swamped in the shallows? In this style of working, we often approach creativity in the outdoors by trying to understand materials in their own terms. What are they trying to express? What can they do? How do they want to be handled? What are their limits and what are their possibilities? We hold them and feel the way that they bend and resist. We try out their capacity to mark, to colour, to connect. In the process, we might say that we develop empathy for them.

Often when people start to create or draw, they try to impose their will upon the task. They have a mental image of what they want to produce and then go out to make it. In this approach to creativity we try not to force things, but, rather, investigate the materials and discover what they are capable of. We collaborate with our media, listening to their capacities and working with their innate tendencies.

This is not a new idea. The great renaissance sculptor, Michelangelo, knew this when he made the oft quoted comment 'I saw the angel in the marble and carved until I set him free.' In his view it was the sculptor's art to discover the statue within the rock rather than forcing the rock to become something which it did not have the capacity to be. Nor was this a whimsical intention. As an artist he had a deep and intimate knowledge of stone, its hardness and its grain, its ability to split beneath the chisel or take a surface. He was able to marry together material and subject. His eye for line and structure and his experience of light and shade, human and non-human forms was educated through the classical geometry of antiquity, but, nevertheless, he was always attentive to his medium. He allowed the stone to lead and guided it into being, as he created his great works of art.

In our workshops we sometimes invite participants to experiment with materials with no thought of the outcome at all. We put chalks and charcoal, pens and pencils for them to use and different kinds of papers and card and we invite them to experiment. What sort of mark does a piece of chalk want to make? Are there different ways to hold it? What happens if it is pressed hard or softly? What about charcoal? How is that different? We invite people to try painting. Experiment with brushes of different sizes, with hands, fingers and other objects, to smear it, spread it, stipple it. We try different colours in different concentrations on different papers. Just as children play with sand and water and paint, we play as adults, and just as children do, we learn their possibilities and limitations. We learn to be receptive and curious rather than to impose.

Nor do we limit ourselves to commercial products. Outdoors we find many things to make marks on paper: a paint tray of earths from orange clay to dark brown loam, textured with peat and humus and moss. We find leaves and grasses that will make green traces and we squash berries to create purples and reds. Crafts people have used natural dyes since humans first began to manufacture cloth. If you want to develop these processes into something more durable, there is plenty of information available on the internet and in books about how to make dyes and paints for fabrics and pottery and so on. But we do not need to make objects which are useful, though this can sometimes be nice to do. We can just go out into the garden or the woods or the parks with paper or boards and use what is around us to make pictures for pleasure and the healing qualities of the process itself.

If we wish, we can even become our own canvasses. From the earliest times, one form of creativity has been body art. People have painted their skin with ochre and ash and woad, adorned themselves with wreaths of leaves and strands of vine and shaped their hair with clay, sculpting it into the waves of the sea or spiking it like porcupines. We can embrace the Earth and allow the Earth to embrace us with its colours and textures and forms. And with this colouration we can embody the environments of the Earth, and the trees, the grasses and the creatures that move about within them. In this way we can grow from our exploration of colour into movement and connection. We can allow the spirit of the wild to flow through us and into us and release our intrinsic wildness.

So in these ways we can connect with our materials, not as masters but as conversationalists. Of course our expressions are hardly original. We have seen too much art and imagery from too many cultures to be innocents in the world. But we can listen to the sounds of our surroundings and become channels for their expression.

Practicalities and approaches

Working outdoors gives scope for many different arts and crafts as well as for drama, music and movement. What we choose to do will depend on the kind of group we are working with, the materials we have available and the spaces where we are working. There are therefore practical issues to consider, so let us look at some general principles.

Managing resources: Working outdoors rarely allows access to the kind of facilities that one might expect in a purpose-built art therapy room. If you are working near to a building such as a country park visitor centre, you may have excellent resources for arts and crafts as many places of this kind specialise in such activities, but if you are taking a group further afield, you will probably be limited to what can be carried in a backpack. This means that it is usually difficult to provide large quantities of materials when you are working in the field, so more pre-planning is necessary. Think about using the many natural resources to hand. These can be used for creative work in conjunction with a few basic resources such as string, secateurs and wire. Consider practicalities. If you want to do drawing and painting outside, paper and paints are vulnerable to weather so you will need waterproof boxes or bags to carry them. You may also need to think about supplying things which you take for granted at home like clean water for brush washing or rubbish bags for discarded paper and other bits. Creating a checklist for each activity is helpful, and if you tend to repeat workshops, you can refine your list over time.

Protecting the environment: Some creative activities involve materials which will, if left behind, cause nuisance and pollution in the environment. Human-made materials should not be left to blow around and installations which are non-biodegradable should generally be dismantled. For this reason, using natural materials for creative work is generally better. It also fosters an appreciation of the intrinsic qualities of things like wood, water and stone. Inspiration for this can be found in the work of artists like Andy Goldsworthy (1998), who generally works using natural materials in situ. There is always a balance to be held in any nature-based work between the benefits of taking people into nature and the destruction caused by doing so. Even if we only use materials found on site, we will almost certainly disrupt insect, plant and animal life and, at some level, our presence will probably be harmful. We need to minimise this.

In this context, it is worth reflecting on the process of deconstruction as well as construction. Sculptures may need to be dismantled at the end of workshops. This can raise issues for group members who feel personally invested in the sculpture that they have made and may be emotionally affected by having to take it down. The activity of deconstruction therefore needs to be given time and done with respect. Generally the deconstruction should be carried out by those who were involved in construction of the sculpture, and time should be given to closure and sharing after the dismantling process is finished.

Interaction with the public: Setting up an easel is the surest way to attract a crowd. It is therefore important to choose a private space in which to work if you intend to do creative work, unless involving the public is part of the process. Some kinds of activity are clearly more obtrusive than others. A writing exercise can easily be done in a public park, whereas dance or drama needs space where the group will not be disturbed. As we saw in the previous chapter, however, even when a place seems private, you may find that members of the public arrive unexpectedly, so the facilitators' role may include protecting the privacy of participants.

Having looked at some general considerations, let us now look at some practical examples of creative work that can be done outdoors. There are obviously many ways of working creatively outdoors, but the following sections describe a few examples, illustrative of the scope of possibilities.

Large scale creative activities

Working outdoors offers opportunities for big scale activities. Groups can work together on projects or use enactment like that described in the previous chapter to explore a theme. They can work collaboratively, building large sculptures with natural objects, or develop performances within a landscape. Sometimes this work is an end in itself. Other times it is part of a longer process, for example they might develop a ceremony to express themes emergent in the group. Often this work draws on myth and story but sometimes it is more personal.

A few years ago, when I was working with a group in France, we spent an afternoon exploring the myth of *Theseus and the Minotaur.* We worked in a clearing in our own woodland. This had previously been used by the group as a home circle and so was familiar to them. I started the session by telling the story of Theseus and Ariadne, then brought out a bag containing balls of coloured wool and invited each participant to take a ball of wool. I instructed them to tie one end of their wool to a nearby tree then go off separately into the thicket surrounding us. This was intended to recall the story of Theseus entering the labyrinth with the silk thread which Ariadne had given him. The participants were to follow their intuition and as far as possible not avoid areas which seemed uncomfortable or off-putting. Whilst in the jungle of fallen branches and thorn bushes, they were to reflect on anything which the experience reminded them of. The participants had about twenty minutes to make their way through the under-growth, climbing over fallen trunks and under low-hanging branches, leaving lines of coloured yarn as they went. When they reached a place where they felt they could rest, they were to sit and continue reflecting until being summoned back to the circle by a bell. Then they were to use the string to retrace their steps, leaving the line in place and not rewinding it.

This first part of the exercise was done in silence. Once everyone was back in the circle, participants were invited to work in pairs. Going back into the thicket together, they were to use the lines of wool to explore each other's paths together. This time they were to talk about the experience as it happened. As each person re-traced their path, accompanied by their partner, the partner took a facilitative role and listened to their reflections. Half-way through the exercise, the pairs swapped roles and explored the second path. At the end, the group returned to the circle to share experiences. Participants had clearly been influenced by the imagery in the story, and this sharing, which was quite lengthy, focused on difficult life experiences and on dark and frightening mental states.

After the sharing, participants worked together, creating a giant spider's web between the trees surrounding the clearing, using the remaining balls of wool. Everyone joined in. We spanned the spaces between branches with lengths of wool then connected them with knotted cross threads. We had spent time the previous day in the nearby meadow watching spiders building webs between the grasses, so this activity was planned to draw the two days' work together.

The latter part of the process felt light hearted, counter-balancing the earlier work. We chatted informally as we created the web. When it was finished, however, we looked up and found ourselves surrounded by an impressive wall of colourful knotted strings. These seemed to define the clearing and felt protective of the group space. It was as if we had built ourselves a spider's web nest. This last activity consolidated the group process and provided some light relief after some difficult personal work.

After we had finished, we reflected on what to do with the wool when we left the clearing. We decided to leave it in situ to rot naturally. In this kind of activity it is good to use natural wool and cotton, as synthetic fibres would have been less bio-degradable.

Weaving

Weaving is a traditional craft which can easily be adapted to working outdoors. We have just seen how a relatively simple large scale weaving was created collectively by a group, providing a way for participants to reconnect after individual and pair work, and allowing them to find integration and closure after an emotionally challenging piece of work. Other weaving activities can be done by individuals, working alone or side by side.

Weaving can be meditative and calming. It can help people slow down and become more aware of their surroundings, particularly if they are using natural materials. Whilst it can be a solitary activity, weaving and other crafts become companionable when people work alongside one another. This is reminiscent of many cultures where women come together to do hand-crafts and chat about their lives and their families. Working side by side, people can engage in conversation if they wish, without feeling pressured to join in if they prefer to stay silent. This can be particularly supportive for groups of people who have common life issues, or who have experienced trauma, especially if they find it difficult to talk about their experiences. Participants can listen to other people's stories and identify with their experiences without having to talk directly about their own. Weaving gives purpose to the gathering, allowing people to converse or not as they feel inclined, and invites intimate sharing because people do not feel pressured.

Weaving and other crafts such as knitting, patchwork or embroidery create products. These things are often taken home. They act as reminders of the group and can become transitional objects, helping participants retain a sense of connection to the group between sessions and after it finishes.

Weaving can incorporate natural materials, either on their own or combined with wool or string. Simple looms can be created using stick frames. These might be rectangular, circular or irregular in shape. Found objects can also be used. I once used a large metal hoop, found in a river in Southern France, which had once been the binding of a barrel, as a weaving frame. I have also used bleached driftwood branches and parts of old wooden boxes. These kinds of frame are rigid and so relatively easy to work on, just requiring a cross-hatching of strings on which to weave. Group leaders may bring ready-made frames of this kind for people to use in order to speed up the process and provide a solid structure for inexperienced participants to work on.

Alternatively it is possible to use two lengths of wood, one as the top and the other as the bottom of the weaving. These are tied so as to hang horizontally in parallel with one another and suspended with string from a branch or beam. The frame, which is similar to basic looms used in many traditional cultures, is tensioned by passing a string which is attached to either end of the lower piece of wood around the weaver's neck or waist.

On these basic frames, warp threads of string or wool are tied in parallel, spaced equidistantly across the breadth of the weaving. These threads need to be strong enough to provide structure for the finished fabric. Various materials can then be woven onto these. Alternatively, the outer frame can be filled with macramé netting in irregular forms or free woven using natural materials. Weaving does not need to follow rules.

A wide variety of materials can be used for weaving, including wool and strips of torn fabric, grass, reeds, twigs, leaves, sheep's wool, lichen and moss. Small stones can be tied into the finished piece with string. These weavings are rich in colour and texture, and can reflect the surroundings in which they were done. Weavings can also reflect therapeutic process by including personally significant objects, scraps of fabric from treasured clothes or furnishings, or things found during group activities. Some, like the spider's web, may be of the moment, ephemeral and left to naturally decay back into the space in which they were created, but others may be taken home and treasured.

Poetry

Many human cultures have produced nature poetry. Although some people resist the idea of writing poetry, if it is approached with sensitivity, this kind of activity can be creative and affirming. There are many ways to initiate therapeutic writing projects. Often they grow out of other activities, for example a meditative reflection, but sometimes they can be an end in themselves.

One way in which I start this kind of work is by focusing on the body sense. After a grounding exercise, I invite participants to explore the area in which we are working, experiencing it through their different senses. I invite them to look at colours and shapes; to touch objects and surfaces and feel rough and smooth, cool and warm and so on; to listen to sounds, human and animal, traffic and birdsong, wind and voices. I invite them to explore the quality of spaces around them and feel their width and narrowness, to smell the air and feel its movement in nostrils and lungs.

After this sense-based exploration, I invite participants to return to the circle and stand with eyes closed. I then suggest that people voice single words to describe what they have experienced. Patterns of image and sound textures start to emerge as we share these impressions. This kind of exercise can be used to build soundscapes and people might sometimes be invited to share non-verbal sounds as well as words. They can then gradually be encouraged to make notes and harmonies, building these up until they create freeform music. Exercises of this kind generally need to be led by example rather than explanation. Other times, though, the focus is on words.

These exercises may simply involve creating spontaneous poetry, but they can be built on if phrases and words which have been used are written down. This can be done individually or collectively. In the latter case, the facilitator can take a lead in shaping the finished poem, or can let the group create it. Words and phrases are strung together, creating a flow of imagery and impressions. If people work individually, their poetry can be shared aloud or kept private according to their level of confidence and their sense of connection in the group.

Whilst this kind of poetry writing is freeform, sometimes we can use structures for writing. Haikus are a popular way of expressing nature imagery (Addiss 2009). A haiku takes a single image or moment and attempts to capture it with clarity and simplicity in a very limited number of words. Haikus follow a fixed pattern of syllables with five syllables in the first line, seven in the second, and five in the last. The longer tanka form couples this three-line verse with a second half, comprising two more lines of seven syllables each, which create a counter-point to the initial haiku. Groups often enjoy using haiku and tanka forms because of their simplicity. Creating the patterning of words is rather like completing a jigsaw and the focus on structure can make the exercise less anxiety provoking. Writing haikus also forces people to distil experiences into their essence and be more focused. Although sometimes self-conscious, this kind of writing helps people think more carefully, pushing them to look more intently and find the right words to convey their experiences.

Changing media, changing perception

The attempt to shape materials into art is rarely a linear process of conception, planning and execution. Rather it is a dialogue with subject and materials through which an artefact evolves. Outcomes are unpredictable. Each attempt to replicate the imagined product is thwarted as ideas are adapted and whatever we create is always a partial expression of what we planned. We represent one story, but others go unspoken. In committing pen to paper or paint to canvas we make choices. Different media bring different areas of experience to the fore, so whilst each encounter is limited by its particular frame, multiple encounters offer cumulative engagement with the material. Just as sectional views of the torso create a three dimensional image in a CT body scan, so too, multiple experiences of phenomena help us see and interact with their complexity.

In 1993, I wrote a book chapter in which I explored how making transitions between different media can be therapeutic (Beech 1993). By using a variety of media sequentially, we can represent the complexity of experiencing. As the process moves from one medium to another, it is as if each stage is a sketch, and moving from story to writing, to painting, to dancing, to voice, each transition provides a new angle on the issue being explored. This way of working offers different perspectives and also allows people to move between different levels of psychological and emotional immersion. Difficult feelings can be explored in depth and then distanced and contained by a shift of medium, as we saw in the example of making the spider's web.

Natalie Rogers, daughter of Carl Rogers, was also interested in using a number of different creative media together in therapeutic work. Her model was based upon the idea that, if creative methods were used sequentially in what she conceptualised as a therapeutic spiral, they would facilitate the flow of experience and participants would develop self-understanding and creativity. Moving from one creative medium to another offered progressive steps in the process of self-discovery and actualisation.

> The creative connection process that I have developed stimulates such self-exploration. It is like the unfolding petals of a lotus blossom on a summer day. In the warm, accepting environment, the petals begin to open to reveal the flower's inner essence. As our feelings are tapped, they become a resource for further self-understanding and creativity. We gently allow ourselves to awaken to new possibilities. With each opening, we may deepen our experience. When we reach our inner core, we find our connection to all beings.
>
> (Rogers 1993: p. 4)

The moves between media can be conceived as a movement towards deeper self-knowledge, but they are also facilitative of a creative process. Each experience becomes the jumping off point for the next. Since mental phenomena which psychotherapy examines are not fixed, but flowing processes, moving from one form of expression to another, creative development also takes place in the psyche. As people become less inhibited by self-consciousness, anxiety or rigidity they start to find new ways to explore and express their experience. Having exhausted habitual responses, they are challenged to respond in new ways and find new resources out of their immediate circumstances with which to create new ways of being.

References

Addiss, S. (2009). *Haiku: An Anthology of Japanese Poems*. Boston: Shambala.

Beech, C. (1993). Looking In, Looking Out: Using Multi-media Approaches in Person-centred Therapy. In D. Brazier (Ed.). *Beyond Carl Rogers: Towards a Psychotherapy for the 21st Century* (pp. 148-166). Constable: London.

Goldsworthy, A. (1998). *Andy Goldsworthy: A Collaboration with Nature*. New York: Harry N. Abrams, Inc.

Rogers, N. (1993). *The Creative Connection: Expressive Arts as Healing*. Palo Alto, CA: Science & Behavior Books.

Schaverien, J. (1992). *The Revealing Image: Analytical Art Therapy in Theory and Practice*. London: Routledge.

Part 5

Global context and wider horizons

13 Environmentally-based therapy in context

Ecotherapy needs to be contextualised in a response to global environmental threat. After examining human tendencies to anthropocentric thinking, individualistic philosophies and consumerist values, this chapter considers Furedi's proposal that therapy itself is deeply enmeshed in cultural developments of recent decades, contributing to current social ills. It then examines alternative perspectives from ecopsychology and Buddhism, including those of Macy and others, suggesting the need for recognition of inter-connection and dependence. The chapter concludes by revisiting The Four Noble Truths, and, in exploring three levels of affliction, showing how fear underlies the current climatic impasse and how facing this may enable positive change.

Despite the fact that working outdoors has been shown to be good for mental health and that a plethora of new approaches are emerging in which therapists and other practitioners are taking people with a variety of mental health problems outdoors, environmentally-based therapies do not sit neatly amongst the categories of psychotherapy and counselling. For many of us in the field, there is a wry appreciation of the fact that our work, like nature herself, is organic and hard to confine. As this book has shown, environmentally-based therapies incorporate a wide range of approaches and span a variety of disciplines, some of which are not generally thought of as therapy at all. Some practitioners operate in specific areas. They might use shamanic practices or therapeutic horticulture, lead wilderness experiences or offer one-to-one counselling outdoors. Others cross boundaries of different approaches in creative and idiosyncratic ways.

Nature is abundant and untidy. Likewise, when we take therapy outdoors, we often find that our neat categorisation of therapeutic modalities and the assumptions which we hold about therapeutic practice are challenged. In the complexity of outdoor environments, we are continually adapting and developing our work in new directions. Just as plants make the best of circumstances and grow towards the light in the best ways that available nutrients can support, so too, nature-based therapies are making use of their varied roots and creating fertile and interesting communities of ideas.

This book presents an overview of approaches to environmental therapy but also offers a model for their integration. The model being proposed unfolds through different fields of psychological enquiry. The first two fields, therapeutic container and the theoretical framework, provide the foundations. These were explored in sections one and two. The remaining sections of this book explore three further fields, representing levels of engagement within therapeutic process. In section three, we looked at the personal dimension, exploring the role of individual history and direct experience in shaping perception of the natural world. In the fourth section, we looked at broader cultural factors which impact on mental states and reflected on the role of myth, ritual and creativity in human process.

This, the final section of the book, explores the broadest level of engagement, and perhaps the most difficult to tackle in the therapeutic arena. We will examine our experience as human beings and as inhabitants of a planet threatened by human activity and we will look at the impact of climatic change and other environmental threats on the field of psychotherapy. We will ask difficult questions about our responsibilities and reflect on the relationship between human and non-human processes. We will examine whether individual psychology can be seen in isolation from our inter-dependence with the planet and look at ways in which therapeutic work can address the human malaise in the face of the karmic consequences of our behaviour towards the ecosystem.

Living at the edge of time

The current generations are witnessing great changes in our planet. Reading statistics collected over the past fifty years and seeing how many climatic and other environmental problems have developed over my lifetime, I feel humbled and scared. I look at my grandchildren and wonder what kind of world they will inhabit in the latter years of this century.

When I was sixteen, the environmental movement was in its infancy. That year, the BBC broadcast a programme in the Horizon series called *Due To Lack of Interest Tomorrow Has Been Cancelled.*[1] This programme had a big impact on me and on my friends. We came to believe that the planet was doomed to destruction through the use of industrial chemicals and other pollutants. We imagined the timescale for our demise to be thirty years, which seemed like an immensity of time in those days, but has, in fact, now long passed. For a while I became deeply involved in campaigning, although I had little idea of how to make any difference through it. I believed fervently that if people just understood the danger we were in, they would do something to stop it, but my pleas and cajoling seemed to fall on deaf ears. Eventually I gave up, feeling defeated by my powerlessness. I got on with life as a student and tried to forget.

Now, after a space of time, I recognise that some of the predictions made in the early seventies were alarmist but also that, forty-five years on, we are indeed facing many of the problems predicted back then, albeit in different forms and sometimes still not affecting our ordinary lives in ways we recognise. Now it is rare for there not to be some item in the news which directly or indirectly alludes to the negative impact of humans on the ecosystem.

Whether it is extreme weather or melting of polar ice-caps, landslides or flooding, chemical spillage or other contamination, human destructiveness is evident daily.

At the same time, living in a western country, privileged enough to have good housing and plentiful food, it is easy to ignore these indications that all is not well. The media create a constant backdrop of news, juxtaposing war and earthquakes with royal romances and celebrity transgressions. We start to turn off and no longer notice specifics in the wallpaper of disasters. Life becomes mundane and television becomes entertainment. Awareness drops away.

We ignore the painful and the frightening because we feel powerless, paralysed by our own reactions. At some level, however, it is hard to be unaware that things are changing. Even if we push the knowledge and the fear into the unconscious, it festers and impacts on our thinking and decision making. It infiltrates our dreams. The fear of global destruction is in the psyche of our age. Often ignored, it is pushed into the shadow consciousness of humanity, the unconscious repository of dark and dangerous mental processes. As with all shadow material, it has the potential to drive us in ignorance towards the brink. The repressed and hidden is often more potent than that which is known and expressed openly. We ignore it at our peril.

This aspect of the psyche has to be part of our field of attention as environmentally-based therapists. Collectively and individually people live under the shadow of environmental calamity, just as, since the last world war, they lived under the shadow of the bomb. Our individual psychologies incorporate fears in different ways, sometimes rising to the challenge of the call to action and sometimes escaping into hedonism or depression, but each person inevitably responds. Maybe too in our work, besides treating the casualties of environmental challenges, we may find ways to contribute to their solution, if such a solution exists.

Anthropocentric thinking

The human species is basically, like other species, self-centred. The needs of humanity are almost invariably placed above interests of other animals and plants. This is not surprising. At a gross level where human life is at stake, few people hold back from environmentally damaging solutions when no other solution can be found. Swamps are drained to stop the spread of mosquito borne diseases and animals are culled if they become a threat to public health. Conservationists argue for particular cases, but no-one lays down their life for a threatened ant hill.

The anthropocentric view which dominates most of human culture places human interests above those of animals or plants or of the ecosystem as a whole. Buddhism has sometimes challenged this assertion of the centrality of humankind, seeing the human realm as one stage in the cycle of rebirth. According to this world-view, respect for animals is important, not just for their intrinsic worth, but also because in other lives, we too may have had four feet or fins or wings. Be kind to all creatures because in some past life, in the infinite aeons of history, they may have been your mother, or you theirs. Thus, for centuries, Buddhists have advocated compassion for life in all its forms. Even this view is basically self-centred, however. We care for animals and other life forms because of an imagined relationship to them, not because, in their own right, these creatures deserve respect.

Other Buddhist perspectives are more holistic, viewing the environment as a system rather than in terms of its individual components. The ecosystem functions as a whole, with complementary patterns of becoming and ceasing, creating and re-creating itself in an eternal process. The image of Indra's Net is used to represent this interconnected whole. In this image, every interstice of the fabric is embellished with a jewel which, in its multi-faceted brilliance, reflects every other jewel. The net stretches out in all directions, a glittering collaboration of elements, each one supporting and reflecting every other. The metaphor of Indra's Net has been used to inspire people to a less self-centred world-view and a more compassionate and skilful relationship to the planet. It is an image which Joanna Macy (1983) and others from the deep ecology movement have drawn on extensively.

Developing ecotherapy practice, we should critique our own approach. If nature is used as a resource for our work, to what extent are we buying into anthropocentric philosophy and using the outdoors to benefit particular people whilst not returning any benefit to the environment itself? Can we hold in mind the planet whilst still responding to individual distress without losing therapeutic integrity? The question is not simple, but, as Indra's Net shows, we are not disconnected and nor are our clients. If we ignore the whole, we do disservice to those we assist by cutting off our work from the root distress which permeates their lives as well as our own.

Individualism and fragmentation

Individualistic thinking has underpinned much that has gone wrong with the world in recent years. In our time, Western society has experienced a steady fragmentation of social groupings. Households have become smaller and more people choose to live alone than ever before. Social values have shifted from the relatively co-operative, mutually supportive culture of the post-war years, in which the residues of wartime spirit focused on building a better world for everyone, to a society based on more individualistic values of competition, achievement and enterprise. Not all change has been bad, of course. Aspects of the old order, which were hypocritical and discriminatory, have, in part, been overturned by the social revolution of the 1960s and 1970s and by subsequent decades of legislative reform, bringing welcome developments in social mobility and anti-discriminatory practice. Sadly, though, the emerging culture of the new millennium is hardly less divided than that of our parents and grandparents, though today's divisions are based increasingly on financial differences rather than the old class structures.

Margaret Thatcher has been credited with the demise of the collective. Her oft quoted comment that 'there is no such thing as society'[2] summarised the changing attitudes of the 1980s and the move away from collective responsibility for the poor and disadvantaged towards more competitive, ruthless attitudes in which people were frequently left to find their own way through difficulties. 'There are individual men and women, and there are families' she continued, and, whilst she did suggest that people care for their neighbours, the primary intent of her message was self-responsibility. Thatcher herself was part of a greater tide of change, however, for people come to power on the waves of collective process, thrown up because they represent something already growing in the wider culture. The social changes of the last few decades have been global as well as national, marking shifting values in Western society as a whole.

The fragmentation of social groupings hasn't only come about through self-interested capitalism. Technological changes have supported people in becoming more isolated. People rely increasingly on home-based entertainment. Initially, television and video drew people away from public entertainment, followed more recently by the growth of social media. Increasing affluence has fuelled increasing technological dependence, compounding individualism. With several televisions in the average household, there is no longer even need to negotiate which channel the family will watch, and, with the popularity of smart phones and tablets, people often spend their leisure time occupying personal cyber worlds, even when in the same room as others. Friendship circles have changed, in some senses becoming bigger and more international, as the online community spans continents, but contact is often limited to sound-bite exchanges, filtered through web-based media. Social places like pubs are closing down for lack of patronage and local societies, which once flourished, now struggle to get members.

We should not be surprised by such changes. Buddhist psychology suggests that, under pressure, people tend to retreat into more rigid behaviour, disconnecting from their surroundings and taking refuge in self-building. They become less trusting and more self-reliant. On the larger scale, this process results in nationalistic movements, but on the small scale it leads families to close ranks and individuals to isolate themselves from others.

Greed culture and commodification

The changes of the last three decades since Thatcher began her assault on the collective power of unions and on the welfare state have, among other things, affected attitudes to wealth. Money has become the primary object of aspiration. Whilst wealth was always important, money is now not only a source of pleasure and status, but also the organising value upon which people assess their worth. To be poor equates with failure, laziness and even immorality. To be rich is prestigious and accords people the highest positions in society, whether political or social. Celebrity culture presents the public with images that celebrate acquisitiveness as an end in itself. The self-made entrepreneur is no longer disparaged as *nouveau riche*, but, rather, is held up as someone to be emulated.

Amid this adulation of wealth, the financial differences between the richest and poorest in society are larger than ever and are increasing steadily. A report published by Oxfam, suggested that 2015 was the year in which the richest 1% of society overtook the rest of the world in terms of assets (Hardoon, Fuentes-Nieva & Ayele 2016). Even allowing for some critiques of this paper, there is little doubt that the social divide between rich and poor is growing steadily and wealth is becoming concentrated in the hands of an increasingly elite group who operate largely internationally, avoiding taxation and calling the tune on many national policies, including those detrimentally affecting the environment.

This move towards greater social difference can only be damaging. According to Pickett and Wilkinson's ground breaking book, *The Spirit Level: Why Equality is Better for Everyone* (2010), societies which have the largest differential between their richest and poorest members perform worst on a number of criteria including mental health, physical health, social provision and community wellbeing, regardless of the country's overall wealth. The main defining factor for positive social change is increasing equality and reducing the gap between rich and poor.

Paradoxically, in parallel with this process, the centralisation of services and the introduction of mechanised systems, mean that ordinary people are not necessarily respected for their specific needs, but are treated more as units and their needs commodified. This commodification permeates many fields in modern culture. A post-industrial phenomenon, it draws on the philosophy of the production line and factory, and, with increasing introduction of computerised systems, extends into fields that previously allowed for personal initiative. We have become numbers on a spread sheet or slots in a timetable.

In its positive aspects, the rise of individualism in the 1960s and 1970s initiated questioning of old authorities. People were no longer prepared to accept poor conditions in work or at home. An emphasis on personal rights fostered, amongst other things, the consumer movement, which, coupled with a litigation culture imported from the United States, empowered people to challenge service providers in all spheres of life. As with many things, however, this development gradually became institutionalised. Organisations began to protect themselves, introducing more and more checks on quality and out-put, so ordinary people were no longer trusted to carry out their work in their own ways. Systems of monitoring were introduced, but were often counter-productive as they tended to lead to the demoralisation of staff.

In education too, a culture of monitoring and certification has led to what appears to be a dumbing down of the values held in educational establishments fifty years ago: of learning for its own sake and the appreciation of subjects like history, philosophy and the classics which, whilst not necessarily economically useful, gave people the tools to think and critique their current age, and, most importantly, gain perspective on current events. In today's education, people are commonly directed to the markers of individual success: material wealth, social status and the pursuit of personal happiness through packaged experiences and products. These values tend to focus people's interests on commercial sources of satisfaction, which in turn diminishes people's sense of connection to their wider environment and to nature.

In this commodified culture, there seems to be increasing fear of the wild and the unmediated experiencing of it. Even when people go outdoors, it is often to participate in packaged experiences of nature, tamed by country parks or fitness activities. As therapists working outdoors, we often contribute to such packages, and may find ourselves working with sponsored schemes and programmes. This is not bad in itself since it makes access to nature possible for people who might otherwise not engage with the outdoors at all, but it is ironic that many of the activities which are now offered as 'getting-into-nature' packages are things which people did as a matter of course a few generations ago.

The changes of the last few decades have been complex. Whilst it would be simplistic to blame economic and political factors for all recent social trends, if not causal, these developments do seem symptomatic of changes in Western society that are replacing family and community interests with economic ones. We are experiencing a global epidemic of grasping, and, as we have seen, grasping is generally rooted in fear. When people feel threatened, they stop relating to one another in real ways, but increasingly resort to stereotypes and functionality in last ditch attempts to assume control. Holding onto a system which is patently unfair and ill-founded, those with power seek more power, leading to the dehumanisation of many aspects of modern society.

Therapy culture

Having explored some social trends of the last few decades, as therapists we must also consider how psychotherapy practice may be being influenced by the philosophies of our times and how we in turn may be influencing society. Interest in psychology has grown in parallel with the social changes of the past few decades. Young adults of the 1980s were dubbed the 'me' generation, riding on the rising culture of personal fulfilment and self-interested introspection which accompanied the quest for material success. The therapy world flourished and proliferated during this time, however, in the 1990s there were recriminations over its more indulgent excesses (Rutter 1990). This led to the evolution of the more muted culture of the therapy world today. Though more understanding of good practice, this an increasingly regulated profession became caught in battles over professional regulation and a scramble for publicly sponsored recognition and funding (Mowbray 1995; Postle 2007).

The psychological therapies have influenced society. They have created changes in the way that ordinary people see themselves and in how the less advantaged are defined. In his book, *Therapy Culture*, Frank Furedi (2003) suggests that the rise of psychotherapy as a force in society has led to a paradigm shift, which increasingly emphasises emotional experience and pathologises life conditions which were previously seen as normal. Furedi considers this change both disempowering and socially divisive, as many people come to believe that they are sick, when really their emotional pain is an ordinary reaction to events and social factors beyond their control.

Whether or not one accepts Furedi's interpretation in its totality, it is evident that, in recent decades, fields as diverse as social policy, education and the media have assimilated the view that psychological factors play a significant part in ordinary human processes. This shift, whilst progressive in some respects, can support mechanisms of social control. Increased access to therapeutic services sometimes becomes linked to less benevolent motives, like getting people off benefits and into work, rather than really engaging with people's underlying problems. In addition, fear of litigation has increased, driving many service providers to adopt conservative approaches to caring as economic pressures create pared down services which fail to deliver the promised support. Increased awareness of mental health issues, changing economic priorities and a culture of solution-based thinking has led increasingly to medicalised approaches to mental health, the latter being fuelled by the rise of large drug companies and the influence of the DSM[3] (Whitaker 2010).

Whilst it is hard to say what is causal and what consequence, the therapy world and the study of human psychology play significant roles in shaping society. The implications of Furedi's proposal are serious. In addition to diminishing people's experiences of loss and trauma to psychological and medical problems, treatable by experts, therapy culture also locates the responsibility for healing collective ills of society and the planet with the individual who is then labelled 'sick' and treated with medication. The weakest and least powerful members of society are often left carrying responsibility for the failings of the bigger system. It is cheaper to treat single mothers for depression than to improve their access to better housing and childcare. It is less troubling to medicate young people for anxiety than to listen to their concerns about environmental change.

Psychology in the global context

Psychology's capacity to enquire into and critique human process has given us understanding of social process and of events from history. It has helped to understand criminal motivation. We have come to appreciate that children go through stages in their development and have particular needs at particular times. We have struggled to make sense of the holocaust and the rise of fascism. We have become more aware of mental distress, the effects of trauma and conditions such as autism, revolutionising their care. At the same time, psychological know-how has been used by the wealthy to exploit market trends and sell merchandise. It has helped authorities to understand and infiltrate movements which the state considered undesirable, and sometimes to torture their enemies more effectively.

Psychotherapy and society mirror one another, and the norms of society penetrate the therapy room. The therapy profession has itself become enmeshed with philosophies of the market place and economic pragmatism. Many therapists today are employed by organisations wholly or partially funded through statutory sources, some within health, educational or employment services, and others in third sector organisations, which bid for contracts from the statutory sector. Within such services, funding is commonly linked to quality assurance, which in turn requires monitoring of outcomes, imposing financially linked targets. In these circumstances, funders' priorities and values, rather than those of professionals or clientele, tend to shape working practice. Other therapists work in private settings which, though experiencing less immediate external control, are still financially constrained in needing to advertise and offer services attractive to the public at large.

Environmental therapies are developing in a time when the environment is under more pressure than ever before in human history. In the last decade we have seen speculation about climate change move from a matter of debate to a reality accepted by all but the most sceptical and financially motivated. Just as individuals may respond to impending crisis with 'business as usual' denial, so too, mirroring society, the psychological professions may fail to engage with these issues, declaring them beyond their remit. If therapists are not to be caught fiddling whilst Rome burns, however, we need to contextualise our work in this greater awareness and recognise that the threat of environmental disaster is not the neurotic delusion of a few, but, rather, something which at some level impinges on the psychology of all our clients. We cannot simply treat the therapy room or the outdoors as oases of healing, unaffected by this bigger picture. Environmentally-based therapies which simply maintain the human-centric position, viewing nature as a resource for therapeutic practice, fail to understand or address this important layer in human psychology.

In these circumstances, as ecotherapists we may want to seek to express concern and find ways to approach environmental questions without alienating those with whom we need to address these matters. If the therapy profession becomes more ecologically consciousness, and environmentally-based therapies become more widely adopted, then we may have the capacity to influence not only therapeutic practice, but also wider developments in society. For this, we need models and philosophies which can be presented to funders and commissioners and others who sanction our work, which offer alternative values and justifications to those of the predominant paradigm.

Philosophies of connection

Whilst some ecotherapy practice is dominated by human-centric philosophies, other approaches are grounded in a view of non-hierarchical inter-relationship between people and the environment. One such philosophy, used in some ecotherapy circles, is biophilia. It has long been recognised in Western philosophy that humans are pre-programmed to connect with nature. Attributed originally to Aristotle, this principle was introduced into modern psychology by Erich

Fromm, the German psychoanalyst and social theorist, who coined the word biophilia to describe the instinctive attraction which all people feel towards life, and particularly to other life-forms (Fromm 1964). The concept was further developed by Edward Wilson in his book *Biophilia* (1984) and has since been widely adopted in certain ecotherapy circles to describe the therapeutic benefits of taking people outdoors. Martin Jordan gives the following description of the hypothesis:

> The biophilia hypothesis suggests human identity and personal fulfilment somehow depend on our relationship with nature, and that the human need for nature is linked not just to the material exploitation of the environment but also to the influence the natural world has on our emotional, cognitive, aesthetic, and even spiritual development.
>
> (Jordan 2009)

The biophilia hypothesis provides a rationale and justification for working outdoors, close to nature and sometimes specifically with animals (Antonioli & Reveley 2005). In its simplicity, the hypothesis says little more than that being close to nature is beneficial to humans. This can be hard to quantify in measurable terms. However, Miles Richardson of the University of Derby has conducted studies and devised methodologies examining the psychological benefits of exposure to nature in limited urban environments, based on the biophilia principle (Richardson, Hallam & Lumber 2015).

Another principle, widely acknowledged in the deep ecology movement, is based on the Buddhist theory of dependent co-arising and represented in the previously mentioned image of Indra's Net. Joanna Macy sees this principle as central to her work. Describing it, she writes: 'The recognition of our essential nonseparateness from the world, beyond the shaky walls erected of our fear and greed, is a Dharma gift occurring in every generation, in countless individual lives.'[4] Macy considers that, inasmuch as people embrace this principle, it will enable humanity to address current global problems. She believes that there are signs that humans are already changing, influenced by their interconnection with the planet, in spite of the psychological disconnection arising out of their fears and greediness.

By making this conscious and recognising their interdependence with one another and with the environment, she believes people will embrace the necessary social changes to save the planet. Because humans are interdependent, no one person is going to retrieve the situation single-handedly, but Macy believes that there are many ways people can contribute to the transformation, which she calls 'The Great Turning' (Macy & Brown 2014). This spiritual revolution, which Macy believes is currently unfolding, has practical consequences. It demands a change of heart and transition from industrial growth models to ones of sustainability, sufficiency and collective enterprise. Individually we may be incapable of making a difference, but together we can create positive change.

Whether or not one accepts Macy's optimistic assertion that 'The Great Turning' is already underway, once prophecies are popularised, they tend to be self-fulfilling. Her work is about turning hearts and minds towards a viable future. Inspiring people with the possibility of change enables change to be brought about. The philosophies of Wilson and Macy both promote environmental solutions rooted in principles of reconnection. Rejecting philosophies of isolationism and grasping, they offer visions of humanity in harmony with the ecosystem, rather than in embattled retreat from it, providing stepping stones to a different way of being.

Dukkha and avoidance

In Chapter 5 we saw how the teaching of The Four Noble Truths explains the way that humans adopt patterns of avoidance in response to existential threats, as typified by sickness, old age and death. Identity-building and delusion, founded on greed and hate-type responses, create the 'shaky walls' referred to by Joanna Macy above. These processes operate at collective, social levels as well as personal ones.

The existential fears driving human psychology, which have always affected people on the personal level, now threaten us collectively. Humanity, in a real way, in the foreseeable future, may face extinction, or at least severe wounding. This is a new situation, and one that we have only experienced over the last few decades. During the Cold War, peoples around the world lived with the threat of nuclear attack, knowing that international crisis could spark the ultimate conflict, destroying the world as we knew it. This threat was acute and frightening, but as the Cold War ended, we became confident that, for the moment, we had peace. Nobody had pushed the button, no harm had been done.

The threat of nuclear war has not disappeared and indeed seems to be increasing again, whilst other dangers seem even more pressing. Humanity is facing crises on many fronts. Behind these, however, we cannot avoid the knowledge that substantive environmental changes are happening at the planetary level and that this may be driving other tensions. Each year brings new record-breaking weather events, and many crises of modern times, whether wars, famines or migrations, may be brought on by failing resources and the impact of human responses to the environmental situation.

These problems will not disappear immediately with any human regime change. Unlike the nuclear threat which is based on something which either happens or does not, climatic and environmental changes are already in process and we can only work to mitigate their effects, not to eliminate them. In the best scenario, much will recover and, although extinctions can never be reversed, we will continue to live on a verdant, life-filled planet. Even this will require sacrifices however. Humans will have to adapt their lifestyles and expectations. In all probability, we will need to adjust to loss on many levels as we face the tragedy which we collectively have precipitated.

Three forms of *dukkha*

Dukkha is inevitable. Our births, as our deaths, are *dukkha* and all the disappointments, losses and tribulations of our lives are also *dukkha.* Knowing this gives rise to fear, and our reaction to fear drives many of the mental processes which cause us trouble. *Dukkha* creates *dukkha.* Suffering is compounded by our attempts to escape it. Recognising this and becoming less avoidant frees us from secondary aspects of suffering. According to the Samyutta Nikaya, *dukkha* has three forms.

> There are these three forms of *dukkha,* my friend: the *dukkha* of pain, the *dukkha* of fabrication, the *dukkha* of impermanence. These are the three forms of *dukkha.*
>
> (Samyutta Nikaya 38.14)

This text offers us a three stage model for understanding how *dukkha* is compounded by our attempts to avoid suffering. The three types of *dukkha* are not separate kinds of *dukkha,* but, rather, three layers of reactivity that construct the ordinary mentality, each conditioned by the previous one. We can summarise the three stages as follows:

- suffering associated with painful events, e.g. birth, sickness, ageing and death
- suffering associated with mental constructs
- suffering associated with wanting things to continue as they are.

Existential suffering is unavoidable. Even the Buddha got old, became sick and died. This suffering is a reality and a noble truth. Coming to terms with *dukkha* takes courage. Accepting impermanence is central to the Buddhist path.

Prior to his enlightenment, the Buddha went into the forest intending to overcome his fears. The account of this process, which immediately preceded his enlightenment, is found in *The Sutta on Fear and Dread,* discussed in Chapter 11 (see also Brazier 2011). Overcoming the pernicious patterns of avoidance which limit our lives involves facing difficult life events, but, as we have seen, humans are generally fearful of facing these things.

As we try to avoid pain, we construct mental 'formations' (*samskaras*) based on our personal patterns of avoidance. These are the source of the second level of suffering. Through processes of attachment and clinging and conditioned patterns of greed, hate and delusion, we build up a sense of identity to engage with the world. Since our root fear is of loss and non-existence, we fear anything that threatens our sense of personal continuity and cling to anything that distracts us from everyday experiences of *dukkha* because they remind us of life's changeability. We ruminate obsessively on things which threaten us and on how to change them and we look to the world around us to reflect our sense of who we are, rejecting things which do not do this, and telling ourselves stories which we have repeated for years, rebuilding scripts which we later enact. These patterns build mental constructs and support the process of 'becoming'.

Through this process we create a sense of a permanent and enduring self. This is conditioned by evidence gathered through selective experiencing of the world. We maintain a rigid world-view so that we can obscure reality. This is maintained because it gives a semblance of structure and reliability to our lives, masking small, every day instances of change and impermanence, and particularly our vulnerability to death. In its extreme, this leads to the third kind of *dukkha*, the all-encompassing fear of any change at all. This final layer of conditioned thinking resists all change. The person clings to pleasant experiences, spoiling them with fear that they will soon be over, or avoids pleasures in case they are lost. Life becomes ever more circumscribed and narrow.

The three level understanding of *dukkha* shows how people become increasingly enmeshed in avoidance, and how this impacts on their lives. Some suffering is inevitable, but because we fear suffering, we actually suffer through our fear, and build psychological defences which make us increasingly frightened of change in any form and of anything which we cannot control by an act of will. We live in a false world of make-believe.

In therapy work we encounter people who experience suffering at all these levels. For some people, the predominant suffering is at the first level, linked to a major loss or life change; a bereavement or serious illness, for example. Their needs are basically to come to terms with what is happening and find courage to face the associated feelings. Other people are suffering at the second level. Concerned with issues of identity and belonging, although their feelings may be triggered by life events, their primary focus is on rebuilding their sense of identity in the new context, disentangling patterns of thinking and stories about the world. A third group of people are locked in the third level of reaction, fearing change in any form. This group may suffer from obsessive-compulsive problems or addictions or live very restricted lives. They may need support to find small ways to make changes so they can start to experience new things without feeling threatened, and gradually build confidence in the world.

Everyone suffers from all of these forms of *dukkha*, but we tend to predominantly live one level or another, depending on the severity of our difficulties at a particular time. All these states are driven by *dukkha*, and all will be helped by discovering a more realistic relationship to impermanence, if this can be achieved.

Three types of *dukkha* and social change

Whilst the three types of *dukkha* can be identified in individual processes, they also manifest in the psychology of our society. Tragedy affects many people. Birth, death, loss and disappointment are common to all of us and we respond collectively as well as individually.

When something awful happens, we can feel isolated and locked into our own grief, yet grief is a universal emotion which has the capacity to bring people together if we can learn to listen to one another and avoid the impulse to withdraw. The tendency to isolation which we so often experience in grief results from the avoidant tendencies, not just in ourselves but also in others, and is not intrinsic to the situation. There is a story in the Buddhist texts of a meeting between the Buddha and Kisagotami, a young woman who came for help because her baby had died. Kisagotami brought her dead child to the Buddha, asking him for a cure. Instead of answering her request directly, the Buddha sent Kisagotami back into the village to find a mustard seed from a house where there had never been a death. This task brought Kisagotami into conversation with many people, and it was through these conversations that she realised the futility of her request, but also the inevitability of death. In the process, she also learned about the commonality of grief.

Recognising that we all experience painful changes and losses in our lives can be comforting, but it can also be disturbing as it confirms to us that there really is no way to avoid reality and that individually and collectively we are subject to mortality and change. As we recognise that changes are happening at a planetary level, the challenge to humanity in directly understanding and facing the real meaning of these events, and responding to the situation in a wise and collaborative way is enormous. People are much more inclined to avoidance, and retreating into individual, everyday activities. Because they feel individually powerless, they are unable to envisage cooperative response.

The three types of *dukkha* suggest that, as we continue to resort to patterns of avoidance, we become more rigid in our thinking and our behaviour becomes more grasping or rejecting. We can therefore predict that, as times get worse, those who are able to will cling onto material resources even more firmly and try to avoid acknowledging the suffering around them by manipulating circumstances and media to their own benefit. Gated communities will flourish. Those who do not have access to material wealth will probably resort to warfare and other forms of conflict, focusing their energy into hatred and violence, or to identities conferred by aligning with strong causes. Those who cannot do either will join the many oppressed peoples, disempowered to the point of personal negation. In this way, at collective levels, people operate within the behavioural *samskaras* of society.

As these processes unfold, and, as these behaviours contribute to declining resources and even greater environmental damage, fear will increase rather than decrease. With fear, people will become more rigid and resistant to change. They will become willing to fight to preserve the current illusions of progress and success even when it becomes obvious this is impossible, because fear of change will become greater than the will to improve things. So it is that countries will close borders and introduce special measures.

Responsible to whom?

To whom are we responsible as therapists? Clearly we have responsibility to the clients and groups with whom we work, but what responsibility do we carry to society as a whole? Do we as therapists have responsibility to the ecosystem, the planet and future generations who will inhabit this beautiful space?

Working in nature, we are thrown back on the immensity of the task which we are taking on. We are faced with the particulars of raw emotion: our own and that of others. We face the collective grief which echoes out of every scenario that comes before us. Working together, we may cry a million tears for our beautiful planet. More than this, though, we need to find ways to act on her behalf.

Environmentally-based therapies are concerned not just with the individual but also with the world which we all inhabit. As participants in the great experiment of history, people cannot be taken out of the sea of life in which they are immersed. As therapists we are better placed than many to be guardians of the psyche of the planet, just as we are there for our individual clients. Thus we have great responsibility.

Notes

1 http://genome.ch.bbc.co.uk/6254d3d38f674b6288acb485fcffdeda
2 Margaret Thatcher quoted in *Women's Own* magazine, 31 October 1987.
3 *Diagnostic and Statistical Manual of Mental Disorders* (DSM), published by the American Psychiatric Association.
4 http://www.joannamacy.net/engaged-buddhism/dependent-co-arising.html

References

Antonioli, C. & Reveley, M. (2005). Randomised Controlled Trial of Animal Facilitated Therapy with Dolphins in the Treatment of Depression. *British Medical Journal*, 331(7527): 1231–1234.

Brazier, C. (2011). *Acorns Among the Grass*. Ropley: Earth Books.

Fromm, E. (1964). *The Heart of Man, Its Genius for Good and Evil*. New York: Harper & Row.

Furedi, F. (2003). *Therapy Culture: Cultivating Vulnerability in an Uncertain Age*. London: Routledge.

Hardoon, D., Fuentes-Nieva, R. & Ayele, S. (2016). *An Economy for the 1%: How Privilege and Power in the Economy Drive Extreme Inequality and How this can be Stopped*. Report: Oxfam International.

Jordan, M. (2009). Back to Nature. *Therapy Today*, April: 28–30.

Macy, J. (1983). *Despair and Power in the Nuclear Age*. Philadelphia: New Society Publishers.

Macy, J. & Brown, M. (2014). *Coming Back to Life* (revised ed). Gabriola Island, BC: New Society Publishers.

Mowbray, R. (1995). *The Case Against Psychotherapy Registration*. London: Trans Marginal Press.

Pickett, K. & Wilkinson, R. (2010). *The Spirit Level: Why Equality is Better for Everyone*. London: Penguin.

Postle, D. (2007). *Regulating the Psychological Therapies*. Ross-on-Wye: PCCS Books.

Richardson, M., Hallam, J. & Lumber, R. (2015). One Thousand Good Things in Nature: The Aspects of Nature that Lead to Increased Nature Connectedness. *Environmental Values*, 24(5): 603–619.

Rutter, P. (1990). *Sex in the Forbidden Zone.* New York: Mandala.

Whitaker, R. (2010). *Anatomy of an Epidemic: Magic Bullets, Psychiatric Drugs, and the Astonishing Rise of Mental Illness in America.* New York: Crown.

Wilson, O. (1984). *Biophilia.* Cambridge, MA: Harvard University Press.

14 Vibrancy

This chapter explores the energetic qualities of people's lives and the way that these are affected by emotional and physical circumstances, looking at how spiritual practice generates and contains energy. After a practical section, exploring issues of safety, risk assessment and working with differently abled participants, the chapter then explores energetic cycles which occur in nature through solar and lunar influences and through hormonal fluctuations, particularly in women's menstrual cycles. It concludes by looking at views on polarity and balance found in Western and Eastern systems of thought, and on variations found within the life journey.

How often do we feel fully alive? When do we feel most energetic? How can we live to our capacity and find pleasure in the process? What slows us down? In this chapter we will explore the ninth element in the Ten Directions model, vibrancy, which is concerned with energy and aliveness. Vibrancy is about challenging ourselves physically, but staying safe in the process. It involves the body-sense, but also the flow of mental energy and emotions. It is about appreciating how we use our energy and how we repress it when we withdraw from situations and from our emotional reactions to them. Vibrancy is concerned with knowing that we are alive and connected to the life flow of others.

There are Buddhist stories about how, on a number of occasions, the Buddha was pursued by Mara, the Lord of Death. Mara tempted the Buddha with many pleasant distractions, including his three beautiful daughters, who tried to seduce the Buddha on the night before his enlightenment. The Buddha repeatedly refused to succumb to these diversions. Instead he stayed wakeful and alert.

The stories of Mara show how the world presents us with many opportunities to dissipate our energy and become psychologically, emotionally and spiritually dead, but how, if we recognise these for what they are, can we choose to live in a more vibrant way? As we have seen in previous chapters, humans have a tendency to avoid things which are unpleasant, and particularly to resist reminders of mortality, in consequence shutting off from things which lead us to feel fully alive. It's a paradox. Through our fear of not existing in the future, we fail to live now. Through anxiety about death we are deadened to the present moment.

Working outdoors puts us in touch with our energetic nature. We generally expend more physical energy outdoors than we do when sitting at home. We engage with the body, and this often brings an immediate sense of aliveness. Outdoor activity can be physically demanding. Hill walking, running, climbing, wild swimming all require physical stamina, strength and fitness. When we reach the top of a mountain or cross a fast flowing river, we know that we are embodied creatures, living in a landscape that is infinitely fascinating and rewarding. We can easily forget this in our urban lives. Even activities which are quieter and more meditative, like a slow walk in the countryside, use muscles and take physical effort. They connect us to the Earth in an immediate and feelingful way. They ground our energy.

Energy and the emotions

The mind and the body are closely linked. Thoughts and feelings evoke physical reactions. The stomach tightens. The shoulders relax. The thighs tense. The jaw unclenches. The heart beats faster. Genitals tingle into life. The eyes dampen. The head aches. We recognise emotions by the physiological symptoms they evoke and consult the wisdom of the felt-sense in our decision making (Gendlin 1978). Conversely, engaging our bodies in activity affects our mental processes. Being outdoors is good for mental health. Participation in sports relieves depression (Rimer *et al.* 2012). Anxiety is reduced by physical work on the land.

Our energy levels are deeply interlinked with our emotional lives in other ways. As we have seen, most of the time people are in some degree of flight from the existential realities of their lives, both in a generalised and specific ways. Avoidant behaviour is the human norm. We distract ourselves with sensory pleasures such as food, sex or activity, involving our bodily processes, and create *samskaras*, the mind-structures based on compulsive grasping or rejection (Brazier 2003). These tie up our mental energy so that we do not function as fully as we might like. This in turn affects our physical energy. People who are depressed find it difficult to get out of bed. Anxiety knots up our muscles and tenses our bodies.

Unconscious processes reduce our available energy. We use energy to repress thoughts and emotions that, at some level, we do not want to feel. As therapists we can sense this. If I am sitting with a client and suddenly, without good cause, start to feel sleepy, I ask myself if this is an indication that something important is being repressed in the session. When difficult memories or uncomfortable thoughts are suppressed, vital energy is diverted into building psychological walls. Whereas healthy mental states are fluid and ever-changing, fear leads people to rigidify their experiencing and creates psychological stagnation. The person becomes tired and listless, and, in more extreme cases, this repressive tiredness can also be experienced by anyone, like the therapist, who is in close psychological contact with them. With experience, as therapists, we come to recognise when we are being invited into this state of not-seeing.

Energy and consumption

Mental states are affected by what we consume. A heavy meal can be comforting but also leave us feeling lethargic or even depressed. Caffeine keeps us alert but can make us jittery or anxious. Fasting or living on a restricted diet brings mental clarity, but will sap energy in the longer term. Alcohol can put us in the party spirit, helping us lose control of inhibitions, but it affects our ability to reason and understand what is going on around us. Most of these effects have a physiological basis, but, since physiology and psychology are closely linked, the reasons why a particular food or drink affects us in a particular way may be complex.

Although most psychotherapists do not discuss diet with their clients, in the broader setting of environmentally-based therapies, it may be more appropriate and useful to reflect on the effects of food on the mentality. These effects can be multi-levelled. Firstly food affects us physically. Good nutrition can be good for mental health. It can stabilise our energy levels and supports our physiology. Secondly, food is symbolic and affects us emotionally. Associated with nurturance and caring, food is the currency of love (Orbach 1978). Thirdly, we are affected by the social and moral contexts of eating. Food production and marketing are often detrimental to those involved in these industries, to animals, and to the environment, and there is much political and social suffering brought about by food inequalities in the world. Whether or not we consciously take these factors to heart, they can affect our reactions to the food that we take in. In her chapter, 'How Much is Enough: Buddhist Perspectives on Consumerism', Stephanie Kaza (2010) discusses similar areas of concern from a Buddhist perspective. Excessive consumption supports identity creation and craving, as well as causing moral harm through the effects of the food industry on animal, plants and humans.

Some foods have particular associations. Childhood favourites like steamed puddings, ice cream and sweets are comforting, in part because they hold memories, and in part because sweet, carbohydrate-rich foods provide immediate, easy calories when we are tired. Other foods, such as salads or fruit, are commonly labelled 'healthy'. People associate them with 'being good' or 'getting slim', enjoying them or not accordingly. By choosing certain foods, we can change our moods and sense of wellbeing pretty much instantaneously. People often punctuate their days with snacks, giving themselves injections of energy and reprogramming their mental states.

Other forms of consumption also affect energy levels. A common stereotype of modern life is the person stretched out in front of the television, only moving from the sofa to fetch drinks and snacks, having lost the energy for more active pursuits and, for the most part, experiencing life through the glass of the screen. This kind of leisure-time consumption provides a kind of anaesthetic against the busyness and frustration of many working lives. Speaking more of avoidance than pleasure, it is contributing to widespread increases in obesity and ill-health, and also affects people's mental states. Moves to get people outdoors in recent years have often arisen out of concern that this kind of lifestyle is sapping the energy of current generations and creating health problems for the future.

Spiritual energy

Psychological and spiritual growth involves liberating energy tied up in defending the psyche. In Buddhist theory, the word used to describe spiritual energy is *virya*. *Virya* is defined as the energy and enthusiasm we bring to spiritual practice, but it is also the strength of will we apply in living our lives with good intent. *Virya* demonstrates our willingness to go the extra mile, throw ourselves into things and stick at them when they become difficult. It is a person's spiritual strength, commitment and moral purpose.

Sometimes we can get the feeling that there is a finite quantity of energy available to us and that we need to protect it and not squander it in case it should run out. Everyday experience shows there is some truth in this idea. If we become tired doing one thing, we will not have the energy to do something else. This is not the whole story, however. Most of us will have had the experience of settling down for the evening, feeling tired after a difficult day and ready to put our feet up, only to receive a phone call with some important news. Whether the news is good, perhaps a job offer or other success, or bad, such as news of a death, the tiredness we felt prior to answering the phone usually disappears instantly. We can understand this phenomenon in terms of the adrenaline release that follows important news, but this understanding does not diminish the fact that we experience a different emotional state, becoming energised and ready to act.

Intensive spiritual practice often involves people pushing themselves mentally and physically over a period of time. It may include fasting, reduced sleep, and long periods of meditation or chanting. During such retreats, practitioners often feel a range of emotions and energy levels, sometimes feeling exhausted, but other times exhilarated. This experience, among other things, teaches us about our energetic and emotional patterns and about how we can live in harmony with them or override them. At the end of a retreat, people often experience feeling high in energy and mood. This is not conserved energy. It is energy generated by the spiritual practice. The challenge at this point is to maintain and use this energy in positive ways rather than dissipating it in distractions. Sometimes it can be daunting to feel so much energy freed up so we automatically seek to quell it.

Some outdoor activities evoke similar intensity to that one might find on an intensive retreat. A solitary experience of the wild, like a solo retreat or vision quest, is often intentionally set up to provide this kind of experience. Long distance treks in difficult country and extreme sports also make physical and psychological demands on people, confronting and challenging them to extend themselves. Undertaking such challenges, people discover their patterns of resistance and their capacity to adapt under pressure. They discover moral strength, trusting their own capabilities and becoming more aware of their limits.

As people work outdoors, they become more attuned to natural environments. They also become more attuned to bodily experience and its energetic variations. Recognising the felt-sense through the therapeutic work helps them develop sensitivity to psychological process and make decisions informed by this intuition. This process brings insight into the interconnectedness of different levels of physical and psychological experience and ways in which these influence one another. Moving towards a more intuitive, embedded way of being, they recognise the fluidity of experience, and become more grounded in the paradigm of impermanence.

Safety and challenge

Working outdoors, there are times when we operate in challenging and even dangerous situations. As facilitators, we are responsible for ensuring appropriate levels of safety for the group and for the conditions. This is usually a matter of finding the right balance between risk and challenge. We have a duty to stay within the limits of our training and adhere to codes of good practice appropriate to the particular activities that we are leading. We also need to have in place the correct professional insurance policy so that we and our clients will be covered in case of an accident. At the same time, we need to be able to offer activities which stretch people.

It is never possible to make all activities completely safe, and trying to do so is often counter-productive. At the same time, being aware of risk factors is an essential part of any preparation. Safety standards in general have improved considerably over the years and lives have been saved as a result. Irresponsible mountaineers, sailors and walkers endanger others as well as themselves, putting the lives of emergency service personnel at risk as they make rescue attempts, often in terrible conditions.

Risk assessment is important to any outdoor activity. This should cover both the work itself and the wider context in which it will take place. Activities should be suited to the level of fitness of the particular group of participants. Leading some activities requires specialist knowledge and training. If you lead wilderness retreats or take people into mountains or other wild terrain, you will probably need specialist training to work in those challenging environments. You should then stay within guidelines and your own fitness frame, co-working with someone reliable who is also qualified. Mostly, though, this book is concerned with work that involves a more every-day level of physical exertion, in situations where help can easily be summoned and in which most people can participate without being excessively challenged. Even here, however, we still need to do risk assessments, holding awareness of our personal limits, of possible dangers, and of the particular needs of others.

Groups need challenge, but activities can be challenging without being dangerous. A long walk in rolling countryside will challenge people who are not used to covering distances on foot, but, unless participants are infirm, they are unlikely to experience health problems beyond a few blisters and aching muscles. A long walk can test people's capacity to cope with mild to moderate discomfort and give them an experience of going beyond their previous limits without putting them at significant risk.

Some challenges are physical, making demands upon a person's energy and physical capacity, but other challenges are psychological. Being alone in the dark, handling spiders or other insects, walking along a narrow cliff path or climbing a tree can all be challenging because they involve facing fears and overcoming previous limitations. When this happens, there is often a release of energy and feeling of excitement and increased confidence, just as when people undertake physical challenges.

Challenges give people confidence and a sense of achievement so long as they are not taken too far out of their comfort zone. If an experience is too uncomfortable, this may just reinforce previous negative associations with the outdoors. Positive encouragement, having the right equipment, camaraderie of the group, and opportunities for debriefing afterwards are all important in making the experience a good one.

Disabilities and special needs

Different people have different levels of energy and different capabilities. These may be related to issues of health, life stage or fitness, as well as to their psychology. Exploring difference may be part of the group process, and it is sometimes appropriate to negotiate activities with the group so that everyone's needs can be accommodated. This works where there is a reasonable level of parity between group members, but it is important that those who are less able do not find themselves feeling discomfited or pressured to push themselves beyond a safe limit. Sometimes, particularly if someone has a disability, those who are less able need some protection. They may be embarrassed by their physical condition, and not want to discuss their limitations, or the reasons for them, with the group. Group leaders may therefore sometimes need to plan activities, taking their requirements into account, without group input.

Working outdoors, it is not always possible to accommodate people with every kind of disability. Some environments and activities, by their nature, exclude those with limited mobility or other physical problems. Access is a major factor. There are now a good number of sites available which have paths suitable for wheelchairs and other adapted facilities such as meeting rooms and toilets, but other places where ecotherapy is practiced are much less accommodating. Rough paths, steep slopes, stiles and other obstacles make the countryside inaccessible to many.

Each person has their own particular capabilities and difficulties. There are many types of disability, bringing different challenges to our work. For example, visual and auditory problems affect people's ability to participate just as much as mobility issues. Usually it is relatively easy to address such needs. It is often a matter of having a conversation with the person concerned, as most people will be able to suggest what they need in order to participate. People with visual disabilities can often join in if offered one-to-one support. Those with hearing loss may need extra help with instructions, knowing when an exercise has ended, and joining in sharing sessions, since voices are more difficult to pick up outdoors.

If therapeutic activities are pre-planned for a group of people who have particular disabilities, then adaptations can be made relatively easily. Individual people should be consulted in advance about their level of need, since it cannot be assumed that everybody with the same disability will require the same level of support. The facilitators should consider practicalities like transport, access to working spaces, toilet and changing facilities, emergency backup in case of difficulties and ratios of helpers and therapists to participants. It is also important to remember that people with limited mobility or ill health may suffer from extremes of weather more than able-bodied people, in part because they are less active. In some cases, if they also have learning difficulties, for example, they may not be able to tell others when they are too cold or too hot.

For those with more severe disabilities, access to the outdoors may be limited to specialist centres. There is still a good range of possible activities: gardening in raised beds, watching birds on feeders, sensory gardens and specialist play equipment can all be accessed by people with multiple difficulties. Once again, assessing people's individual needs and capacities is important. A good deal of work has been done adapting tools and facilities so participation can be active and satisfying. In other situations, such as residential homes, hospitals or hospices, you may need to find ways of taking nature indoors. Here, there may be issues of infection control and other medical considerations, but the benefits of exposure to nature in such circumstances are high.

Some disabilities are psychological. People with severe mental health problems often benefit hugely by being outdoors, and can be involved in gardening, sports and other outdoor projects, whereas other types of ecotherapy activity, such as those involving therapeutic group sessions or long periods of isolation, may not be suitable. Some people may also struggle if activities involve unpredictable elements and may find cooperation with others difficult. Their presence may then be inhibiting for the group. Pre-selection of participants is therefore important for ecotherapy events which may attract people with mental health problems so that, if participants are known to be psychologically fragile, activities can be kept suitably structured.

As with many aspects of this work, planning needs to include appraisal of the group for whom activities are intended and a realistic assessment of their capabilities. Facilitators may wish to meet the potential participants in advance of a first session, or at least to enquire whether they have any particular physical or psychological needs through a questionnaire. If participants have special needs, facilitators then need to include these specifically when conducting their risk assessment, making a detailed inspection of the space to be used and an inventory of potential hazards. They can then make a realistic assessment of whether adaptations can be made in order to include particular people.

Adaptation is not always possible. Advance information can give potential participants clear indications of what would be involved in participating so that they can decide whether or not to participate, but ultimately it is the group leaders' responsibility to ensure, as far as they are able, that they do not accept people into a group who will not be able to participate at a level that ensures psychological and physical safety for themselves and others.

Natural cycles

Since the earliest times, humans have been conscious of cyclical processes which govern all life-forms on this planet. People devised megalithic structures to calculate the turning seasons and calibrate the passing of days so as to be able to understand the yearly patterns of changing day lengths and weather conditions. These observations were important to early farmers, helping them discern times for the planting and harvesting upon which their survival depended. They were also important to their spiritual life, and many monuments that we still see today were used for seasonal rituals as much as for pragmatic purposes.

Our planetary experience is of cycles within cycles. The Earth circles the sun and the moon circles the Earth. Patterns of light and dark, day and night and the seasons of the year all unfold in an interlocking dance. People are accustomed to such changes. In temperate latitudes, periods of warmth and sunshine alternate with colder times when the world is dark and many of the processes of life fall into dormancy. Only in equatorial areas are these annual changes less evident.

The solstices and the equinoxes hold the four quarters of the year. These days, celebrated through much of history, represent the turning of seasons: spring equinox, summer solstice, autumn equinox and winter solstice at the darkest time of all. Growing up within the cycle of light times and dark times has a profound effect upon the human psyche. The experiences of these changes are deeply ingrained in our culture and in the mythology that we have generated. They help us understand our own processes of growth and decline, but they are not merely metaphors, for the physicality of these changes in the world around us impinges on our body experience and we respond in a variety of ways, some of which seem grounded in our animal nature.

Some effects are psychological. Others can be attributed to practicalities. We wear more clothing in winter and feel the restriction of heavier garments on our bodies. Other effects seem to be physiological. Being indoors, with central heating and artificial lighting, to some extent insulates us from the experience of winter, but at the same time can exacerbate the problem since, confined to an office or a house, we do not experience even the limited winter sunlight. In the 1980s, seasonal affective disorder was recognised as a condition affecting peoples in higher latitudes. This made sense of the depression that some people feel in winter when light levels diminish. Many people find winter difficult, however. The dark evenings and the colder climate seem to encourage us to spend more time indoors and sleep for longer. Without the bright light of the morning sun to wake us, we feel sluggish and reluctant as we get up for work, or we lie in bed for longer if we do not have to. It is not hard to believe that we, like the dormice and the bears, are designed to hibernate.

In summer, conversely, long days and warmer temperatures draw people outdoors. The body feels different, more flexible in lighter clothing, and for most people moods become positive and more sociable. Not everybody has the same reaction to the seasons, however. Some people love winters and find summers times of anxiety and stress. Longer term groups and individual work may span the seasons, allowing us to reflect on idiosyncratic reactions to changing energies. We can observe the greening of woods and fields in spring and the autumnal mists and fruitfulness as the year moves towards its turning, and we can feel, reflected in them, our own processes of growth and maturation.

Other cycles also affect us psychologically and physiologically. The Earth turns on her axis, night following day and day following night. The sun appears to move across the sky, reaching its zenith at noon before sinking into the western sunset at evening. Birds awaken in the dawn chorus. Owls and bats fly in the evening twilight. The human body also passes through a daily pattern of hormonal cycles, instigating wakefulness or sleeping, digesting or fasting. As we become sensitive to these body processes, realising just how powerful these diurnal patterns are, we can find ways to work with them rather than against them. I have found, for example, that there are periods of the day in which I write more effectively: early morning, and late evening. If I can plan my work to accommodate these periods, I find that it goes better and that I am more productive.

Sleep is affected by these daily patterns. It can be disrupted by changes in the clock, either through inter-continental travel or daylight saving measures, causing us considerable distress and upsetting bodily functions such as digestion or alertness. The body-clock can also be affected by lifestyle changes such as shift work or having babies, though our body cycles can be trained and people acclimatise to different patterns of sleep. Humans are adaptable. For example, today most of us in the West expect an uninterrupted night of sleep, but there is considerable evidence that in Elizabethan times people slept in two distinct sections, broken by a period of activity.

Of all the different cycles affecting our planet, however, the one which has perhaps been most mysterious to human beings throughout history is that of the moon. In her waxing and waning, the moon's face changes over the period of a month, turning our nights from times of total darkness to those when the light is so bright that one can see one's shadow cast on the ground. These changes have fascinated peoples since prehistoric times, giving rise to folklore and iconography that is both cultural and spiritual. In Buddhism, the cycle of the moon has been used by different traditions to create calendars for religious activities. Full moon and new moon in particular are designated as *Uposatha* days, when monastics and lay people conduct extra practices and take on additional disciplines.

The moon is also associated with the female Buddha, Quan Shi Yin, who is widely venerated throughout the Chinese Buddhist world (Palmer & Ramsay 1995). The embodiment of compassion, Quan Shi Yin is often represented against a deep blue night sky, superimposed upon a full moon and rising above the ocean waves, with which she is also associated. It is to her that people call in their suffering, and she is said to shed an ocean of tears for the sorrows of the world, weeping for *The Great Grief*, the suffering of humankind and of our planet down the ages. This association between moon and sea, recurring in mythology of different cultures, is founded on reality, for the moon's circuit round the Earth causes the ocean tides, creating the twice daily rise and fall of the seas and impacting on our coasts and beaches. Synchronising with solar cycles, these tides are amplified at the equinox to create the high and low extremities.

The lunar cycle influences us on different levels. The moon is very visible from the Earth, affecting humans and animals significantly. Before street lighting, there was an immense difference between full moon and no moon. More subtly, too, the image of the moon has infiltrated our folklore, seeming to speak of quieter and wilder aspects of human experience, connecting us to the unconscious world of dreams, the feminine, and the dangerous. The time of full moon has often been thought of as charged with supernatural energies, the time of lunatics and mad dogs, witches and magic.

Working outdoors, we can observe the phases of the moon and explore these associations and energies in ourselves. Tuning in to our embodied sense of daytime and nighttime, we notice the influence of sunset and moonrise, the coolness of moonlight or the silky darkness of a moon-free night, studded with stars. We feel the temperature change as sunlight fades into the crisp sharpness of night and we let our eyes adjust to the silver-grey light. Such times bring instinctive wariness. Our senses are sharpened and our attention drawn to any movements. We find shapes in the shadows and hear the sounds of night-time amplified. We become aware of animals rustling in the undergrowth and owls calling among the trees. We feel dew condensing onto grass stems and on our skin, and smell the scent of night flowers in the air.

The cycles of nature are fundamental to our ecosystem, shaping its daily and seasonal variations. Living within this ever-changing process, we experience the constant flow of transitional spaces which they create. Winter becomes spring becomes summer. Morning becomes noontide becomes afternoon and evening. Rain gives way to sunshine and the dampness evaporates back into the air in wisps of mist that dance above the tarmac of the road. Gently nature accustoms us to impermanence and the natural cycles of birth, death, decay and re-generation. Gently we let go our need for certainty.

Women's cycles

We live on a planet in the constant flow of cyclical process. The cycles of nature surround us, and we also experience these cycles of life as part of our embodied experience. Winter to summer, day to night, our bodies respond to the physical environment with hormonal fluctuations. In particular, for women, for many of our years, the patterns of our lives are not linear or static, but move and flow in ever changing rhythms. We do not, for the most part, control these processes, but rather, live our lives in relationship to them. Though modern medical science has produced artificial hormones to moderate and suppress our natural cycles, these have their difficulties, and, in any case, do not change our basic make-up.

It is almost certainly not coincidental that women's menstrual cycles follow the same pattern as the moon. Like the tide within us, the cycling between ovulation and menstruation unfolds over around twenty-eight days. So for a portion of our lives, we are in tune with lunar energy in deeply embodied ways. Of course, we are not always in sync with the moon herself. In our modern disconnection, we have long since parted company with this ancestral influence. Sometimes though, in contact with nature and living more in the moonlight, women will attune again to this ancient harmony.

The menstrual cycle is not only a series of bodily changes, the waxing and waning of the uterus as it prepares for ovulation and then (if the egg is left unfertilised to tumble from the body, an empty, unused piece of DNA) weeps its lining as the flow of blood. It is also a flow of changing emotions and varying energy levels, hormone driven in part, but also, perhaps arising from the women's sense of deep connection to the life cycle itself. Different women will experience these changes differently, and some will identify more strongly than others with the mythology growing up in modern times around menstruation. *The Wise Wound* by Penelope Shuttle and Peter Redgrove (1978) was one of the first books to explore menstruation in terms of its mythic and psychological meanings, challenging taboos still around in society of the time. They, and others who followed, saw the long associations between menstruation and being unclean as symptomatic of misogynistic cultures which sought to confine women's creativity and freedom. To them, ovulation was the time when women were socialised as potential mothers and wives, compliant, fertile and ready for impregnation. The time when women bled, however, was the time of the lone, independent, strong woman who, fired with pre-menstrual clarity and power, expressed her own story. In the decades following publication of this classic, some women's groups took up the cause, reclaiming the traditional menstrual hut as a place for women to be together and support one another.

Whether or not women identify with these particular interpretations, understanding and appreciating the changing patterns of mood and sensation of different stages in the cycle is part of the process of tuning in to our bodies. It is also part of attuning to our energetic patterns. Through this process, we become more aware of the flow of energies which hold us, neither under our control nor separate from us. We resist or yield to these energies as each month we circle through patterns of birth and death, creation and destruction. We learn that nothing is permanent and the life force can be trusted.

Over a lifetime, women go through many transformations. Puberty, menarche, pregnancy, birth, breastfeeding and menopause reshape and reinvent the body and the identity (Friedman & Moon 1997). Whilst men plough a relatively steady path from puberty to death, women accommodate change and, in the process, experience events which, if heeded, reflect universal life patterns. This changeability has often, in history, led women to be treated as inferior, crazy victims of unsteady constitutions, like nature, labelled wild and dangerous. Though to the rational, linear mind of modern man, the power of nature, embodied in women, seems incomprehensible and frightening, this flowing, changing trajectory may give women connection to the sources of life, and perhaps special insight into the needs of our planet. Having cradled babies in the womb, women know both the fragility and robustness of life.

Polarities and balance

Humans tend to think in terms of opposites. From earliest childhood we learn to distinguish one thing from another, defining meaning in terms of what things are not as much as what they are. Perception is based on discrimination. A cat is not a dog. A daffodil is not a lily. Acquiring knowledge involves gaining ever finer categories. We begin by distinguishing animals from inanimate objects. Dogs are different from horses. Later we learn to recognise a poodle from a husky. The ability to discriminate makes us look more carefully at details in our surroundings, but also leads us to give differential attention, favouring one thing over another.

As we grow, we learn to give moral values to different elements. Experience is divided into good and bad, beautiful and ugly. We rank phenomena according to status. This becomes a habit so that we frequently find ourselves choosing one thing over the other. We like this book and dislike that one. We prefer tea to coffee. When we cannot choose we are confused and discomforted. Which chocolate bar to buy? Which lover?

As we distinguish good from bad and right from wrong, objects often become linked and grouped together. Concepts like light, sun, strong, cheerful, rational, linear, awakened, male, are contrasted with their perceived opposites: darkness, moon, weak, melancholy, irrational, cyclical, dreaming and female (Totton 2011). These collections of associations may vary person by person, but, nevertheless, some groupings seem to resonate in many different cultures. We may even come to identify with one group or another, developing positive or negative feelings about ourselves as a result. Sometimes we rewrite the script we are given and other times we claim it is our own.

Western thought is often based on conflicting opposites, maybe originating from Judaeo-Christian roots, and mirroring the fundamental battle between good and evil. Eastern thought, on the other hand, particularly influenced by Taoist philosophy, emphasises the need for balance between polarities. Taoism understands the universe in terms of wholeness within which opposing principles exist in balance. These fundamental polarities, known as Yin and Yang, are complementary qualities permeating all other polarities found in nature. Light and dark, male and female, rock and water are all examples of Yin and Yang.

Psychodynamic theory, particularly originating from Melanie Klein and Ronald Fairburn, identifies a psychological process known as splitting. This unconscious polarisation of experience within the self and in relationships occurs when a person has not developed the psychological resources to cope with contradictory aspects of inter-personal relating. Mature relationships are complex, with some aspects of the other person's behaviour and personality feeling positive whilst other aspects feel negative, but for some people this ambivalence is too difficult to contain. They tend to separate the two sets of feelings, projecting them differentially onto others. Splitting is an unconscious defensive strategy. It may involve attributing good and bad characteristics to the same person on different occasions, and behaving towards them in ways alternating between idealisation and denigration. Alternatively it can involve projecting opposite qualities onto different people, perhaps inviting 'secret' confidences from one person, characterised as 'good' whilst blaming the other, characterised as 'bad'. Co-facilitators are well advised to take into account these patterns when running groups, since some degree of splitting or polarisation in the group's view of its leaders, one good, one bad, is very common.

People manage anxiety by separating the world into polarities. They feel psychologically in control of their surroundings by categorising their experience of them. In Buddhist terms, polarisation is described by the term 'dualistic thinking'. We create an unenlightened world-view by separating the world into 'me' and 'everything else' or 'mine' and 'not mine', and these processes are upheld by attraction and aversion responses and notions of good and bad. Seeing aspects of our surroundings in terms of polarities, we subtly identify with one thing and differentiate ourselves from the other, reducing anxiety, but also reducing our energy.

The mature relationship is one in which complexity and ambiguity can be accepted. In furthering the wellbeing of the planet we need therefore to take care that we do not, ourselves, fall into polarised views. It is too easy to idealise green lifestyles and philosophies and denigrate those with whom we disagree. If, however, we cannot relate to and live in harmony with the majority of the population because we see their behaviours and lifestyles as damaging, then we become part of the problem. Polarisation perpetuates dynamics which have created global problems down the ages. People and situations are complex and the solutions to the world's problems must address this complexity with understanding rather than judgement.

Life journey

Many human experiences are cyclical. We flow between opposite and complementary ways of being. Waking and sleeping, hungry and satiated, agitated and peaceful, happy and sad, our lives alternate between known experiences, revisiting and renewing patterns which are familiar. Such repetitious patterns occur in nature and in ourselves, so we recognise them both within us and in the world. Other processes are progressive and linear, at least as we experience them. Of these, the life journey is perhaps the fundamental example.

Experientially, our lives come out of oblivion and return to it at their close, but, whilst we can see processes of life and death following natural cycles of departure and return, personally, we often experience life in terms of a line with a beginning and an ending. This line is divided into a series of stages, some of which are commonly recognised: infancy, childhood, adolescence, young adulthood, middle-age, maturity and old age. Other times we measure our lives idiosyncratically, in terms of relationships, locations and activities: new careers and new partners, children and grandchildren. In traversing these stages, our embodied experience changes dramatically, as do our energy levels. Children are lively but adolescents sleep till noon. Faculties are affected by illness, accidents, childbearing and time. Sometimes we exercise and look after our health, but other times we allow our bodies to become flaccid and unfit. We live in different locations, do different jobs, and have different lovers. Our relationships with our bodies are coloured by psychological factors such as depression or anxiety, and energy can be suppressed by things that are going on in our lives.

Exploring the changing pattern of energy levels over a lifetime can be an emotional process. In living, a part of us is always moving closer to death and signs of decline may become evident. Sometimes accidents or illness irrevocably damage the body, changing our physical capabilities in ways which we know we will not be able to reverse. When this happens, we may enter a period of grieving, passing through stages of denial, sadness, anger and acceptance. As time goes on, we may discover new limitations, starting to fear the future and extrapolate experiences of present limitations and pain into our imagined old age.

On the other hand, if our lives become more engaged with the outdoors, and we become more physically active, we may find ourselves feeling more energetically connected as a result. As we work with emotional issues and free up psychic energy which has been trapped in processes of repression, we may find ourselves less tired and start to feel more alive as our energy and enthusiasm grow. We may start to experience the vibrancy of our surroundings and of ourselves and appreciate that we are part of a bigger pattern of cycles that flows inexorably forwards.

References

Brazier, C. (2003). *Buddhist Psychology*. London: Constable Robinson.

Friedman, L. & Moon, S. (Eds.). (1997). *Being Bodies: Buddhist Women on the Paradox of Embodiment*. Boston: Shambala.

Gendlin, E. (1978). *Focusing*. New York: Everest House.

Kaza, S. (2010). How Much is Enough: Buddhist Perspectives on Consumerism. In R. Payne (Ed.), *How Much is Enough: Buddhism, Consumerism, and the Human Environment*, (pp 39–62). Somerville, MA: Wisdom.

Orbach, S. (1978). *Fat is a Feminist Issue*. London: Paddington Press Ltd.
Palmer, M. & Ramsay, J. (1995). *Kwan Yin : Myths and Prophesies of the Chinese Goddess of Compassion*. San Francisco: Thorsons.
Rimer, J., Dwan, K., Lawlor, D., Greig, C., McMurdo, M., Morley, W. & Mead, G. (2012). Exercise for Depression. *Cochrane Database Systematic Review*, 11 July.
Shuttle, P. & Redgrove, P. (1978). *The Wise Would: Menstruation and Everywoman*. UK: Littlehampton Book Services Ltd.
Totton, N. (2011). *Wild Therapy: Undomesticating Inner and Outer Worlds*. Ross on Wye: PCCS Books.

15 Embedded living

This final chapter explores the role of ecotherapy in a world threatened by multiple environmental issues, examining the place of therapists in mediating psychological and social factors. Whilst needing to maintain therapeutic neutrality, ecotherapy may assist change by reconnecting people to nature, and also in supporting activists, preventing burnout. Therapists can offer ways of understanding resistance and supporting change. This chapter explores the need for spiritual transformation, as presented by Paul Maiteney. It concludes with reflections on two distinctly Buddhist responses: The International Dharma Teachers' Statement on Climate Change, written by One Earth Sangha (published in full as an appendix) and Naikan practice reflecting on gratitude and responsibilities to the Earth.

Psychotherapy only exists within the greater frame of human process. Humans only exist by grace of our planetary conditions. Our planet only exists through coincidences of astronomical forces and the laws of physics. Whatever beliefs we use to make sense of our shared predicament, we are indeed small players in a great mystery which is life.

This book has, by and large, concerned itself with the minutiae of therapeutic process and the details of human psychology. We have looked at therapeutic interventions which can be used in the outdoors and at some of the theoretical and philosophical perspectives which can underpin this kind of therapeutic work. This in itself is an ambitious agenda, and, in covering a broad spectrum of methodologies and theories, we have at times, of necessity, been limited to signposting areas which are dealt with in more detail elsewhere. In particular our exploration has been grounded in Buddhist psychology, though we have also used other sources to complement and expand this core material.

The final element in the Ten Directions model, embedded living, contextualises our work in the larger frame. It incorporates questions of lifestyle and green agendas as well as looking at our place as humans in the ecosystem. Viewed from the planetary perspective, this element is the most important and needs to be integrated through all of our work. At the same time, in other ways, it is the most difficult element to include, since it is most at odds with traditional Western psychotherapeutic practice, being concerned with lifestyles change, politics and other practicalities as much as with events in the therapy room.

As we have already discussed, our individual psychology cannot be separated from our involvement in the greater order of global inhabitants or from the implications of human culpability in current environmental problems. Our individual mind-sets are influenced by and interrelated with these collective elements. People today, at some level, hold awareness of the seriousness of the human situation. We cannot avoid the news headlines or the evidence of our eyes as we witness small instances of larger scale changes. Last year daffodils bloomed in England before Christmas. What an un-thought of experience. But life continues and our lifestyles are busy as ever.

Since the majority of the population do not spend time consciously reflecting on environmental issues, inevitably fears and anxieties about the future remain, for the most part, in the unconscious of society. They nevertheless shape individual and collective psychologies. Our work as environmentally-based therapists may, in part, be to make conscious these emotions and bring people face-to-face with uncomfortable facts and their reactions to them. Thus we can help people understand the malaise gripping so many in Western society, and break pernicious cycles of avoidance which drive overconsumption and isolationism. Also, by fostering a different relationship to the natural world in people we work with, inviting them to be a part of nature rather than living in alienation from it, we can support practices which heal not only individuals, but also society and the planet.

Therapeutic work is concerned with psychology rather than activism, and the overtly political is generally outside our remit as practitioners. Aligning with particular positions compromises the neutrality that therapists must adopt so as to be empathically available to clients of all backgrounds, and promoting particular viewpoints is likely to break the therapeutic alliance upon which we depend. Grounding our work in the bigger picture is, therefore, generally implicit rather than explicit. On the other hand, from this bigger perspective, the profession's silence on these global matters seems collusive with the pathology of our times, giving us a responsibility to address them in some way.

It is our role as therapists to enquire into truth and to allow that truth to speak for itself, whether that truth is about individual process or global realities. Whilst precedent suggests we should work at the level of individual experience and neurosis, we are also in a position to acknowledge the interdependence of the person with systems in which they operate. Buddhist psychology offers us models which place the individual in relationship to collective and universal processes, giving us concepts to describe the complexity of human conditions. In addition, the working styles described in this book are varied, in some cases incorporating approaches which are community-based or systems orientated. Not everybody practicing ecotherapy identifies with the psychotherapy professions and many of us are crossing boundaries and experimenting with different ways of working therapeutically in nature.

Whether or not we overtly discuss green lifestyles or the politics of global environmentalism, by staying open to these matters and keeping ourselves informed about them, we will support those with whom we work therapeutically and be open to their concerns about the global situation. More importantly, by working outdoors with people and helping them to reconnect with nature we may create conditions for changing awareness, attitude and behaviour and ultimately benefit the planet.

Points of impact

Over the past decade, people have been encouraged to live, to a greater or lesser degree, in ways that reduce damage to the environment. Fuel economy and recycling have become part of ordinary life, and, whether or not individuals take action in these areas, few can be unaware that refuse collections and the price of petrol at the pump are changing to accommodate the green agenda. For those who are concerned, there are many other ways to 'make a difference'. Organic food, green energy and environmentally friendly travel and so on are all relatively easily acquired by those with financial resources to do so.

At the same time, for most people, change only happens when financially rewarded or when the alternative, not changing, becomes too difficult or the focus of too much public disapprobation. For many people, the dots between collecting empty cartons and the future of the planet are never joined up. Most people get on with their lives without ever thinking that their children and grandchildren may not enjoy the same lifestyle that they do. The myth of progress and growth is pervasive. Even though, at some level, most people are aware of the threat hanging over us all, for the majority it remains well buried beneath everyday concerns.

Because those who make substantial changes of lifestyle are in the minority, the impact of individual changes of lifestyle is small in practical terms, and is effective primarily in influencing social norms rather than in saving particular resources. There is always a vanguard of people willing to initiate new practices. These may be adopted by the rest of the population at a later date, in part inspired by their examples and in part by pressure of legislation. Those people willing to 'be the change', letting go some modern comforts for the higher good, perhaps gain some sense of personal virtue, or at least a feeling that, in the face of impotence, they are doing something. These people are often guinea pigs for society, trying out experimental technologies and testing new products before they are sold more widely.

Real change, however, needs to happen on a global scale. As the world faces wholesale extinctions and erosion of resources, destruction of environments and catastrophic changes to weather systems, saving plastic bottles alone will not be enough to save humanity. From this perspective, even national policy is evidently not sufficient. Some parts of Europe, such as the Netherlands and Scandinavia, have instituted green policies on scales which the rest of the world can only envy, but these changes will have little overall effect if neighbouring countries produce toxic waste and large-scale emissions. More environmentally responsible countries, like green-minded individuals, function more as test-grounds and examples for the rest of us. Meanwhile, international agreements become fraught with difficulties as countries jostle to maintain their economic and political positions and the lifestyles which their people have come to expect, and multinational companies become adept at moving from place to place, exploiting loopholes in legislation and maximising profits.

Knowing these things, it can be hard to know how best to make a difference. People feel paralysed by the enormity of the problem and complexity of the situation, wondering whether it is better to put energy into insulating or campaigning. Whilst both have value, and people find their own balance between them, sometimes it feels as if we ricochet between possible courses of action, powerless on all fronts. Working on the front line of green politics can be demoralising, and environmentally-based therapists have a potential role in supporting activists. For those caught up in campaigning on a daily basis with scant resources, often feeling socially isolated and disapproved of for their positions, the pressure of caring can become unbearable. Creating supportive networks for activists can help to prevent burnout and socially active Buddhists have a role to play in this. Ken Jones, author of *The New Social Face of Buddhism* (2003), offered 'barefoot retreats' for activists for many years and Joanna Macy has also worked to address the despair felt by many involved in political activism (Macy 1983; Macy & Brown 2014).

Awareness raising

Working therapeutically with people outdoors, as we ourselves hold awareness of the relationship between human activity and degradation of the ecosystem, both in our lifestyles and in our ways of thinking, we may naturally invite questions among those with whom we work about lifestyle and environmental impact. It is not, however, generally appropriate for us as therapists to actively promote particular positions or question the choices that people make. Our role remains therapeutic, and our work should not be hijacked by political or activist agendas. This neutrality sometimes feels difficult to maintain, however.

The need for neutrality highlights paradoxes within our therapeutic work. On the one hand in order to maintain the therapeutic alliance, keeping empathy for those we work with is paramount. This means remaining non-judgemental even if their lifestyle is very different from our own. Not only do we need our clients to believe that we are 'on their side' but also we need to be able to put aside our prejudices because, if we are basically critical, we will not be able to offer any real depth of relationship. On the other hand, when we know that a particular behaviour leads to mental health problems, it may be difficult to remain neutral in this way. If a client's lifestyle is having a bad effect upon his psychological state, whether through use of alcohol, drugs, pornography or other addictive habits, the therapist is unlikely to support this continuing self-destructive behaviour even though she may empathise with the reasons he indulges in it. Yet, as environmentally aware therapists, we do not generally express our concerns at the choices being made by those with whom we work, even though we may be aware that these behaviours are having a negative impact both on the planet and on the person who is going to be living with the consequences.

In many ways, the solution to such dilemmas is in our commitment to the truth. Whilst it is inappropriate for us to suggest or impose our views, facts can be explored, and, if our views are based on more than prejudice, the truth will become apparent. This is pragmatic as well as ethical. People act on evidence and a change of heart. The client is autonomous and will probably not abandon his addiction because the therapist disapproves, however if the therapist is broadly supportive but curious about the behaviour, he may realise the effect which his behaviour is having when he starts to seriously investigate its consequences in terms of impact on his wellbeing and that of others. To instigate a therapeutic enquiry of this kind, one needs to approach the questions with an open mind oneself and not manipulate the situation. Even though we might have a strong conviction that a client's behaviour is unhelpful, we need to retain our capacity to be wrong. We need to keep open the window of not knowing (Chisholm & Harrison 2016).

Conversation about climatic change and environmental damage can begin with direct experience of the landscape in which we work. We may notice the flowering of daffodils in mid-winter or early buds appearing on the trees. This year, as our ecotherapy group worked in the garden at the end of January, many spring bulbs were already in bloom. It was impossible not to notice that things were different from previous years. Situations like this can spark conversations. We compare things going on now with what we remember from the past and talk about changes. Often these conversations take place in the between times, in coffee breaks and lunchtimes, when people casually remark on the strangeness of such phenomena. As group therapists, we can notice people's concerns and reintroduce them into sessions, exploring the feelings and reactions that might be glossed over in the lightness of ordinary chat. Drawing on these ordinary observations, we can explore the issues of climate change in more depth.

Sometimes we deliberately introduce an exercise or activity which is provocative to stimulate discussion. The M1 motorway runs near to our centre in Leicestershire and there is a field path which we sometimes use which runs beneath the carriageway beside the River Soar. The motorway bridge is supported on massive concrete pillars and the crossing point beneath it is a large, rather bleak space where little grows. Sometimes we deliberately take groups there to work.

It is a strange, in-between space, flanked by fields and brambles, with an expanse of dusty gravel and clay running down to the river, which is dark and rather muddy in the shadow of the bridge. There is graffiti on the pillars and the mud banks sloping up to the foundations of the road have skid marks where they have been used by youngsters for skateboarding. When we go there, participants usually react strongly. For some people, the space is edgy, a reminder of teenage escapades, and the places where they hung out, away from adult curiosity. For other people, the place feels desolate, threatening and uncomfortable. We explore the contrast between the green, life-filled fields on either side of the motorway and the incongruous area of lifeless ground beneath it, experiencing in microcosm the destructiveness of human impact. A place of this kind provokes discussion of environmental issues, and allows feelings of many kinds to be expressed. We listen to the constant roar of traffic overhead, and participants sometimes recognise that they themselves have driven over the bridge on their way to and from the programme or on other occasions. In this simple situation, the complexity of the modern world is exemplified.

Working outdoors can also make us aware of our use of resources. Often we are restricted to the equipment and sustenance that we can carry for the day or longer. When we wild camp on our yearly Ten Directions intensive, facilities are limited and we do not have access to a mains water supply. All our food is carried from the nearest parking space to the camping area, a five minute walk uphill, which, although not far, is long enough to remind us only to take what we really need. Toilet facilities are dug into the hillside and for water we collect the rain in barrels, carry jerry cans from the nearest house, or use water from a small stream nearby. Food is cooked on wood fires, for which wood must be foraged. Staying alive requires work.

Yet even in these limited circumstances, we still depend on shops for basic supplies of food and other necessities. We sleep in tents and wear clothing, both of which have been manufactured. When it rains hard, we are grateful for a shelter, roofed with polycarbonate sheeting. Even when apparently living a simple life away from civilisation, we are dependent on others and on industrial processes and transportation. At the same time, this period of living away from many of the modern resources teaches us that much of what we regard as essential to everyday life is not as necessary as we assume. We become more appreciative and less profligate.

Issues of judgement and resistance

Those who campaign for local measures to ameliorate environmental change often become frustrated by the lack of support from the general public. Although some people try to live in principled ways, reducing their carbon footprints by cutting down travel, minimising fuel bills and eating ethically, they often have difficulty in persuading others to do likewise. This can lead to feelings of isolation and disaffection and can mean that some activists become ghettoised, operating in small circles of like-minded people and avoiding mainstream activities. They may become hostile to others and blame the rest of humanity for the ills which they see going on around them. In particular they may demonise certain groups of politicians or multinationals as the perpetrators of the damage which is being inflicted on the ecosystem.

If people are to effect change on a scale large enough to have any impact on the environment, however, they need to engage with society at a wider level and not simply speak to the converted. This can be difficult because it means engaging with those whose views are seen as being part of the problem. It may even, at top levels, mean engaging with those parties who have been major players in the destructive processes of industrialisation and consumption, the politicians and the heads of corporations. Some conversations will inevitably be confrontational. On the whole, though, engagement will be more effective where there is dialogue and each side can develop a level of empathy for the other's position. This is hard, not only because it means exposing oneself to opposite arguments, disagreement and sometimes ridicule, but also because it can dilute the sense of identity which comes from being with like-minded people. As we have seen, identity is frequently formed in opposition so engaging meaningfully with 'the enemy' can undermine the security which comes from solidarity and difference. Without the certainty of holding onto a position, our fear and confusion in the current global situation can become overwhelming.

At the same time, campaigns which rely on evoking fear or guilt, or which are proscriptive and dogmatic, are often counter-productive, particularly when aimed at the general public. This has been recognised for some time in fields of public health and safety. People are generally psychologically programmed to react against authoritarian messages and to resist knowledge which induces too much anxiety. Even where a person conforms out of feelings of guilt or shame, their longer term commitment to the new behaviour is likely to be undermined by conflicted emotions. People are more likely to adopt lifestyle changes if their motivation is based on first-hand evidence and positive reward. It therefore makes sense to promote benefits of a change of behaviour, rather than giving warnings about dreadful consequences of continuing the status quo. In addition, people are more likely to act in ways that they see as being in their own interests. These strategies work because they are in tune with the psychology of grasping and avoidance. People avoid those things which frighten or disturb them and seek things which are pleasant and comforting, and particularly things which will reinforce the positive sense of self. For example, people are more likely to take up cycling because they believe it will make them feel better, lose weight and achieve a healthier image, than they are to do so because they have been made to feel guilty for driving their cars unnecessarily and fear the consequences of car use in terms of climate change.

The situation on this planet will not be resolved by one group of people judging another. Only by recognising that all of us play our part in what is happening will we make changes for the future. In this, it is important that, on the one hand, we do not become consumed by self-blame, whilst, on the other hand, we realistically take responsibility for our part in what is going on. Viewing the situation in terms of the collective whole, we can work together to find collective solutions. The groups we work with provide a microcosm of society. We will find blame and judgement in our midst as well as towards outside parties. Facing these dynamics honestly and working through differences rather than avoiding them can be a first step in learning to work with judgement on the larger scale. This does not mean that we should avoid negative feelings, however. It can be important to explore feelings of powerlessness and anger towards those who seem to hold the keys to change. This helps people form resolve and cohesion and make sense of the problems that we face individually and collectively. Anger can release energy which is otherwise repressed and rage can be a positive agent for change if harnessed in ways that avoid excessive hostility. Having recognised our rage, however, we need to move on beyond the politics of blame and recognise that we too carry culpability and have agency in creating a different future.

This is not to say that all inhabitants of the planet share equal responsibility for the situation in which we find ourselves. Clearly some societies and some individuals consume more than others and have greater power to inflict their will upon the rest of humanity. For this reason, abandoning judgemental views is not straightforward. We need to develop our capacity for critical thinking and speaking out, but we also need to become skilful in how we do so and avoid rushing to blame. We can take systemic views of situations and appreciate the wider conditions which support individuals and groups in behaving as they do. We can also recognise our own fallibility, both in the ways we contribute to the problems, and in the ways in which, if we were in the same position as leaders of government and industry, we might well be drawn into justifying similar strategies. Judgement creates resistance and is rarely a skilful strategy for change. Whether we operate at the local level, promoting greener lifestyles, or globally, engaging with major campaigns, we can understand the situations which concern us holistically, and appreciate that offering positive incentives for change is likely to be more effective than adopting a purely confrontational stance.

Change as spiritual transformation

Nature relies upon achieving equilibrium, although, being in a state of constant flux, the basis of this equilibrium is constantly changing. Particular ecosystems remain in place because they are based upon complex webs of checks and balances. Carnivores multiply dependent upon the food chain, and the food chain is sustained by a finite supply of basic foodstuffs, that is, plants or simple organisms. When populations overreach the capacity of their environment, they generally die off through starvation, in-fighting and weakness. Animals are driven by impulses to feed and reproduce. These often lead to intra-species and interspecies conflict and survival of the fittest means the demise of the weaker members of the group. Individuals are sacrificed for the good of the whole community. Where change occurs, nature can be ruthless, eliminating those creatures that are not able to adapt.

As humans, we are still governed by animal instincts for survival. Our most basic fight or flight responses make us pugnacious or avoidant. We are programmed to eat when food is available, even if we do not really need the nourishment, and to look after those who share our genetic inheritance before considering the needs of those from different families. Indeed, we are biased towards those of similar genetic constitution in many ways. This probably underlies many people's choice of partner, for many of us are attracted to people of similar facial types to ourselves. This also probably underlies the tendency of humans towards racism. These animal traits are generally overlooked for humans seek to place themselves above others on the evolutionary ladder, and, rather than aspiring to be top dog in the animal kingdom, have often viewed themselves as different entities, possessors of souls and not subject to the same instincts.

Two hundred years ago, the Romantic Movement swept through the intelligentsia of Europe, introducing a change of attitude to nature and the countryside. This movement was in part a reaction to the large scale industrialisation which had taken place in the previous century. It advocated a return to a simpler, nature-based lifestyle. Figures like Jean-Jacques Rousseau described the nobility of the natural life, and, from his work, there grew a spirit which was expressed in art, literature, social theory and many other areas of life. The Romantic Movement took inspiration from nature, and particularly used natural phenomena as metaphors to explore the relationship between the human and the divine. Against the power of the elements, people were small, insignificant players, standing in awe of influences beyond their knowledge. We should be humble, the movement warned, for we dabble with forces of nature at our peril.

Despite placing humans in the wider arena of natural forces, however, the Romantic Movement did not equate humans with animals. Founded in a Judaeo-Christian tradition, it placed man in relationship to God, formed in His image, rather than to the birds and beasts of the field over whom he was given dominion. The Romantic Movement still influences some modern views of our relationship to the natural world and many of those who write about working in nature draw on its spirit, seeking in nature both a return to native innocence and a mirror of the divine. In the light of new levels of industrialisation and urbanisation the dream of 'getting back to nature' still motivates many of those involved in offering environmentally-based therapies. On the other hand, we also find sceptical elements in the modern view, which reject the Romantic ideal for its simplification of our situation and notions of human supremacy. If we recognise our animal drives for what they are, the prospect of a harmonious future becomes ever more distant.

Recognising the voracity of our animal nature can be sobering. Whilst the idea of a return to nature has been romanticised, the reality is that to really take our place in nature would be to embrace those instincts which we aspire to overcome, our greediness, self-centredness and impulses to harm others, as the basis of who we are. This is uncomfortable. Humans do not always live up to their higher ideals, and our rhetoric tends to mask our more basic impulses which seek personal and familial survival at the expense of others. In his chapter in the anthology, *Vital Signs*, Paul Maiteney (2012) suggests that reverting to our animal nature is not necessarily something to which humans should aspire.

Nature is not as gentle as we might like to think, and apparent harmony of the animal world is only achieved through hard won fights or through the ravages of starvation and disease which commonly follow over-population of a particular species. Balance is maintained by dividing hunter and prey, top dog and pack. If we transcend our violence and destructiveness, as Maiteney proposes, it will be through finding other qualities within the human psyche that go beyond these instincts. It will require a spiritual leap forward in which we discover higher principles than mere survival on which to base our lives.

On the other hand, our actualisation as humans cannot be separated from our part in the ecosystem, and recognising our embodied selves, and the dependence of those bodies on the web of life which surrounds us, is vital to our future on this planet. Only by appreciating that we are not the central components of the system, but bound to live in sympathetic resonance with it, a part of a system to which we must relate with respect and openness (Kidner 2001; Fisher 2002) will we find our niche.

Dharma teachers' statement

In January 2014, the One Earth Sangha,[1] a Buddhist environmental activist group, launched *The Earth as Witness: International Dharma Teachers' Statement on Climate Change*, and invited Dharma teachers around the world to sign. This statement acknowledges the impact of climate change as it is already unfolding and affecting our planet, and draws on the Buddhist teachings to offer insights into the roots of the environmental catastrophe and suggests ways that our situation might be addressed.

The statement firstly outlines real changes already happening to the planet and the consequences that they are having and will have in the future for people and ecosystems. It contextualises these events in terms of the Buddhist approach to suffering. Only by recognising the truth of *dukkha*, however painful, can people start to move forward. The first step in approaching the problem of climate change therefore must be to recognise the First Noble Truth and acknowledge that suffering exists.

> As a starting point, the Dharma states that to formulate meaningful solutions to any problem we must first acknowledge the truth of our suffering...Only by recognizing these truths can we adopt a meaningful path toward solutions.
>
> (ibid.)

As we have discussed, recognising the reality of affliction is fundamental to the Buddhist path. It is our failure to take on board just how bad things are that prevents us from doing something about our situation. It is also this failure that leads us to create further suffering by compounding our misery with various escapist tendencies. The statement does not avoid the truth, but rather iterates the consequences of a rise of 2°C in global temperatures. These outcomes it considers to be highly likely, given the current state of the environment and of human activity, and indeed, since the statement's publication in 2014, we have seen temperatures continue to rise towards this figure.

The statement continues by showing how the Buddhist understanding, based on the Second Noble Truth, the arising of craving, suggests that the roots of affliction are to be found in the grasping, aversion and delusion which arise in response to our craving. This throws light on the current scientific analysis that climate change is caused by human activity, and particularly the workings of the industrialised nations, appropriating land in order to extract fuel and other resources in a way that is careless of the needs of the environment or of peoples displaced by them.

The statement suggests that it would be possible to learn from our experience of impending disaster, but that it is only by being faced by reality in its rawest manifestations that people will awaken to this possibility of change. In this way, climate change has something to teach us about ourselves. *Climate change is perhaps humanity's greatest teacher yet about how these mental forces, when unchecked in ourselves and our institutions, cause harm to other people and the living environment.* The statement thus sees the ecological crisis as an opportunity for spiritual and social growth. By being faced by the consequences of our actions, writ big on the global stage, humanity will be forced to take notice and learn other ways of living within the biosphere. *By learning from our mistaken beliefs and activities, we can create more equitable, compassionate and mindful societies that generate greater individual and collective wellbeing while reducing climate change to manageable levels.*

The statement proposes a solution based upon the three pillars of Buddhism, which it lists as wisdom, ethics and mindfulness. We need to find the wisdom to see how difficulties of life arise out of our human patterns of avoidance: greed, hatred and delusion. We need the ethics to moderate our actions so that they are based on moral principles and to practice right action rather than engaging in self-motivated grasping. We need mindfulness so that we can act with awareness and sobriety rather than impulsiveness. With this change of perspective, a new order would become possible. This order, based on principles of the Buddhist path, would ensure a future for the planet and for all those who live on it.

Naikan

There is a form of Buddhist therapy, developed in Japan, called Naikan. This therapy was originated by a Japanese Jodo Shinshu practitioner called Yoshimoto Ishin. Ishin developed Naikan based on his own experience of an ascetic practice of introspection, *mishirabe*, which he had practiced as a young man and found beneficial. He invented Naikan as a more accessible practice for ordinary people. It involves reflecting on our relationships with significant people in our lives, and particularly focuses on the practitioner's primary relationships with parents and other caregivers from childhood (Krech 2002; Reynolds 1986). The purpose of this practice is to help the person to see parents and other carers in new ways, letting go habits of framing experience in terms of personal stories and learning to view those experiences in ways that are more objective and appreciative.

Traditionally Naikan is done as an intensive retreat, taking place over a week or so, but more recently, both in Japan and in the West, it has been adapted as a therapy. This has made it more accessible for clients who do not wish to undertake retreats as it is offered in more regular therapeutic formats with shorter sessions on a weekly basis. Besides changing the format of sessions, the focus of the questions which Naikan uses can also be varied, allowing practitioners to explore other situations and relationships that are important in their lives, including current ones. Although the primary questions generally remain the same in all these applications, subsidiary questions, continuing the central areas of enquiry, are sometimes added.

In the traditional Naikan life-review, the practitioner begins by reflecting on the earliest period of his life from birth to three years old. He starts by focusing on the relationship with his mother or the person who took on the mothering role, using a standard set of questions. These are:

- What did this person do for me? (e.g. she fed me, washed me, played with me)
- What did I do for this person in return? (e.g. I hugged her, I folded my clothes)
- What trouble did I, or my presence, cause her? (e.g. she sat with me when I was sick, I always refused to eat tomatoes).

The practitioner is instructed to work from memory, to be concrete and specific in what he recalls, and to focus on what actually happened rather than trying to rationalise or justify his answers. In particular he is told not to speculate on psychological factors which might have been involved, but to stay focused on memories of events and, when these were not forthcoming, knowledge of what must have been the case. Where there is no memory, the practitioner is told to look for evidence based on what they know from other sources about what it is like to care for a small baby, or about the history of the time in which they grew up. For example, not too long ago, in Britain it would have been normal for women to have to stop working when a new baby arrived, so he might surmise that she gave up her job before he was born.

The practitioner can deduce that meals must have been cooked. He might think about what this would have involved in terms of the mother's workload and the facilities and resources available to her at the time. He might be asked to calculate how many hours a day she spent cooking and what this cost her in energy and effort. In the same way, the practitioner is invited to think about other tasks which were involved in looking after a baby such as washing clothes, changing and cleaning the child, getting up at night and so on. He is asked to reflect on the financial outlay which having a baby might have involved and on what he knows about the economic circumstances of the family at the time. In recalling or imagining these things, he is reminded not to speculate on his mother's motivation or the spirit in which these tasks were done, but to stick to facts.

When Naikan is done as an intensive retreat, the person who is leading the event goes to each participant in turn, inviting them to report back on the memories that they have recalled and the deductions that they have made. The leader will not usually comment on what is said, except to encourage the participant to continue reflecting. Thus each participant is given a lot of space to explore memories and to think about what really happened in their early life. As the process continues, he is repeatedly challenged to go on looking more closely at the reality of the experience, constantly questioning his assumptions and biases.

After a while, maybe half a day, reflecting on the first three years of life, participants are told to move on and reflect the next phase of their lives, between three and six years. After further time, they go on to the next phase, six to nine years, and so on. The important thing about Naikan is that it is about exploring reality and reaching a deeper appreciation of how it was for the other person to be relating to oneself. When this happens, the practitioner starts to appreciate that the parent or carer truly is a separate person with their own life experiences. He sees that he was dependent upon them but that the parents had their own stories which were unfolding in their own ways, separate from him. They were real people, not just functional objects in his world.

The Naikan method is not intended to involve blaming anyone, and although people sometimes feel regret and even remorse when undertaking a Naikan retreat, by the end, most people predominantly feel appreciation and gratitude and a sense of release. Although the Naikan questions can seem quite shocking and even harsh when compared with Western therapies, most people experience the approach as evoking positive feelings of having been cared for and even loved. It is not for everyone, but it does offer a way of working which some people find deeply transformative.

Whilst the traditional Naikan retreat focuses on family relationships, Naikan questions can be adapted and we can use them to reflect on other aspects of our lives. In particular, in environmental work, we can use the Naikan questions to look at our relationship with the Earth. I have introduced these questions on a number of occasions on environmentally-based retreats and training programmes and have found them very moving to work with. So in conclusion of this book, let us go together outdoors and engage with the questions which link us deeply to our mother, the Earth. Let us reflect on the question not only of our birth-rights but also our birth-obligations.

We can take a walk into a quiet, peaceful place. We can spend time sitting, perhaps at the foot of a tall tree, leaning against its strong trunk, listening to the sounds around us and enjoying what we hear. We can take time, for we have as long as we need to do this exercise. If we wish we can spend all day on it. Let us be honest and thoughtful, looking deeply into our memories. Let us be concrete in our answers, stripping away the embroideries of the ego. Let us look into what is true. So, taking the traditional Naikan questions we can ask ourselves:

What has the Earth given to me?
What have I given to the planet?
What trouble have I caused to the planet?

Note

1 http://www.oneearthsangha.org/articles/dharma-teachers-statement-on-climate-change/

References

Chisholm, R. & Harrison, J. (Eds.). (2016). *The Wisdom of Not Knowing*. Axminster: Triarchy Press.

Fisher, A. (2002). *Radical Ecopsychology: Psychology in the Service of Life*. Albany: State University of New York Press.

Jones, K. (2003). *The New Social Face of Buddhism*. Somerville, MA: Wisdom.

Kidner, D. (2001). *Nature and Psyche: Radical Environmentalism and the Politics of Subjectivity*. Albany: State University of New York Press.

Krech, G. (2002). *Naikan: Gratitude, Grace and the Japanese Art of Self-Reflection*. Berkeley: Stone Bridge Press.

Macy, J. (1983). *Despair and Power in the Nuclear Age*. Philadelphia: New Society Publishers.

Macy, J. & Brown, M. (2014). *Coming Back to Life* (revised ed). Gabriola Island, BC: New Society Publishers.

Maiteney, P. (2012). Longing to be Human: Evolving Ourselves in Healing the Earth. In M. Rust & N. Totton (Eds.), *Vital Signs: Psychological Responses to Ecological Crisis* (pp. 47–60). London: Karnac.

Reynolds, D. (1986). *Constructive Living*. Honolulu: Kolowalu Books.

Appendix

The following statement is reprinted by kind permission of One Earth Sangha from their web site (www.oneearthsangha.org).

The Earth as Witness: International Dharma Teachers' Statement on Climate Change[1]

Today humanity faces an unprecedented crisis of almost unimaginable magnitude. Escalating climate change is altering the global environment so drastically as to force the Earth into a new geological age. Unprecedented levels of suffering for all life on Earth, including human, will result. Significant reductions in greenhouse gases and other actions will be needed to reduce climate change to manageable levels. But more fundamental changes are also needed, and this is where we can draw guidance from the rich resources of the Buddha's teachings, the Dharma. This statement briefly describes core Buddhist insights into the root causes of the climate crisis and suggests ways to minimize its potentially tragic consequences.

As a starting point, the Dharma states that to formulate meaningful solutions to any problem we must first acknowledge the truth of our suffering. As shocking and painful as it may be, we must recognize that without swift and dramatic reductions in fossil fuel use and major efforts to increase carbon sequestration, global temperatures will rise close to or beyond 2 degrees C. This increase will lead to injury and death for millions of people worldwide and the extinction of many of the Earth's species. Millions more will experience severe trauma and stress that threaten their physical, emotional, and psychological well-being. These stresses will, in turn, trigger social and political unrest. In a grave injustice, low-income communities, poor nations, and people systematically subjected to oppression and discrimination, who contributed little to climate change, will initially be harmed the most. Even worse, as frightening as it is, if we fail to make fundamental changes in our energy, manufacturing, transportation, forestry, agricultural, and other systems along with our consumption patterns with utmost urgency, in mere decades irreversible climate shifts will occur that undermine the very pillars of human civilization. Only by recognizing these truths can we adopt a meaningful path toward solutions.

The Dharma teaches us the origin of our suffering. The majority of the world's climate scientists are unequivocal that on the external physical plane climate change is caused by the historic and ongoing use of fossil fuels and the greenhouse gases they generate when burned. Destructive land management practices such as clearing forests also contribute by reducing nature's capacity to sequester carbon. The Dharma informs us, however, that craving, aversion, and delusion within the human mind are the root causes of vast human suffering. Just as these mental factors have throughout history led to the oppression, abuse, and exploitation of indigenous peoples and others outside the halls of wealth and power, craving, aversion, and delusion are also the root causes of climate change. Climate change is perhaps humanity's greatest teacher yet about how these mental forces, when unchecked in ourselves and our institutions, cause harm to other people and the living environment. Led by industrialized nations, the desire for evermore material wealth and power has resulted in the reckless destruction of land and water, excessive use of fossil fuels, massive amounts of solid and toxic waste, and other practices that are disrupting the Earth's climate. However, by acknowledging and addressing these internal mental drivers, we can begin to resolve the external causes of climate change.

The Dharma offers hope by teaching us that it is possible to overcome the detrimental forces of craving, aversion, and delusion. We can use the climate crisis as a catalyst to acknowledge the consequences of our craving for more and more material wealth and the pursuit of power and realize we must change our assumptions, attitudes, and behaviors. We can use the climate crisis as a catalyst to educate ourselves about planetary processes so we understand that the Earth has ecological limits and thresholds that must not be crossed. By learning from our mistaken beliefs and activities, we can create more equitable, compassionate, and mindful societies that generate greater individual and collective wellbeing while reducing climate change to manageable levels.

Finally, the Dharma describes a pathway of principles and practices we can follow to minimize climate change and the suffering it causes. The first principle is wisdom. From this point forward in history we must all acknowledge not only the external causes of climate change, but the internal mental drivers as well, and their horrific consequences. To be wise we must also, individually and as a society, adopt the firm intention to do whatever is necessary, no matter what the cost, to reduce the climate crisis to manageable levels and over time re-stabilize our planet's climate.

The second Dharma principle is ethical conduct, which is rooted in a compassionate concern for all living beings in the vast web of life. We need to make a firm moral commitment to adopt ways of living that protect the climate and help restore the Earth's ecosystems and living organisms. In our personal lives, we should recognize the value of contentment and sufficiency and realize that, after a certain modest level, additional consumption, material wealth, and power will not bring happiness. To fulfill our wider moral responsibility, we must join with others, stand up to the vested interests that oppose change, and demand that our economic, social, and political institutions be fundamentally altered so they protect the climate and offer nurturance and support for all of humanity in a just and equitable manner. We must insist that governments and corporations contribute to a stable climate and a healthy environment for all people and cultures worldwide, now and in the future. We must further insist that specific scientifically credible global emission reduction targets be set and means adopted to effectively monitor and enforce them.

The third Dharma training, and the one that makes all of the others possible, is mindfulness. This offers a way to heighten our awareness of, and then to regulate, our desires and emotions and the thoughts and behaviors they generate. By continually enhancing our awareness, we can increasingly notice when we are causing harm to others, the climate, or ourselves, and strengthen our capacity to rapidly shift gears and think and act constructively. Mindfulness increases awareness of our inherent interdependency with other people and the natural environment and of values that enhance human dignity rather than subordinate people, animals, and nature to the craving for more material wealth and power.

As we each awaken to our responsibility to follow the path described in the Dharma to help us protect and restore the planet and its inhabitants, we may feel awed by the immensity of the challenge. We should take heart, however, in the power of collective action. Buddhists can join with others in their Sanghas, and our Sanghas can join hands and hearts with other religious and spiritual traditions as well as secular movements focused on social change. In this way we will support each other as we make the necessary shifts in perspectives, lifestyles, and economic and institutional systems required to reduce climate change to manageable levels. History shows that with concerted, unified, collective effort, changes that at one time seemed impossible have time and again come to pass.

When we come together to celebrate our love for the natural world and all of the beings that inhabit it, and when we take a stand to counter the forces of craving, aversion, and delusion, we reclaim our own inner stability and strength and live closer to the truth, closer to the Dharma. Together, we can seek to ensure that our descendants and fellow species inherit a livable planet. Individually and collectively, we will be honoring the great legacy of the Dharma and fulfill our heart's deepest wish to serve and protect all life.

Note

1 http://www.oneearthsangha.org/articles/dharma-teachers-statement-on-climate-change/

Previous books by Caroline Brazier

Brazier, C. (2003). *Buddhist Psychology*. London: Constable Robinson
Brazier, C. (2007). *The Other Buddhism: Amida Comes West*. Ropley: O-Books
Brazier, C. (2009). *Guilt: an exploration*. Ropley: O-Books
Brazier, C. (2009). *Listening to the Other*. Ropley: O-Books
Brazier, C. (2009). *Other-Centred Therapy: Buddhist Psychology in Action*. Ropley: O-Books
Brazier, C. (2011) *Acorns Among the Grass: Adventures in Ecotherapy*. Ropley: Earth Books

For further information about the Ten Directions Training Programme in ecotherapy and other Tariki courses and events please see www.buddhistpsychology.info

Index